Phil
8.99

D0220012

AN INQUIRY INTO THE ORIGINAL OF OUR
IDEAS OF BEAUTY AND VIRTUE

San Diego Christian College
2100 Greenfield Drive
El Cajon, CA 92019

NATURAL LAW AND
ENLIGHTENMENT CLASSICS

Knud Haakonssen
General Editor

Francis Hutcheson

17/.2
H973i

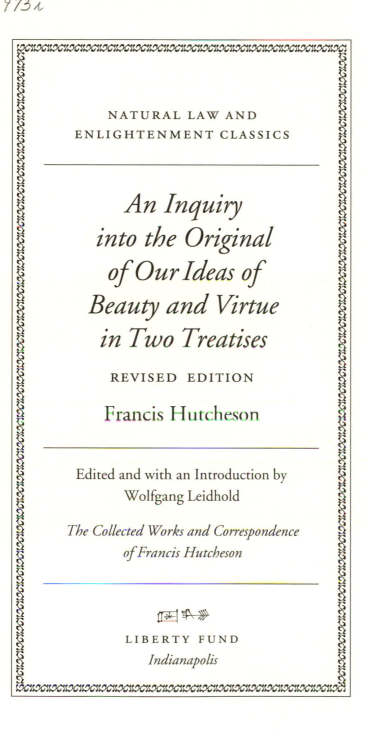

NATURAL LAW AND
ENLIGHTENMENT CLASSICS

An Inquiry
into the Original
of Our Ideas of
Beauty and Virtue
in Two Treatises

REVISED EDITION

Francis Hutcheson

Edited and with an Introduction by
Wolfgang Leidhold

*The Collected Works and Correspondence
of Francis Hutcheson*

LIBERTY FUND
Indianapolis

This book is published by Liberty Fund, Inc., a foundation established to encourage study of the ideal of a society of free and responsible individuals.

The cuneiform inscription that serves as our logo and as the design motif for our endpapers is the earliest-known written appearance of the word "freedom" (*amagi*), or "liberty." It is taken from a clay document written about 2300 B.C. in the Sumerian city-state of Lagash.

© 2004, 2008 by Liberty Fund, Inc.

All rights reserved

Printed in the United States of America

C   10 9   8   7   6   5   4   3   2   1
P   10 9   8   7   6   5   4   3   2   1

Frontispiece: Detail of a portrait of Francis Hutcheson by Allan Ramsay (ca. 1740–45), oil on canvas, reproduced courtesy of the Hunterian Art Gallery, University of Glasgow.

Library of Congress Cataloging-in-Publication Data
Hutcheson, Francis, 1694–1746.
An inquiry into the original of our ideas of beauty and virtue:
in two treatises/Francis Hutcheson;
edited and with an introduction by Wolfgang Leidhold. Rev. ed.
p.   cm.—(Natural law and enlightenment classics)
Includes bibliographical references and index.
ISBN 978-0-86597-773-0 (hb: alk. paper)—ISBN 978-0-86597-774-7 (pbk.: alk. paper)
1. Ethics, Modern—18th century.   2. Aesthetics—Early works to 1800.
I. Leidhold, Wolfgang, 1950–   II. Title.
BJ1005.H88 2008
171'.2—dc22   2008015089

LIBERTY FUND, INC.
8335 Allison Pointe Trail, Suite 300
Indianapolis, Indiana 46250-1684

CONTENTS

INTRODUCTION

Liberty and Happiness

The political dimension of liberty is at least twofold: civil liberties and independence. The former is a matter of the political order of a country; the latter, of freedom from foreign domination. Liberty and happiness can be related to each other as they were in the third section of the "Virginia Bill of Rights," from 6 June 1776:

> That government is or ought to be instituted for the common benefit, protection and security of the people, nation or community; of all the various modes and forms of government, that is best which is capable of producing the greatest degree of happiness and safety and is most effectually secured against the danger of maladministration; and that when any government shall be found inadequate or contrary to these purposes, a majority of the community has an indubitable, inalienable and indefeasible right to reform, alter or abolish it, in such manner as shall be judged most conducive to the public weal.

The preceding section puts forward a short argument: The right to reform, alter, or abolish government is founded on the judgment of whether such government is adequate or contrary to its main purpose, namely the greatest degree of happiness and safety of the community. The argument has a philosophical background. The criterion of "producing the greatest degree of happiness" is part of the principal maxim of utilitarian ethics. The right of resistance against inadequate government, on the other hand, is part of the liberal creed. In the eighteenth century the Scottish philosopher Francis Hutcheson (1694–1746), in his *Inquiry into the Original of Our Ideas of Beauty and Virtue* (London,

ix

1725), linked the two sides of the argument for the first time.[1] There he even coined the phrase, "That action is best, which procures the greatest happiness for the greatest numbers."[2]

Hutcheson's philosophy became part of the ideas that formed the American polity. In the eighteenth century his books were imported to America and his philosophy was well known through his students and learned visitors to Scotland—among them was Benjamin Franklin in 1759. Hutcheson's ideas even became part of the colonial curriculum.[3] The *Inquiry*, which is published here in a new edition, was the book that established Hutcheson's reputation as a philosopher.

The Argument of the *Inquiry*

Already in this early work, Hutcheson detailed some of his political ideas.[4] However, his main task was examining the foundations of his aesthetic, moral, and political philosophy. This was done in two treatises, one dealing with the principles of aesthetics,[5] the other with those of ethics and, to some extent, their political consequences.[6] In both treatises

1. For Hutcheson's biography, see W. R. Scott, *Francis Hutcheson, His Life, Teaching and Position in the History of Philosophy* (Cambridge: Cambridge University Press, 1900; reprint, New York: A. M. Kelley, 1966). Also see the brief overview of Hutcheson's early life and writings in the editor's introduction to Hutcheson, *An Essay on the Nature and Conduct of the Passions and Affections, with Illustrations on the Moral Sense* (1728), ed. Aaron Garrett (Indianapolis: Liberty Fund, 2003).

2. The formula was first used by Gottfried Wilhelm Leibniz in a critical remark on Samuel Cocceji's thesis *De Principio Juris Naturalis Unico, Vero, et Adaequato* (Frankfurt: Schrey/Hartmann, 1699); see Joachim Hruschka, pp. 166–69.

3. For the impact of Hutcheson's philosophy in Europe and America, see the introduction to Hutcheson, *Über den Ursprung unserer Ideen von Schönheit und Tugend*, ed. Wolfgang Leidhold (Hamburg: Meiner, 1986), pp. xi–xiv.

4. Especially in the second and the third editions of the *Inquiry*, 1726 and 1729, respectively.

5. On Hutcheson's aesthetic philosophy, see the works and articles of Peter Kivy, Caroline Korsmeyer, E. Michael, and M. Strasser, listed in "References and Further Reading" (p. xix of this volume).

6. For discussion of Hutcheson's central ideas, see "References and Further Reading" (p. xix of this volume), especially the works and articles of Giovanni de Crescenzo, William K. Frankena, Knud Haakonssen, Peter Kivy, Wolfgang Leidhold, David Fate Norton, D. D. Raphael, Jane Rendall, and William Robert Scott; still

the structure of the argument is similar: (1) Our ideas have their origin in our perceptions and are received by senses. (2) For different perceptions we have different senses. (3) Perceptions are founded in certain qualities of the objects perceived. (4) These qualities we can describe in a maxim or formula. Hutcheson's theory in both treatises therefore is a complex of three related components: a subjective sense, an objective foundation, and an analytical formula. Hutcheson presents the outline of his theory of perception in the first treatise.

The First Treatise

Hutcheson's theory of perception starts with the ideas of John Locke.[7] For Locke all materials of reason and knowledge come "from experience" and our senses are "the first step and degree towards knowledge, and the inlet of all the materials of it."[8] Hutcheson accordingly defines different senses as the powers "of receiving . . . different Perceptions" (I. I. §§ I, II) and maintains that we also acquire the material for our aesthetic and ethical knowledge by some sort of perception. However, what is the specific quality we perceive in aesthetic perceptions? Here Hutcheson relies on Shaftesbury. Shaftesbury's analysis of aesthetic perception is based on the Platonic concept of *form* (*forma* is the Latin version of the Greek Platonic term *idea*). Beauty then is the "outward form" of things, reflecting the "inward form" of some "forming power."[9] Accordingly Hutcheson defines beauty as a "form" or as "Figures . . . in which there is Uniformity amidst Variety" (I. II. § III).

Hutcheson implies that form and uniformity cannot be perceived by the normal senses but by a special sense only. Therefore he expands the

---

valuable as a basic bibliography is T. E. Jessop. For a wider British context, see Isabel Rivers.

7. Locke is mentioned in the *Inquiry,* I. I. § VII. Here and in the following the *Inquiry* is quoted by treatise, section, and article; for example, "I. I. § VII" means first treatise, first section, article seven.

8. John Locke, *Essay Concerning Human Understanding,* II. I. § 2; see II. IX. § 15.

9. See J. V. Arregni and P. Arnau, "Shaftesbury: Father and Critic of Modern Aesthetics," *British Journal of Aesthetics* 34 (1994): 350–62.

notion of experience beyond the confines of the ordinary five senses. *Form* or *uniformity* then is the particular *quality in objects* that is the "Foundation or Occasion of the Ideas of Beauty among Men" (I. II. §§ I, II). Beauty is our perception or knowledge of this objective quality, and in accord with his definition of "sense" as the power of perceiving these objective qualities, he assumes a special *sense of beauty*. This sense is but one of a group of "internal senses," which include among others the "good Ear" or "sense of harmony" (I. VI. § IX). The formula by which the objective form in things themselves can be described is, as already noted, "uniformity amidst variety." With these words Hutcheson paraphrases Shaftesbury's concept of beauty. As in his analysis of moral actions, Hutcheson thinks that aesthetic phenomena are capable of a mathematical analysis, which he sketches in his study of "original or absolute beauty" (title of I. II.).

After delineating his theory of aesthetic knowledge, Hutcheson in the remaining chapters of the first treatise develops a general aesthetic theory. This theory of beauty is not limited to a theory of art but extends to a general, almost cosmological theory. This becomes clear when we look at his basic distinction of original or absolute beauty from comparative or relative beauty at the end of the first section. Absolute beauty we "perceive in Objects without comparison to any thing external, of which the Object is suppos'd an Imitation, or Picture" (I. I. § XVI). Examples of such beauty are the works of nature (such as heaven and earth, plants and animals); the harmony of music; some works of art, when their beauty, as in architecture or gardening, is not an imitation of something else. Even theorems, such as those in mathematics, can in the absolute sense be beautiful. Relative beauty is "founded on a Conformity, or a kind of Unity between the Original and the Copy" (I. IV. § I). Instances here are poetry and painting and the creation as a whole—since in the beauty of the effects it reflects the design and wisdom of its cause, which is God the Father as the Creator (I. V.).

It is the general theory of perception as developed in the first treatise that forms the basis of the similar argument in the second. We may assume that Hutcheson wanted first to establish the idea of additional senses in a field that was not as controversial as that of moral philosophy.

The Second Treatise

The moral controversy is found right in the title of the book. In the first edition we read that Hutcheson wants to defend Shaftesbury's ideas against the author of the *Fable of the Bees,* that is, Mandeville. The two names reflect the clash between the "benevolent" and the "selfish" system. The first position argues that men have by nature moral principles, the second that these principles are but a political invention that is socially useful and based only on self-love or self-interest. Shaftesbury taught that *social affections* were the foundation of morals and that a *moral sense* was the origin of our moral ideas.[10] Where Shaftesbury speaks of "social affections" as the foundation of morals, Hutcheson prefers the Christian concept of "love" as "benevolence." The logical structure of the second treatise is similar to the first. Again we can discern three major components: an objective foundation, which here is benevolence; a particular sense, which is the moral sense; and the analytical formula of "the greatest happiness for the greatest numbers."

LOVE OR BENEVOLENCE AS THE FOUNDATION OF THE MORAL GOOD

In the second treatise, Hutcheson wants to establish the notion of a moral sense as the "Original of our Ideas of . . . Virtue" and love or benevolence as the particular quality we perceive in virtue:

> The Affections which are of most Importance in Morals, are Love and Hatred: All the rest seem but different Modifications of these two original affections. (II. II. § II)

Since Hutcheson wanted to follow Locke's theory of knowledge (as in the first treatise), he had to analyze love or benevolence in accordance

---

10. See Anthony Ashley-Cooper, Third Earl of Shaftesbury, *Characteristics of Men, Manners, Opinions, Times,* ed. Philip Ayres, 2 vols. (Oxford: Clarendon, 1999), I, pp. 55–57, 62ff., 93–101, 196–274. Also see Stanley Grean. The term *moral sense* was first used by Thomas Burnet, a student of Ralph Cudworth, in his discussion of John Locke, cf. Ernest Tuveson.

with Locke's ideas. According to Locke, all materials of experience consist either of simple ideas or of complex ideas, which are composed of simple ideas. Complex ideas can be real or they can be fictitious (being put together by the imagination or by reason). However, neither imagination nor reason can invent simple ideas. Therefore, only simple ideas necessarily represent something real. If Hutcheson thinks benevolence is the objective foundation of morals, he must show what simple ideas constitute it.

Locke had defined love by the simple ideas of pleasure and pain.[11] Love for him is the subjective pleasure of something and is identical with self-love. This definition of love is compatible only with the selfish system. Hutcheson wants to avoid just that. Therefore he distinguishes two versions of "good" and "evil," that is, natural and moral good or evil. A natural good is perceived only in inanimate beings. This perception is one of advantage or disadvantage, of pleasure or pain. A moral good is perceived in rational agents since "they study the interest, and desire the Happiness of other Beings." Our moral relationship with rational agents then is twofold: (1) a moral perception and (2) a moral affection or desire. The moral perception is generally called "approbation" or "disapprobation"; the desire is generally named "love" and "benevolence" or "dislike" and "hate" (II. Introduction; II. I. § I; II).

Hutcheson defines love by the "simple idea of desire." In the first edition of the *Inquiry* the terminology is not yet quite consistent; refinements are added later.[12] In the *Essay* he defines love as the "desire" for the happiness of others and addresses *desire* as a simple idea (*Essay*, p. 64).[13] In contrast to Locke,[14] Hutcheson considers desire to be an act of the will. This is consistent with the Christian idea of love. Love in

---

11. See Locke, *Essay*, II. XX. § 4.

12. Here the reader is confronted with an irritating number of terms used to describe love: affection, intention, sentiment, design, disposition, inclination, motive, determination, instinct, even passion, see *Inquiry* (first edition 1725), 104, 107, 112, 119, 131, 137, 143; "passion": 132, 134, 141, 175ff.

13. The same argument is added to the third and the fourth editions of the *Inquiry* (II. II. § IV and § V).

14. Locke, *Essay*, II. XXI. §§ 28ff.

the Christian sense of *benevolence* is not an emotion or a feeling, but an act of the will.[15] Otherwise, the words of the Sermon on the Mount—"Thou shalt love thy neighbor as thyself" (Matthew 19:19)—would become a very strange commandment: a feeling cannot be commanded. A contemporary Christian author, Richard Cumberland (1631–1718), knew this very well.[16]

THE MORAL SENSE AS THE
ORIGIN OF MORAL IDEAS

While benevolence is the foundation of the moral good, the moral sense is the source of moral ideas, of approbation and disapprobation. Hutcheson concedes that the moral sense is a "secret sense" (II. Introduction; II. I. § III). That means the existence of such a sense is not immediately known and calls for an indirect proof. On the basis of his theory of perception he demonstrates that there are distinct moral perceptions and concludes that there must be a distinct sense:

> since the Definition agrees to it, viz. a Determination of the Mind, to receive any Idea from the Presence of an Object which occurs to us, independent on our Will. (II. I. § I)

---

15. On the Christian idea of love see M. C. D'Arcy, *The Mind and Heart of Love* (London: Faber and Faber, 1944); J. Burnaby, *Amor Dei: A Study of the Religion of St. Augustine* (London: Hodder and Stoughton, 1947); V. Warnach, "Agápe, Not Eros—or Caritas," *Anglican Theological Review,* 37 (1955): 67–73; most comprehensive: Ceslaus Spicq, *Agapè dans le Nouveau Testament: Analyse de textes,* 3 vols. (Paris: Gabalda, 1958–59). A good introduction is C. S. Lewis, *The Four Loves,* 21st ed. (Glasgow: Collins, 1981).

16. See R. Cumberland, *A Treatise of the Law of Nature* (London: Phillips, Knapton, 1727; first edition in Latin, London, 1672), 42. For Hutcheson the conceptual situation was rather complicated, and it took him a while to clarify it. Finally, in the fourth edition of the *Inquiry* the definition of love is given the most precise wording. Here Hutcheson identifies the "Desire of the Good of Others" with the Aristotelian "ὄρεξις βουλευτική," translating it as a "settled Disposition of the Will, or a constant Determination, or desire to act . . . , or a fixed Affection toward a certain Manner of Conduct." Since the foundation of morals sometimes had been called an "instinct," he at the same time defines "instinct" as an "Essential or Natural Disposition of the Will, an Affectionate Determination" (p. 195).

For Hutcheson, the particular moral perception is approbation. We perceive a "moral good" when a person acts from benevolence, and this "(excites) . . . Approbation or Perception of moral Excellence." The "natural good," on the other hand, raises the "Desire of Possession toward the good Object." Hutcheson emphasizes that approbation should not be mixed up with the "Opinion of Advantage," and later on throughout the first and the following chapters he strengthens his position with a number of instances. That the perception of approbation or moral excellence is different from other perceptions is for Hutcheson a matter of evidence.[17] Evidence for him seems to be a proof from experience, which cannot be supported by other sufficient reasons (II. I. § I).

THE GREATEST HAPPINESS FOR
THE GREATEST NUMBERS

To be sure, the moral quality of actions is not the same in all cases. Sometimes we approve one act more than another, or we may have to choose between different options. To clarify the difference, we have to analyze the object of perception, that is, the moral quality itself. In this case we would make a judgment about moral quality. This is what Hutcheson does with his maxim of the greatest happiness for the greatest numbers. In the third section Hutcheson introduces the formula:

> that Action is best, which procures the greatest Happiness for the greatest Numbers; and that, worst, which, in like manner, occasions Misery. (II. III. § VIII)

The formula is based on the moral sense, the objective moral quality, and a rational procedure, namely a comparison of the varying moral qualities of actions. The subsequent judgment is based on the moral sense that still performs a leading role. In the earlier editions, the presentation of the maxim was followed by a number of mathematical algorithms that, however, are omitted in the fourth edition. Hutcheson states in the preface to the latter that he had left out the mathematical expressions since they "appear'd useless, and were disagreeable to some

17. Hutcheson uses the word *evidence,* for example, in *Inquiry* II. I. § I.

Readers" (4th ed., Preface, p. xxi; see Preface, note 38, in the Textual Notes of the present edition). The term "happiness" is defined as a "natural good." To be sure, the greatest good turns out to be benevolence itself (II. III. § XV) or the "Possession of good moral Qualities" (II. VI. § I). The greatest happiness for Hutcheson cannot be found in wealth and external pleasures, but virtue is "the chief Happiness in the Judgment of all Mankind" (II. VI. § II).

POLITICAL PERSPECTIVES:
HAPPINESS AND LIBERTY

Hutcheson's moral philosophy has a political perspective.[18] This becomes clear in phrases like the "common good" or "public interest" that he uses throughout the *Inquiry*. Especially in its final chapter he treats the basic questions of political order. His main subjects are the corruption of human nature, prudence, rights, and the form of government. The political problem emerges right from the center of Hutcheson's moral philosophy. Since virtue is the highest form of happiness, and virtue is based on benevolence and benevolence in turn on the will, then only people who can exert their will autonomously (in other words, who are free in a political sense) can be happy.[19] Liberty therefore becomes a central political idea. At the same time, liberty can provide difficulties: it may happen that people do not follow the path of virtue.

What shall we do if the moral foundation is weak and if the moral ideas are insufficient? The argument is based on the insight that not all citizens may be virtuous all the time. Although the moral sense and all good reasons may point toward a virtuous life, human nature is open to corruption because men are free. Man is moved by two opposing principles, love and self-love, and is free to follow either. Therefore liberty

18. See Wolfgang Leidhold, *Ethik und Politik bei Francis Hutcheson* (Freiburg, Munich: Alber, 1985), especially chaps. 6–10.

19. See Hutcheson, *A System of Moral Philosophy,* 2 vols. (London, 1755), vol. 1, 102, and his *Synopsis metaphysicae* (1744), II. 2. 3, translated in *Logic, Metaphysics, and the Natural Sociability of Mankind,* ed. James Moore and Michael Silverthorne (Indianapolis: Liberty Fund, 2006), 129–30. On love and free will, see *Ethik und Politik,* 72–125.

and happiness sometimes counteract each other. It is difficult to determine the prevailing motive, benevolence or self-love, particularly in public life (II. III. § XII). The polity therefore can be based not on good intentions but on good results. Government can rest only on *prudence,* not on moral perceptions. The importance of prudence as opposed to moral reflections is typical for both the republican tradition of James Harrington and the Whig tradition, and Hutcheson was close to both.[20] Accordingly, the moral sense must be supplemented by an external motive to "beneficent Actions . . . for the publick Good . . . to counterballance those apparent Motives of Interest." This external motive is "a Law with Sanctions" (II. VII. § I). For Hutcheson the transfer and restriction of liberty therefore is the central question of political order and of the limits of government:

> Men have [the Right] to constitute Civil Government, and to subject their alienable Rights to the Disposal of their Governours, under such Limitations as their Prudence suggests. And as far as the People have subjected their Rights, so far their Governours have an external Right at least, to dispose of them, as their Prudence shall direct, for attaining the Ends of their Institution; and no further. (II. VII. § VIII)

To be acceptable, liberty and its restriction must be in balance with happiness. If a government assumes all rights from its people and neglects the "publick Good of the State" altogether, it is called despotism. For Hutcheson a "Despotick Government" is directly inconsistent with his idea of a civil government (II. VII. § X). With despotism, liberty and happiness are at stake. In such cases, Hutcheson advocates a right of resistance (II. VII. § X). And later on he argued that this is *"When it is that colonies may turn independent."*[21]

Wolfgang Leidhold

---

20. See Caroline Robbins and Charles Blitzer, *An Immortal Commonwealth* (New Haven: Yale University Press, 1960), and J. G. A. Pocock, ed., *The Political Works of James Harrington* (Cambridge: Cambridge University Press, 1977).

21. Hutcheson, *A System of Moral Philosophy,* 2 vols. (Glasgow: Foulis, 1755), vol. 2, 308.

REFERENCES
AND FURTHER READING

Arregni, J. V., and P. Arnau. "Shaftesbury: Father and Critic of Modern Aesthetics." *British Journal of Aesthetics* 34 (1994): 350–62.

Blackstone, William T. *Francis Hutcheson and Contemporary Ethical Theory.* Athens, Ga.: University of Georgia Press, 1965.

Bredvold, Louis J. "The Invention of the Ethical Calculus." In *The Seventeenth Century: Studies in the History of English Thought and Literature from Bacon to Pope,* by Richard Foster Jones and Others, Writing in His Honour, 165–80. Stanford, Calif.: Stanford University Press, 1951.

Campbell, Roy H., and Andrew S. Skinner, eds. *The Origins and Nature of the Scottish Enlightenment.* Edinburgh: J. Donald, 1982.

Carey, Daniel. *Locke, Shaftesbury, and Hutcheson: Contesting Diversity in the Enlightenment and Beyond.* Cambridge: Cambridge University Press, 2006.

Crescenzo, Giovanni de. *Francis Hutcheson e il suo tempo.* Turin: Taylor, 1968.

Cumberland, Richard. *A Treatise of the Law of Nature.* Ed. Jon Parkin. Indianapolis: Liberty Fund, 2005.

Frankena, William K. "Hutcheson's Moral Sense Theory." *Journal of the History of Ideas* 16 (1955): 356–75.

Grean, Stanley. *Shaftesbury's Philosophy of Religion and Ethics: A Study of Enthusiasm.* Athens, Ohio: Ohio University Press, 1967.

Haakonssen, Knud. *Natural Law and Moral Philosophy: From Grotius to the Scottish Enlightenment.* Cambridge: Cambridge University Press, 1996.

Hruschka, Joachim. "The Greatest Happiness Principle and Other Early German Anticipations of Utilitarian Theory." *Utilitas* 3 (1991): 165–77.

Jensen, Henning. *Motivation and the Moral Sense in Francis Hutcheson's Ethical Theory.* The Hague: Nijhoff, 1971.

Jessop, T. E. *Bibliography of David Hume and of Scottish Philosophy.* London: A. Brown and Sons, 1938.

Kail, P. J. E. "Hutcheson's Moral Sense: Realism, Scepticism and Secondary Qualities." *History of Philosophy Quarterly* 18 (2001): 57–77.

Kivy, Peter. *The Seventh Sense: A Study of Francis Hutcheson's Aesthetics and Its Influence in Eighteenth-Century Britain.* 2nd rev. ed. Oxford: Oxford University Press, 2003.

Korsmeyer, Carolyn Wilker. "The Two Beauties: A Perspective on Hutcheson's Aesthetics." *Journal of Aesthetics and Art Criticism* 38 (1979/80): 145–51.

Leidhold, Wolfgang. *Ethik und Politik bei Francis Hutcheson.* Freiburg, Munich: Alber, 1985.

McCosh, James. *The Scottish Philosophy, Biographical, Expository, Critical, from Hutcheson to Hamilton.* London: Macmillan, 1875. Reprint, Hildesheim: Olm, 1966.

Michael, E. "Francis Hutcheson on Aesthetic Perception and Aesthetic Pleasure." *British Journal of Aesthetics* 24 (1984): 241–55.

Moore, James. "The Two Systems of Francis Hutcheson: On the Origins of the Scottish Enlightenment." In *Studies in the Philosophy of the Scottish Enlightenment,* edited by M. A. Stewart, 39–59. Oxford: Oxford University Press, 1990.

———. "Utility and Humanity: The Quest for the *Honestum* in Cicero, Hutcheson and Hume." *Utilitas* 14 (2002): 365–86.

Norton, David Fate. "Francis Hutcheson in America." *Studies on Voltaire and the Eighteenth Century* 154 (1976): 1547–68.

———. "Hutcheson on Perception and Moral Perception." *Archiv für Geschichte der Philosophie* 59, no. 2 (1977): 181–97.

Raphael, David Daiches. *The Moral Sense.* London: Oxford University Press, 1947.

Rendall, Jane, ed. *The Origins of the Scottish Enlightenment 1706–76.* Basingstoke: Macmillan, 1978.

Rivers, Isabel. *Reason, Grace, and Sentiment: A Study of the Language of Religion and Ethics in England 1660–1780.* 2 vols. Cambridge: Cambridge University Press, 1991, 2000.

Robbins, Caroline. *The Eighteenth-Century Commonwealthman.* Indianapolis, Ind.: Liberty Fund, 2004.

———. " 'When It Is That Colonies May Turn Independent': An Analysis of the Environment and Politics of Francis Hutcheson (1694–1746)." *William and Mary Quarterly,* 3rd ser., 11 (1954): 214–51.

Roberts, T. A. *The Concept of Benevolence.* London, Basingstoke: Macmillan, 1973.

Scott, William Robert. *Francis Hutcheson, His Life, Teaching and Position in the History of Philosophy.* Cambridge: Cambridge University Press, 1900. Reprint, New York: A. M. Kelley, 1966.

Sloan, Douglas. *The Scottish Enlightenment and the American College Ideal.* New York: Teachers College Press, 1971.

Stephen, Leslie. *History of English Thought in the Eighteenth Century.* 3rd ed. 2 vols. London: Murray, 1927.

Strasser, M. "Hutcheson on Aesthetic Perception." *Philosophia* 21 (1991/ 1992): 107–18.

Turco, Luigi. "Sympathy and Moral Sense: 1725–1740." *British Journal for the History of Philosophy* 7 (1999): 79–101.

Tuveson, Ernest. "The Origins of the 'Moral Sense.'" *Huntington Library Quarterly* 11 (1947–48): 241–59.

White, Morton. *The Philosophy of the American Revolution.* New York: Oxford University Press, 1978.

NOTE ON THE TEXT

This volume is the revised edition of Hutcheson's *Inquiry into the Original of Beauty and Virtue* prepared for the series Natural Law and Enlightenment Classics. The first edition was sold out by mid-2006. Since then, more variants among the four different editions from the author's lifetime have been discovered, misprints and errata of the first edition have been compiled, and the entire text has been revised and edited anew. In the paragraphs following, an asterisk (*) indicates the additional versions that have now been taken into account.

The Editions

During Hutcheson's lifetime, four different editions of the *Inquiry into the Original of Beauty and Virtue* were published. These editions are chronologically referred to as A, B, C, and D. The texts of B, C, and D not only contain corrections but also introduce alterations and additions by the author. A separate booklet titled *Alterations and Additions* was published in 1726 "by the Author" (i.e., Hutcheson); it is listed below (after A3) by this title. The present edition is based on the second edition (B) from 1726; it presents the variants of the other editions and of the aforementioned *Alterations and Additions* in a critical apparatus. The second edition was chosen for its philosophical relevance. Although the later editions display further additions and corrections, these are mostly of philological importance.

Several *versions* of the first edition (A) and fourth edition (D) exist. In the eighteenth century it was common practice to intervene in the process of printing to correct misprints and to introduce changes. In many cases some copies containing uncorrected sheets or leaves were sold nevertheless. That practice produced at least three versions of the first edition and four versions of the fourth. Arabic numerals are used to mark the variants (A1, A2, A3; D1, D2, D3, D4); whenever all four versions of the fourth edition are identical, they are referred to as D (without an Arabic numeral). So far no additional versions of editions B and C have been discovered.

A1: The first edition was published in London in 1725: "Printed by J. Darby in Bartholomew Close, for Will. and John Smith on the Blind Key in Dublin; and sold by W. and J. Innys at the West End of St. Paul's Churchyard, J. Osborn and T. Longman in Pater-Noster-Row, and S. Chandler in the Poultry."

Copies used for editing A1: (a) University of Aberdeen, Queen Mother Library, shelf mark pi 1929 Hut i; (b) British Library, shelf mark 526.k.22 (reprinted in facsimile as volume 1 of *Collected Works of Francis Hutcheson,* edited by Bernard Fabian, 7 vols., Hildesheim, 1969, 1971; also available as a digital facsimile from Eighteenth Century Collections Online, http://www.gale.com/EighteenthCentury/); (c) University of Oxford, Bodleian Library, shelf mark 8° Z 80 Jur.; (d) Cambridge University Library, Rare Books Department, shelf mark Hh.15.63. Other copies (not seen except for the photocopied title page): (e) University of Birmingham, Main Library, Special Collections, shelf mark Wigan B 1501.I7; (f) University of Glasgow, Special Collection, shelf mark Sp. Coll. 986.[1]

*A2: This version of the first edition was published in London in 1725. It differs from A1 in three instances and from A3 in two: (a) The title page does not display the paragraph referring to Shaftesbury, Mande-

---

1. Referring to the copy of A1 from the British Library as reprinted in the *Collected Works,* ed. B. Fabian (Hildesheim: Olms, 1969, 1971), vol. 1, Thomas Mautner (in Francis Hutcheson, *On Human Nature,* ed. T. Mautner, Cambridge: Cambridge University Press, 1993, p. 170) lists three misprints in the quotation from Cicero on the title page (*factisve* for *factisque; conservandum* for *conservandam; cernerentur* for *cerneretur*). Only the second one of these could be verified. Referring to the copy of A1 from the Bodleian Library at Oxford he lists a missing word (*tanquam*) in the same quotation, which allegedly is displayed in the British Library copy; in fact it is missing in all versions of the first edition. It is introduced with the second edition (B) only.

ville, and the "attempt to introduce a mathematical calculation in sub-
jects of morality" and instead displays the subtitles of the two treatises:
"I. Concerning Beauty, Order, Harmony, Design." and "II. Concerning
Moral Good and Evil." (b) In the last paragraph of the title page the
first names of the printer and the booksellers are printed in full except
for the last one, and one name (T. Longman) is omitted: "Printed by
John Darby in Bartholomew Close, for William and John Smith on the
Blind Key in Dublin; and sold by William and John Innys at the West
End of St. Paul's Churchyard, John Osborn in Pater-Noster-Row, and
Sam. Chandler in the Poultry." (c) Finally, on page 216, line 31 it displays,
as does A3, "appears" instead of the plural "appear": "Our Misery and
Distress appears immediately in our Countenance. . . ."

Copies used for editing *A2: (a) National Library of Scotland, Edinburgh, shelf mark RB.s.916; other copies (not seen except for the photocopied title page and page 216): (b) Warwick University, Special Collections, shelf mark B 1501.16; (c) McGill University Library, Montreal,
Rare Book Division, McLennan Building, shelf mark BJ604 H8 1725.

*A3: This version of the first edition was published in London in 1725.
It differs from A1 in two instances: (a) In the last section of the title page,
containing the names of the printer and the booksellers, the first book-
seller (William and John Smith on the Blind Key in Dublin) is printed
as "WIL." (*one* "L" instead of two): "Printed by J. Darby in Bartholomew
Close, for Wil. and John Smith on the Blind Key in Dublin; and sold
by W. and J. Innys at the West End of St. Paul's Churchyard, J. Osborn
and T. Longman in Pater-Noster-Row, and S. Chandler in the Poultry."
(b) On page 216, line 31 an "appears" is displayed as in A2: "Our Misery
and Distress appears immediately in our Countenance. . . ."

Copies used for editing *A3: (a) University of Aberdeen, Special Libraries and Archives, shelf mark GY 1571 Hut; (b) Yale University, Beinecke Rare Book and Manuscript Library, shelf mark K8 H97 b725;
(c) Harvard University, Houghton Library, Special Collections (facsimile printed by microfilm/xerocopy in 1985 by University Microfilm International, Ann Arbor, Michigan), shelf mark EC7 H9706 725i, facsimile obtained from Staatsbibliothek Preußischer Kulturbesitz, Berlin,
registration number 701276.

Alterations and Additions, Made in the Second Edition of the Inquiry into Beauty and Virtue, by the Author [i.e., Francis Hutcheson], [no place, no printer] 1726 [reprinted in: Francis Hutcheson, *Collected Works,* ed. B. Fabian, pp. 277–308]. Copy used for editing: British Museum, shelf mark 116.i.18.

B: The second edition "corrected and enlarg'd" was published in London in 1726: "Printed for J. Darby, A. Bettesworth, F. Fayram, J. Pemberton, C. Rivington, J. Hooke, F. Clay, J. Batley, and E. Symon."

Copies used for editing B: (a) British Library, shelf mark 8413.b.6 (also available as a digital facsimile from Eighteenth Century Collections Online); (b) Yale University, Beinecke Rare Book and Manuscript Library, shelf mark BJ1005 H88 (reprinted by Garland Publishers, New York, 1971).[2]

C: The third edition "corrected" was published in London in 1729: "Printed for J. and J. Knapton, J. Darby, A. Bettesworth, F. Fayram, J. Pemberton, J. Osborne and T. Longman, C. Rivington, F. Clay, J. Batley, and A. Ward."

Copies used for editing C: (a) British Library, shelf mark 526.k.23 (also available as a digital facsimile from Eighteenth Century Collections Online); (b) Deutsche Zentralbibliothek für Wirtschafts wissenschaften, Kiel (Germany), shelf mark I 14829.

*D1: The first version of the fourth edition was published in London in 1738: "Printed for D. Midwinter, A. Bettesworth, and C. Hitch, J. and J. Pemberton, R. Ware, C. Rivington, F. Clay, A. Ward, J. and P. Knapton, T. Longman, R. Hett, and J. Wood."

Copies used for editing *D1: (a) University of Edinburgh, Main Library, Special Collections, shelf mark D.S.g.1.33; (b) University of Oxford, Bodleian Library, shelf mark Godw. Octavo. 534; (c) Dartmouth College, Hanover, New Hampshire, Baker-Berry Library, shelf mark B1604.H8 1738.

2. The Garland reprint (New York, 1971) of this work reports a *wrong* shelf mark (K8.H97 b726) of Yale University Library as its original source; K8.H97 b726 refers to a copy of the *third* edition (C) of 1729 (both books are located in the Beinecke Rare Book and Manuscript Library).

D2: The second version of the fourth edition was also published in London in 1738: "Printed for D. Midwinter, A. Bettesworth, and C. Hitch, J. and J. Pemberton, R. Ware, C. Rivington, F. Clay, A. Ward, J. and P. Knapton, T. Longman, R. Hett, and J. Wood." While D1 is largely a reset version of C, D2 differs considerably from both. These changes are not exhausted by the "Additions and Corrections &c." and "Small Alterations designed for this Edition" added at the end, after p. 304. At the beginning of this appendix Hutcheson remarks:

> This edition having been inadvertently cast off, before the Author's corrections were obtained, a few sheets have been cancelled where it was necessary, and some few additional paragraphs or notes are here subjoined, with some few corrections of the Expressions referred to their proper pages and lines, where the reader may make a mark.

Since the appendix is not paginated, the pages here are counted consecutively, starting from the last numbered page of the text itself. Textual notes refer to this appendix as Corrigenda and indicate the page number: for example, *D2* [*Corrigenda, p. 310*].

Copies used for editing D2: (a) Princeton University, Rare Books and Special Collections: shelf number (F) 6102.349.11 (the only original copy of D2 identified until now); (b) an unidentified copy of the D2 edition reprinted in 1969 by Gregg International Publishers Limited, Westmead, Farnborough, Hants., in England. The reprint gives no information on the original source; the publisher no longer exists.

D3: The third version of the fourth edition was also published in London in 1738 and "Printed for D. Midwinter, A. Bettesworth, and C. Hitch, J. and J. Pemberton, R. Ware, C. Rivington, F. Clay, A. Ward, J. and P. Knapton, T. Longman, R. Hett, and J. Wood."

Version D3 differs from D2 in several instances: (a) A new sixth article in Treatise II, section 3 was added. (b) After the identical "Additions and Corrections &c.," a paragraph with "Directions to the Bookbinder" was added, stating: "In the Preface, Cancel from p. 15 to the End. In the Work, Cancel from p. 9 to 17. From 29 to 39. From 57 to 59. From 173 to 179. From 185 to 203. From 217 to 223. From 253 to 255. From 287 to 293." (c) In the D3 version the page numbers 179 and 180 are used twice.

Copies used for editing D3: (a) Staatsbibliothek Preußischer Kultur-besitz, Berlin, shelf mark 50MA15122; (b) Universität Bonn, Universi-täts- und Landesbibliothek, shelf mark B 743.

*D4: The fourth version of the fourth edition was also published in London in 1738 and "Printed for D. Midwinter, A. Bettesworth, and C. Hitch, J. and J. Pemberton, R. Ware, C. Rivington, F. Clay, A. Ward, J. and P. Knapton, T. Longman, R. Hett, and J. Wood."

Version D4 differs from all other versions of the fourth edition: (a) From the title page to p. 28 it is identical with D3, (b) from p. 29 to p. 38 with D1, and (c) from p. 39 to the end again with D3. (d) A misprint displayed in D3 on p. 220 (last line: *Maultiplicity*) is corrected (*Multi-plicity*). Because D4 differs from other versions in only these respects, it is not documented separately in the textual notes.

Copy used for editing D4: British Library, shelf mark 8411.m.57 (the only original copy of D4 identified so far; also available as a digital fac-simile from Eighteenth Century Collections Online).

A fifth edition was published posthumously in London in 1753: "Printed for R. Ware, J. and P. Knapton, T. and T. Longman, C. Hitch and L. Hawes, J. Hodges, J. and J. Rivington, and J. Ward." This edition has been found to be a close version of D3. There is no evidence that Hutcheson had any hand in preparing this edition, which appeared six years after his death. Accordingly it has not been documented in the textual notes.

Editorial Intervention in the Main Text

In spelling and punctuation the present edition is based on the text of the second edition, except in cases of obvious misprints, which were silently corrected. Differences in spelling and punctuation displayed in other editions have been annotated on those occasions where, in the judgment of the editor, such variants may be of intellectual relevance. The typography has been standardized and ignores Hutcheson's, or his printer's, liberal use of italics and small capitals. There are no other silent editorial deletions or additions. The page breaks of the second edition are indicated by square brackets [ ]: for example, the text of page 215 begins after [215].

The editor's explanatory notes are marked by lowercase Roman numerals (i, ii, iii, etc.). Textual notes are marked by Arabic numerals. The textual notes state the differences between the text of B and the other editions. In all cases, the editions are cited in the alphanumeric order given above (A1, A2, A3, C, D1, D2, D3), followed by the page and the text. For example, $C(p.\ 2)$, $D(p.\ 2)$: *great* means that in edition C, on page 2, and in edition D, on page 2, a word (or phrase) was changed into *great*. When a new passage was inserted, a single superscript number refers to the note giving the new passage.

When alterations of the text occur, in addition to the Arabic superscript, pairs of double vertical bars indicate the beginning and the end of a passage that was changed. For example, ‖[4] *we enjoy the Delights of Virtue*‖ means that beginning with ‖[4] and ending with ‖ the words "we enjoy the Delights of Virtue" were altered as shown in note 4. In some cases there are changes within changes. Here the Arabic numerals for footnotes are supplemented with lowercase letters to indicate the beginning and the end of the respective variants. For example, ‖[3a] *amiable or disagreeable Ideas of Actions, when they* ‖[4b] *shall*[b]‖ *occur to our Observation*[a]‖ means that one changed passage starts after ‖[3a] and ends at [a]‖ and that another variant affecting only the word "shall" was inserted between ‖[4b] and [b]‖.

ACKNOWLEDGMENTS

First of all I would like to thank Elisabeth Schreiber and Andreas Kamp, who—together with Christine Unrau, Fotios Amanatides, Johannes Clessienne, Hermann Halbeisen, Felix Krafft, Dirk Neumann, and Alexander Scheufens—revised the text and contributed to the task with many hours of research. I am much indebted to Christoph Fehige for his critical remarks and to Thomas Mautner and Luigi Turco (again!), who helped with a lot of information to fill many gaps and to locate additional copies of rare books.

The scientists and staff of the libraries with whom we have worked were extraordinarily helpful. Without their nonbureaucratic help, a timely completion of the revised edition would have been a futile attempt. I would like to express thanks especially to Peter X. Accardo (Harvard University), Polly Armstrong (Stanford University), Anne Bertling (English Seminar, Universität Münster), Patricia Boyd (Edinburgh University), Irene Danks and Eoin Shalloo (National Library of Scotland), June Ellner (University of Aberdeen), Lydia Ferguson (Trinity College Dublin), Helen Ford and Peter Larkin (University of Warwick), Ivana Frian (University of Birmingham), Michelle Gait (University of Aberdeen), Ruth Greenwood (British Library), Helen J. Hills (Cambridge University), Kathryn James (Yale University), Josie Lister and Dunja Sharif (Bodleian Library, Oxford), Robert MacLean (Glasgow University), Raymond L. Marcotte (Dartmouth College), Margaret Sherry Rich (Princeton University), Richard Virr (McGill University, Montreal), Christine Weidlich (Universitätsbibliothek, Bonn), and Christiane Wiese (Staatsbibliothek Preußischer Kulturbesitz, Berlin).

Last but not least, I am very much indebted to Laura Goetz and Knud Haakonssen, who supported our work with great patience and professional advice.

W. L.

AN INQUIRY INTO THE ORIGINAL OF OUR
IDEAS OF BEAUTY AND VIRTUE

An Inquiry into the Original of Our Ideas of Beauty and Virtue;

In Two Treatises.

|| ¹ I. Concerning Beauty, Order, Harmony, Design.
II. Concerning Moral Good and Evil. ||
The Second Edition, Corrected and Enlarg'd.

Itaque eorum ipsorum quae aspectu sentiuntur, nullum
aliud animal pulchritudinem, venustatem, convenientiam
partium sentit. Quam similitudinem natura ratioque ab
oculis ad animum transferens, multo etiam magis
pulchritudinem, constantiam, ordinem in consiliis,
factisque conservandum putat. Quibus ex rebus conflatur &
efficitur id quod quaerimus honestum: Quod etiamsi
nobilitatum non sit, tamen honestum sit: quodque etiamsi à
nullo laudetur, naturâ est laudabile. Formam quidem ipsam
& ||² tanquam|| faciem honesti vides, quae si oculis
cerneretur, mirabiles amores excitaret sapientiae.

—Cic. *de Off.* lib. I. c. 4.ⁱ

London: 1726.

---

i. Translation: "And so no other animal has a sense of beauty, loveliness, harmony
in the visible world; and Nature and Reason, extending the analogy of this from the
world of sense to the world of spirit, find that beauty, consistency, order are far more
to be maintained in thought and deed. It is from these elements that is forged and
fashioned that moral goodness which is the subject of this inquiry—something that,
even though it be not generally ennobled, is still worthy of all honour; and by its own
nature, it merits praise, even though it is praised by none. You see here the very form

To His Excellency, John, Lord Carteret,[ii]
Lord Lieutenant of Ireland.

May it please your Excellency,

When I publish'd these Papers, I had so little Confidence of their Success, that I was unwilling to own them; and [iv] what I was unwilling myself to own, I durst not presume to inscribe to any great Name.

Your Excellency's favourable Reception of them, soon put me out of all Fears about their Success with the wiser and better Part of the World; and since this has given me Assurance to own them, I humbly presume to inscribe them in this second Edition to your Excellency, that I may have at once an Opportunity of expressing the sincerest Gratitude for the Notice you were pleas'd to take of me, and have the Pleasure also of letting the [v] World know that this small Work has your Excellency's Approbation.

The Praise bestow'd by Persons of real Merit and Discernment, is allow'd by all to give a noble and rational Pleasure. Your Excellency first made me feel this in the most lively manner; and it will be a Pleasure as lasting as it is great: 'twill ever be matter of the highest Joy and Satisfaction to me, that I am Author of a Book my Lord Carteret approves.

I know, my Lord, that much of your Commendation [vi] is to be attributed to your own Humanity: you can entirely approve the Works of those alone, who can think and speak on these Subjects as justly as

---

and as it were the face of Moral Goodness; and if it could be seen with the physical eye, it would awaken a marvellous love of wisdom." Cicero, *De officiis,* trans. Walter Miller, Loeb Classical Library (Cambridge, Mass.: Harvard University Press, 1975), 14–17.

ii. John Carteret, First Earl Granville (1690–1763), English orator, diplomat, and statesman, member of the House of Lords since 1711, Lord Lieutenant of Ireland 1724–30.

your self; and that is what few, if any, even of those who spend their Lives in such Contemplations, are able to do. In the Conversation, with which your Excellency has been pleas'd to honour me, I could not, I own, without the utmost surprize, observe so intimate an Acquaintance with the most valuable Writings of contemplative Men, Antient, and Modern; so just a Taste of what is excellent in the ingenious Arts, [vii] in so young a man, amidst the Hurry of an active Life. Forgive me, my Lord, that ‖⁴I‖ mention this part of your Character: 'tis so uncommon that it deserves the highest Admiration; and 'tis the only one which an obscure Philosopher, who has receiv'd the greatest Obligations from your Excellency, can with any Propriety take notice of.

Those other great Endowments which have enabled you, even in Youth, to discharge the most difficult Employments, with the highest Honour to your self, and Advantage to your Country, I dare not presume to de-[viii]scribe. He who attempts to do Justice to so great and good a Character, ought himself to be one of uncommon Merit and Distinction: and yet the ablest Panegyrist would find it difficult to add any thing to your Excellency's Fame. The Voices of Nations proclaim your Worth. I am,

> May it please your Excellency,
>> Your most obliged,
>>> Most obedient, and
>>>> Most devoted humble Servant,

Dublin,
June 19.
1725.

> Francis Hutcheson. [ix]

THE PREFACE

There is no part of Philosophy of more importance, than a just Knowledge of Human Nature, and its various Powers and Dispositions. Our late Inquirys have been very much employ'd about our Understanding, and the several Methods of obtaining Truth. We generally acknowledge, that the Importance of any Truth is nothing else than its Moment, or Efficacy to make Men happy, or to give them the greatest and most lasting Pleasure; and Wisdom denotes only a Capacity of pursuing this End by the best Means. It must surely then be of the greatest importance, [x] to have distinct Conceptions of this End it self, as well as of the Means necessary to obtain it; that we may find out which are the greatest and most lasting Pleasures, and not employ our Reason, after all our laborious Improvements of it, in trifling Pursuits. It is to be fear'd indeed, that most of our Studys, without this Inquiry, will be of very little use to us; for they seem to have scarce any other tendency than to lead us into speculative Knowledge it self. Nor are we distinctly told how it is that Knowledge, or Truth is pleasant to us.

This Consideration ‖5put‖ the Author of the following Papers ‖6upon‖ inquiring into the various Pleasures which Human nature is capable of receiving. We shall generally find in our modern philosophick Writings, nothing ‖7further‖ on this Head, than some bare Division of them into Sensible, and Rational, and some trite [xi] Common-place Arguments to prove the ‖8latter more‖ valuable than the former. Our sensible Pleasures are slightly pass'd over, and explain'd only by some Instances in Tastes, Smells, Sounds, or such like, which Men of any tolerable Reflection generally look upon as very trifling Satisfactions. Our rational Pleasures have had much the same kind of treatment. We are seldom taught any other Notion of rational Pleasure than that which we have upon reflecting on our Possession, or Claim to those Objects, which may be Occasions of Pleasure. Such Objects we call advantageous; but Advantage, or Interest, cannot be distinctly conceiv'd, till we know what ||⁹those|| Pleasures are which advantageous Objects are apt to excite; and what Senses or Powers of Perception we have ||¹⁰with respect to|| such Objects. We may perhaps ||¹¹find|| such an Inquiry of more importance in Morals, to prove what we call the Reality of Virtue, or [xii] that it is the surest Happiness of the Agent, than one would at first imagine.

In reflecting upon our external Senses, we plainly see, that our Perceptions of Pleasure, or Pain, do not depend directly on our Will. Objects do not please us, according as we incline they should. The presence of some Objects necessarily pleases us, and the presence of others as necessarily displeases us. Nor can we by our Will, any otherwise procure Pleasure, or avoid Pain, than by procuring the former kind of Objects, and avoiding the latter. By the very Frame of our Nature the one is made the occasion of Delight, and the other of Dissatisfaction.

The same Observation will hold in all our other Pleasures and Pains. For there are many other sorts of Objects, which please, or displease us as necessarily, as material Objects [xiii] do when they operate upon our Organs of Sense. There ||¹²is scarcely any Object which our Minds are employ'd about, which is|| not thus constituted the necessary occasion of some Pleasure or Pain. Thus we ||¹³find|| our selves pleas'd with a regular Form, a piece of Architecture or Painting, a Composition of Notes, a Theorem, an Action, an Affection, a Character. And we are conscious that this Pleasure necessarily arises from the Contemplation of the Idea, which is then present to our Minds, with all its Circumstances, although some of these Ideas have nothing of what we ||¹⁴call|| sensible Perception in them; and in those which have, the Pleasure arises from some Uniformity, Order, Arrangement, Imitation; and not from the simple Ideas of Colour, or Sound, or mode of Extension separately consider'd.

These Determinations to be pleas'd with ||¹⁵any Forms, or Ideas [xiv] which occur to our Observation,|| the Author chuses to call Senses; distinguishing them from the Powers which commonly go by that Name, by calling our Power of perceiving the Beauty of Regularity, Order, Harmony, an Internal Sense; and that Determination to ||[16]be pleas'd with the Contemplation of those|| Affections, Actions, or Characters of rational Agents, which we call virtuous, he marks by the name of a Moral Sense.

His principal Design is to shew, "That Human Nature was not left quite indifferent in the affair of Virtue, to form to it self Observations concerning the Advantage, or Disadvantage of Actions, and accordingly to regulate its Conduct." The weakness of our Reason, and the avocations arising from the ||[17]Infirmity|| and Necessitys of our Nature, are so great, that very few ||[18]Men could ever have|| form'd those [xv] long Deductions of Reason, which ||[19]shew|| some Actions to be in the whole advantageous to the Agent, and their Contrarys pernicious. The Author of Nature has much better furnish'd us for a virtuous Conduct, than ||[20]our|| Moralists seem to imagine, by almost as quick and powerful Instructions, as we have for the preservation of our Bodys. ||[21]He has made Virtue a lovely Form, to excite our pursuit of it; and has given us strong Affections to be the Springs of each virtuous Action.||

This moral Sense of Beauty in Actions and Affections, may appear strange at first View. Some of our Moralists themselves are offended at it in my Lord Shaftesbury,[iii] so much ||[22]are they|| accustom'd to deduce every Approbation, or Aversion, from rational Views of ||[23]Interest||, (except it be merely in the simple Ideas of the external Senses) and have such a Horror at innate Ideas, [xvi] which they imagine this borders upon. But this moral Sense has no relation to innate Ideas, as will appear in the second Treatise. [24]Our Gentlemen of good Taste can tell us of a great many Senses, Tastes, and Relishes for Beauty, Harmony, Imitation in Painting and Poetry; and may not we find too in Mankind a Relish for a Beauty in Characters, in Manners? ||[25a]I doubt we have made Phi-

---

iii. Anthony Ashley Cooper, Third Earl of Shaftesbury (1671–1713), was educated under the supervision of John Locke but was not a follower of his philosophy. Hutcheson used the collection of Shaftesbury's works in *Characteristicks of Men, Manners, Opinions, Times,* 3 vols. (London, 1711). According to the subtitle of the first edition of the *Inquiry* (see note 1 on the title page), Hutcheson's intention was to defend Shaftesbury's views against Mandeville's *Fable of the Bees.*

losophy, as well as Religion, by our foolish management of it, so austere and ungainly a Form, that a Gentleman cannot easily bring himself to like it; and those who are Strangers to it, can scarcely bear to hear our Description of it. So much ||²⁶ᵇit isᵇ|| changed from what was once the delight of the finest Gentlemen among the Antients, and their Recreation after the Hurry of publick Affairs!ᵃ||

In the first Treatise, the Author perhaps in some Instances has gone too far, in supposing a greater Agree-[xvii]ment of Mankind in their Sense of Beauty, than Experience ||²⁷will|| confirm; but all he is solicitous about is to shew, "That there is some Sense of Beauty natural to Men; ||²⁸that we find|| as great an Agreement of Men in their Relishes of Forms, as in their external Senses which all agree to be natural; and that Pleasure or Pain, Delight or Aversion, are naturally join'd to their Perceptions." If the Reader be convinc'd of ||²⁹such Determinations of the Mind to be pleas'd with Forms, Proportions, Resemblances, Theorems,|| it will be no difficult matter to apprehend another superior Sense, natural ||³⁰also|| to Men, determining them to be pleas'd with Actions, Characters, Affections. This is the moral Sense, which makes the Subject of the second Treatise.

The proper Occasions of Perception by the external Senses, occur to us as soon as we come into the [xviii] World; ||³¹whence|| perhaps we easily look upon these Senses to be natural: but the Objects of the superior Senses of Beauty and Virtue generally do not. It is probably some little time before Children ||³²reflect||, or at least let us know that they reflect upon Proportion and Similitude; upon Affections, Characters, Tempers; or come to know the external Actions which are Evidences of them. ||³³Hence|| we imagine that their Sense of Beauty, and their moral Sentiments of Actions, must be entirely owing to Instruction, and Education; whereas it ||³⁴is as|| easy to conceive, how a Character, a Temper, as soon as they are observ'd, may be constituted by Nature the necessary occasion of Pleasure, or an Object of Approbation, as a Taste or a Sound; ||³⁵tho it be sometime before these Objects present themselves to our Observation.|| [xix]

||³⁶The first Impression of these Papers was so well receiv'd, that the Author hopes it will be no offence to any who are concern'd in the Mem-

ory of the late Lord Viscount Molesworth,[iv] if he lets his Readers know that he was the Noble Person mention'd in the Preface to the first Edition, and that their being published was owing to his Approbation of them. It was from him he had that shreud Objection, which the Reader may find in the first Treatise;* besides many other Remarks in the frequent Conversations with which he honour'd the Author; by which that Treatise was very much improved beyond what it was in the Draught presented to him. The Author retains the most grateful Sense of his singular Civilitys, and of the Pleasure and Improvement he received in his Conver-[xx]sation; and is still fond of expressing his grateful Remembrance of him: but,

Id cinerem, & Manes credas curare sepultos.[v]

To be concern'd in this Book can be no honour to a Person so justly celebrated for the most generous Sentiments of Virtue and Religion, deliver'd with the most manly Eloquence: yet it would not be just toward the World, should the Author conceal his Obligations to the Reverend Mr. Edward Syng;[vi] not only for revising these Papers, when they stood in great need of an accurate Review, but for suggesting several just Amendments in the general Scheme of Morality. The Author was much

---

iv. Robert Molesworth, a wealthy Irish merchant, politician, diplomat, and author (1656–1725), with short interruptions a member of both the English and Irish Parliaments for about thirty years. He was one of the most prominent radical Whigs of his time. At the end of 1722 Molesworth retired to Dublin, where he founded a philosophical and literary circle. Hutcheson was a member of the group.

* Sect. v. Art. 2. the last Paragraph.

v. Translation: "Thinkest thou that dust or buried shades give heed to that?" Virgil, *Aeneid,* bk. 4, l. 34, in *Eclogues, Georgics, Aeneid I–VI,* trans. H. Rushton Fairclough, revised ed., Loeb Classical Library (Cambridge, Mass.: Harvard University Press, 1935).

vi. Edward Synge (1692/94?–1762) was successively bishop of Clonfert, Cloyne, Firns, and Elphin. He was a friend of Berkeley and probably a member of Molesworth's circle in Dublin, where a lasting friendship with Hutcheson developed. Hutcheson's son dedicated his father's posthumous *System of Moral Philosophy* (London, 1755) to Bishop Synge. As Synge demonstrated in a sermon from 25 October 1725 (the anniversary of the Irish rebellion), later published as *The Case of Toleration,* he was a liberal and tolerant Anglican.

confirm'd in his Opinion of the Justness of these Thoughts, upon find-
ing, that this Gentleman had fallen into the same way of thinking before
him; and will ever look upon his Friendship [xxi] as one of the greatest
Advantages and Pleasures of his Life.

To recommend the Lord Shaftesbury's Writings to the World, is a
very needless Attempt. They will be esteemed while any Reflection remains among Men. It is indeed to be wished, that he had abstained from
mixing with such Noble Performances, some Prejudices he had receiv'd
against Christianity; a Religion which gives us the truest Idea of Virtue,
and recommends the Love of God, and of Mankind, as the Sum of all
true Religion. How would it have moved the Indignation of that ingenious Nobleman, to have found a dissolute set of Men, who relish
nothing in Life but the lowest and most sordid Pleasures, searching into
his Writings for those Insinuations against Christianity, that they might
be the less restrained from their Debaucherys; when at the same time
their low Minds are [xxii] incapable of relishing those noble Sentiments
of Virtue and Honour, which he has placed in so lovely a Light!‖

Whatever Faults the Ingenious may find with ‖³⁷this Performance,
the Author‖ hopes no body will find any thing in it contrary to Religion
or good Manners: and he shall be well pleased if he gives the learned
World an occasion of examining more thorowly these Subjects, which
are, he presumes, of very considerable Importance. The chief Ground
of his Assurance that his Opinions in the main are just, is this, That as
he took the first Hints of them from some of the greatest Writers of
Antiquity,ᵛⁱⁱ so the more he has convers'd with them, he finds his Illustrations the more conformable to their Sentiments.

‖³⁸In the former Edition of this Book there were some Mistakes in
one or two of the Instances borrowed [xxiii] from other Sciences, to a

---

vii. Hutcheson was familiar with Plato, Aristotle, Cicero, and probably with
Plotinus. See the quotation from Cicero on the title page (from *De officiis,* book 1,
§§ 14, 15). Also see Plato on the perception of beauty in *Phaedrus* (250d) and Aristotle's *Nicomachean Ethics,* II, 9 (1109b, 20–26) and III, 6 (1113a, 23–35) as well as
Politics, I, 11 (1253a, 16–19). On this topic, see E. H. Olmsted, "The 'Moral Sense'
Aspects of Aristotle's Ethical Theory," *American Journal of Philology* 69 (1948): 42–
61. See Plotinus, *On Beauty* (Ennead I. 6).

perfect Knowledge of which the Author does not pretend; nor would he now undertake that this Edition is every way faultless. He hopes that those who are studious of the true measures of Life, may find his Ideas of Virtue and Happiness tolerably just; and that the profound Connoisseurs will pardon a few Faults, in the Illustrations borrow'd from their Arts, upon which his Arguments do not depend.‖ [xxiv]

THE CONTENTS[i]

i. The page numbers used in the Contents are those of the present Liberty Fund
edition.

15

TREATISE II

∞ ‖[1]TREATISE I ∞

viz.

An Inquiry Concerning Beauty, Order, &c.[1]‖

An Inquiry ||²Concerning Beauty, Order, &c.||

⋙ SECTION I ⋘

*Concerning some Powers of Perception, distinct
from what is generally understood by Sensation.*

To make the following Observations understood, it may be necessary to premise some Definitions, and Observations, either universally acknowledg'd, or sufficiently prov'd by many Writers both ancient and modern, concerning our Perceptions called Sensations, and the Actions of the Mind consequent upon them.

Art. ||³I||. Those Ideas ||⁴which|| are rais'd in the Mind upon the presence ||⁵ Sensation.|| of external Ob-[2]jects, and their acting upon our Bodys, are call'd Sensations. We find that the Mind in such Cases is passive, and has not Power directly to prevent the Perception or Idea, or to vary it at its Reception, as long as we continue our Bodys in a state fit to be acted upon by the external Object.

II. When two Perceptions are entirely different from each other, or agree   Different in nothing but the general Idea of Sensation, we call the Powers of re-   Senses. ceiving those different Perceptions, different Senses. Thus Seeing and Hearing denote the different Powers of receiving the Ideas of Colours and Sounds. And altho Colours have ||⁶vast|| Differences among themselves, as also have Sounds; yet there is a greater Agreement among the most opposite Colours, than between any Colour and a Sound: Hence we call all Colours Perceptions of the same Sense. All the several Senses seem to have their distinct Organs, except Feeling, which is in some degree diffus'd over the whole Body.

The Mind how active. III. The Mind has a Power of compounding Ideas, ||⁷which|| were receiv'd separately; of comparing ||⁸their|| Objects by means of the Ideas, and of observing their Relations and Proportions; of enlarging and diminishing its Ideas at pleasure, or in any certain Ratio, or Degree; and of considering separately [3] each of the simple Ideas, which might perhaps have been impress'd jointly in the Sensation. This last Operation we commonly call Abstraction.

Substances. IV. The Ideas of ||⁹Substances|| are compounded of the various simple Ideas jointly impress'd, when they presented themselves to our Senses. We define Substances only by enumerating these sensible Ideas: And such Definitions may ||¹⁰raise an Idea clear enough|| of the Substance in the Mind of one who never immediately perceiv'd the Substance; provided he has separately receiv'd by his Senses all the simple Ideas ||¹¹which|| are in the Composition of the complex one of the Substance defin'd: But if ||¹²there be any simple Ideas which he has not receiv'd, or if he wants any of the Senses necessary for the Perception of them, no Definition can raise any simple Idea which has not been before perceived by the Senses.||

Education. Instruction. V. ¹³ Hence it follows, "That when Instruction, Education, or Prejudice of any kind, raise any Desire or Aversion toward an Object, this Desire or Aversion must be founded upon an Opinion of some Perfection, or of some Deficiency in those Qualitys, for Perception of which we have the proper Senses." Thus if Beauty be desir'd by one who has not the Sense of Sight, the Desire must be rais'd by some [4] apprehended Regularity of Figure, Sweetness of Voice, Smoothness, or Softness, or some other Quality perceivable by the other Senses, without relation to the Ideas of Colour.

Pleasure. Pain. VI. Many of our sensitive Perceptions are pleasant, and many painful, immediately, and that without any knowledge of the Cause of this Pleasure or Pain, or how the Objects excite it, or are the Occasions of it; or without seeing to what further Advantage or Detriment the Use of such Objects might tend: Nor would the most accurate Knowledge of these things vary either the Pleasure or Pain of the Perception, however it might give a rational Pleasure distinct from the sensible; or might raise a distinct Joy, from ||[14]a|| prospect of further Advantage in the Object, or Aversion, from ||[15]an|| apprehension of Evil.

VII. The ||[16]simple|| Ideas rais'd in different Persons by the same Object, are probably ||[17]some way|| different, when they disagree in their Approbation or Dislike; and in the same Person, when his Fancy at one time differs from what it was at another. This will appear from reflecting on those Objects, to which we have now an Aversion, tho they were formerly agreeable: And we shall generally find that there is some accidental Conjunction of a disagreeable Idea, [5] which always recurs with the Object; as in those Wines ||[18]to|| which Men acquire an ||[19]Aversion||, after they have taken them in an Emetick Preparation: ||[20]In this case|| we are conscious that the Idea is alter'd from what it was when that Wine was agreeable, by the Conjunction of the Ideas of Loathing and Sickness of Stomach. The like Change of Idea may be insensibly made by the Change of our Bodys, as we advance in Years, ||[21]or when we are accustomed to any Object,|| which may occasion an Indifference ||[22]toward|| Meats we were fond of in our Childhood||[23a]; and may make some Objects cease to raise the disagreeable Ideas, which they excited upon our first use of them. ||[24b]Many of our simple Perceptions are disagreeable only thro the too great Intenseness of the Quality: thus moderate Light is agreeable, very strong Light may be painful; moderate Bitter may be pleasant, a higher Degree may be offensive. A Change in our Organs will necessarily occasion a Change in the Intenseness of the Perception at least; nay sometimes will occasion a quite contrary Perception: Thus a warm Hand shall feel that Water cold, which a cold hand ||[25c]shall[c]|| feel warm[ab]||.

We shall not find it perhaps so easy to account for the Diversity of Fancy ||[26a]about more complex Ideas of Objects, ||[27b]in which we regard[b]|| many Ideas of different Senses at [6] once; as ||[28c]in[c]|| some Perceptions of those call'd primary Qualitys, and some secondary, as ex-

Different
Ideas.

plain'd by Mr. Locke:[i] for instance, in the different Fancys about
Architecture, Gardening, Dress. Of the two former we shall offer something in Sect. VI. As to Dress, we may generally account for the Diversity
of Fancys from a like Conjunction of Ideas: Thus[a]||, if either from any
thing in Nature, or from the Opinion of our Country or Acquaintance,
the fancying of glaring Colours be look'd upon as an evidence of Levity,
or of any other evil Quality of Mind; or if any Colour or Fashion be
commonly us'd by Rusticks, or by Men of any disagreeable Profession,
Employment, or Temper; these additional Ideas may recur constantly
with that of the Colour or Fashion, and cause a constant Dislike to them
in those who join the additional Ideas, altho the Colour or Form be no
way disagreeable of themselves, and actually do please others who join
no such Ideas to them. But there ||[29]does not seem to be any|| Ground
to believe such a Diversity in human Minds, as that the same ||[30]simple||
Idea or Perception should give pleasure to one and pain to another, or
to the same Person at different times; not to say that it seems a Contra-
diction, that the same ||[31]simple|| Idea should do so. [7]

Complex
Ideas.   VIII. The only Pleasure of Sense, ||[32]which|| ||[33]our|| Philosophers seem
to consider, is that which accompanys the simple Ideas of Sensation: But
there are ||[34]vastly|| greater Pleasures in those complex Ideas of Objects,
which obtain the Names of Beautiful, Regular, Harmonious. Thus every
one acknowledges he is more delighted with a fine Face, a just Picture,
than with the View of any one Colour, were it as strong and lively as
possible; and more pleas'd with a Prospect of the Sun ||[35]arising|| among
settled Clouds, and colouring their Edges, with a starry Hemisphere, a
fine Landskip, a regular Building, than with a clear blue Sky, a smooth
Sea, or a large open Plain, not diversify'd by Woods, Hills, Waters, Buildings: And yet even these latter Appearances are not quite simple. So in
Musick, the Pleasure of fine Composition is incomparably greater than
that of any one Note, how sweet, full, or swelling soever.

----

i. John Locke (1632–1704) developed the theory of simple and complex ideas, and
of primary and secondary qualities in *An Essay Concerning Human Understanding*
(London, 1690), bk. 2, "Of Ideas," and bk. 4, "Of Knowledge and Opinion."

IX. Let it be observ'd, that in the following Papers, the Word Beauty is **Beauty.** taken for the Idea rais'd in us, and a Sense of Beauty for our Power of receiving this Idea. Harmony also denotes our pleasant Ideas arising **Harmony.** from Composition of Sounds, and a good Ear (as it is generally taken) a Power of perceiving this Pleasure. In the following Sections, an Attempt is made [8] to discover "what is the immediate Occasion of these pleasant Ideas, or what real Quality in the Objects ordinarily excites them."

X. It is of no consequence whether we call these Ideas of Beauty and **Internal Sense.** Harmony, Perceptions of the External Senses of Seeing and Hearing, or not. I should rather chuse to call our Power of perceiving these Ideas, an Internal Sense, were it only for the Convenience of distinguishing them from other Sensations of Seeing and Hearing, which men may have without Perception of Beauty and Harmony. It is plain from Experience, that many Men have in the common meaning, the Senses of Seeing and Hearing perfect enough; they perceive all the simple Ideas separately, and have their Pleasures; they distinguish them from each other, such as one Colour from another, either quite different, or the stronger or fainter of the same Colour, ||^{36}when they are plac'd beside each other, altho they may often confound their Names, when they occur a-part from each other; as some do the Names of Green and Blue:|| they can tell in separate Notes, the higher, lower, sharper or flatter, when separately sounded; in Figures they discern the Length, Breadth, Wideness of each Line, Surface, Angle; and may be as capable of hearing and seeing at great distances as any men [9] whatsoever: And yet perhaps they shall ||^{37}find|| no Pleasure in Musical Compositions, in Painting, Architecture, natural Landskip; or but a very weak one in comparison of what others enjoy from the same Objects. This greater Capacity of receiving such pleasant Ideas we commonly call a fine Genius or Taste: In Musick we seem universally to acknowledge something like a distinct Sense from the External one of Hearing, and call it a good Ear; and the like distinction we ||^{38}should|| probably acknowledge in other ||^{39}Objects||, had we also got distinct Names to denote these Powers of Perception by.

XI. [40] There will appear another Reason perhaps ||[41] afterwards||, for call-
ing this Power of perceiving the Ideas of Beauty, an Internal Sense, from
this, that in some other Affairs, where our External Senses are not much
concern'd, we discern a sort of Beauty, very like, in many respects, to
that observ'd in sensible Objects, and accompany'd with like Pleasure:
Such is that Beauty perceiv'd in Theorems, or universal Truths, in general Causes, and in some extensive Principles of Action.

XII. Let ||[42a] every one here consider, how different we must suppose the
Perception to be, with which a Poet is transported upon the Prospect of
any of those Objects [10] of natural Beauty, which ravish us even in his
Description; from that cold lifeless Conception which we ||[43b] imagine
in[b]|| a dull Critick, or one of the Virtuosi, without what we call a fine
Taste. This latter Class of Men may have greater Perfection in that
Knowledge, which is deriv'd from external Sensation; they can tell all
the specifick Differences of Trees, Herbs, Minerals, Metals; they know
the Form of every Leaf, Stalk, Root, Flower, and Seed of all the Species,
about which the Poet is often very ignorant: And yet the Poet shall have
a ||[44c] vastly[c]|| more delightful Perception of the Whole; and not only the
Poet but any man of a fine Taste. Our External ||[45d] Senses[d]|| may by
measuring teach us all the Proportions of Architecture to the Tenth of
an Inch, and the Situation of every Muscle in the human Body; and a
good Memory may retain these: and yet there is still something further
necessary, not only to make ||[46e] a man[e]|| a compleat Master in Architec-
ture, Painting or Statuary, but even a tolerable Judge in these Works; or
||[47f] capable of receiving[f]|| the highest Pleasure in contemplating them. [a]||
Since then there are such different Powers of Perception, where what
are commonly called the External Senses are the same; since the most
accurate Knowledge of what the External Senses discover, ||[48] often does||
not give the Pleasure of Beauty or Harmony, which yet one of a good
Taste will en-[11]joy at once without much Knowledge; we may justly
use another Name for these higher, and more delightful Perceptions of
Beauty and Harmony, and call the Power of receiving such Impressions,
an Internal Sense. The Difference of the Perceptions seems sufficient to
vindicate the Use of a different Name, ||[49] especially when we are told in
what meaning the Word is applied.||

XIII. [50] This superior Power of Perception is justly called a Sense, because of its Affinity to the other Senses in this, that the Pleasure ||[51]does not arise|| from any Knowledge of Principles, Proportions, Causes, or of the Usefulness of the Object; ||[52]but strikes us at first with the Idea of|| Beauty: nor does the most accurate Knowledge increase this Pleasure of Beauty, however it[53] may super-add a distinct rational Pleasure from prospects of Advantage, or ||[54]from|| the Increase of Knowledge.*

Its Pleasures necessary and immediate.

XIV. [55] And further, the Ideas of Beauty and Harmony, like other sensible Ideas, are necessarily pleasant to us, as well as immediately so; neither can any Resolution of our own, nor any Prospect of Advantage or Disadvantage, vary the Beauty or Deformity of an Object: For as in the external Sensations, no View of Interest will [12] make an Object grateful, nor ||[56]View of|| Detriment, distinct from immediate Pain in the Perception, make it disagreeable to the Sense; so propose the whole World as a Reward, or threaten the greatest Evil, to make us approve a deform'd Object, or disapprove a beautiful one; Dissimulation may be procur'd by Rewards or Threatnings, or we may in external Conduct abstain from any pursuit of the Beautiful, and pursue the Deform'd; but our Sentiments of the Forms, and our Perceptions, would continue invariably the same.

XV. [57] Hence it plainly appears, "that some Objects are immediately the Occasions of this Pleasure of Beauty, and that we have Senses fitted for perceiving it; and that it is distinct from that Joy which arises ||[58]from Self-love|| upon Prospect of Advantage." Nay, do not we often see Convenience and Use neglected to obtain Beauty, without any other prospect of Advantage in the Beautiful Form, than the suggesting the pleasant Ideas of Beauty? Now this shews us, that however we may pursue beautiful Objects from Self-love, with a view to obtain the Pleasures of Beauty, as in Architecture, Gardening, and many other Affairs; yet there must be a Sense of Beauty, antecedent to Prospects ||[59]even of|| this Advantage, without which Sense, these Objects would not be thus [13] Advantageous, nor excite in us this Pleasure which constitutes them ad-

This Sense antecedent to and distinct from prospects of interest.

* See above, Art. 6.

vantageous. Our Sense of Beauty from Objects, by which they are constituted good to us, is very distinct from our Desire of them when they
are thus constituted: Our Desire of Beauty may be counter-ballanc'd
by Rewards or Threatnings, but never our Sense of it; even as Fear of
Death, ||⁶⁰or Love of Life,|| may make us ||⁶¹chuse and|| desire a bitter
Potion, or neglect those Meats which the Sense of Taste would rec-
ommend as pleasant; ||⁶²and yet no prospect of Advantage, or Fear of
Evil, can|| make that Potion agreeable to the Sense, or ||⁶³Meat|| dis-
agreeable to it, ||⁶⁴which was|| not so antecedently to this Prospect.
||⁶⁵Just in the same manner as to|| the Sense of Beauty and Harmony;
that the Pursuit of such Objects is frequently neglected, from prospects
of Advantage, Aversion to Labour, or any other Motive of ||⁶⁶Self-love||,
does not prove that we have no Sense of Beauty, but only that our Desire
of it may be counter-ballanc'd by a stronger Desire||⁶⁷: So Gold out-
weighing Silver, is never adduc'd as a proof that the latter is void of
Gravity||.

XVI.⁶⁸ Had we no such Sense of Beauty and Harmony; Houses, Gardens, Dress, Equipage, might have been recommended to us as conve-
nient, fruitful, warm, easy; but never as beautiful: ||⁶⁹ᵃAnd in Faces I see
no-[14]thing ||⁷⁰ᵇwhichᵇ|| could please us, but Liveliness of Colour, and
Smoothness of Surface:ᵃ|| And yet nothing is more certain, than that all
these Objects are recommended under quite different Views on many
Occasions: ||⁷¹And no Custom, Education, or Example could ever|| give
us Perceptions distinct from those of the Senses which we had the use
of before, or recommend Objects under another Conception than grateful to* them. But of the Influence of Custom, Education, Example,
upon the Sense of Beauty, we shall treat below.†

Beauty,
Original or
Comparative.

||⁷³XVII.|| ||⁷⁴Beauty|| is either Original or Comparative; or, if any like
the Terms better, Absolute, or Relative: Only let it be ||⁷⁵observ'd||, that
by Absolute or Original Beauty, is not understood any Quality suppos'd

---

* See Art. ||⁷²5||.
† Sect. 7.

to be in the Object, ||⁷⁶which|| should of itself be beautiful, without relation to any Mind which perceives it: For Beauty, like other Names of sensible Ideas, properly denotes the Perception of some Mind; so Cold, ||⁷⁷Hot||, Sweet, Bitter, denote the Sensations in our Minds, to which perhaps there is no resemblance in the Objects, ||⁷⁸which|| excite these Ideas in us, however we generally imagine ||⁷⁹that there is something in the Object just like our Perception||. The Ideas of Beauty and [15] Harmony being excited upon our Perception of some primary Quality, and having relation to Figure and Time, may indeed have a nearer resemblance to Objects, than these Sensations, ||⁸⁰which|| seem not so much any Pictures of Objects, as Modifications of the perceiving Mind; and yet were there no Mind with a Sense of Beauty to contemplate Objects, I see not how they could be call'd beautiful. We therefore by* Absolute Beauty understand only that Beauty, which we perceive in Objects without comparison to any thing external, of which the Object is suppos'd an Imitation, or Picture; such as that Beauty perceiv'd from the Works of Nature, artificial Forms, Figures||⁸², Theorems||. Comparative or Relative Beauty is that which we perceive in Objects, commonly considered as Imitations or Resemblances of something else. These two Kinds of Beauty employ the three following Sections. [16]

---

* This division of Beauty is taken from the different Foundations of ||⁸¹Pleasure|| to our Sense of it, rather than from the Objects themselves: for most of the following Instances of relative Beauty have also absolute Beauty; and many of the Instances of absolute Beauty, have also relative Beauty in some respect or other. But we may distinctly consider these two Fountains of Pleasure, Uniformity in the Object it self, and Resemblance to some Original.

Of Original or Absolute Beauty.

Sense of Men. I. Since it is certain that we have Ideas of Beauty and Harmony, let us examine what Quality in Objects excites these Ideas, or is the occasion of them. And let it be here observ'd, that our Inquiry is only about the Qualitys ||¹which|| are beautiful to Men; or about the Foundation of their Sense of Beauty: for, as was above hinted, Beauty has always relation to the Sense of some Mind; and when we afterwards shew how generally the Objects ||²which|| occur to us, are beautiful, we mean ||³that such Objects are|| agreeable to the Sense of Men: ||⁴for as there are not a few|| Objects, which seem no way beautiful to Men, ||⁵so we see a variety of|| other Animals ||⁶who|| seem delighted with them; they may have Senses otherwise constituted than those of Men, and may have the Ideas of Beauty excited by Objects of a quite different Form. We see Animals fitted for every Place; and what to Men appears rude and shapeless, or loathsom, may be to them a Paradise.

II. That we may more distinctly discover the general Foundation or Occasion of [17] the Ideas of Beauty among Men, it will be necessary to consider it first in its simpler Kinds, such as occurs to us in regular Figures; and we may perhaps find that the same Foundation extends to all the more complex Species of it.

Uniformity with Variety. III. The Figures ||⁷which|| excite in us the Ideas of Beauty, seem to be those in which there is Uniformity amidst Variety. There are many Conceptions of Objects ||⁸which|| are agreeable upon other accounts, such

28

as Grandeur, Novelty, Sanctity, and some others, ||⁹which shall be mention'd hereafter.*|| But what we call Beautiful in Objects, to speak in the Mathematical Style, seems to be in a compound Ratio of Uniformity and Variety: so that where the Uniformity of Bodys is equal, the Beauty is as the Variety; and where the Variety is equal, the Beauty is as the Uniformity. This ||¹⁰will be plain from Examples.||

First, the Variety increases the Beauty in equal Uniformity. The Beauty of an equilateral Triangle is less than that of the Square; which is less than that of a Pentagon; and this again is surpass'd by the Hexagon. When indeed the Number of Sides is much increas'd, the Proportion of them to the Radius, or Diameter of the [18] Figure, ||¹¹or of the Circle to which regular Polygons have an obvious Relation,|| is so much lost to our Observation, that the Beauty does not always increase with the Number of Sides; and the want of Parallelism in the Sides of Heptagons, and other Figures of odd Numbers, may also diminish their Beauty. So in Solids, the Eicosiedron surpasses the Dodecaedron, and this the Octaedron, which is still more beautiful than the Cube; and this again surpasses the regular Pyramid: The obvious Ground of this, is greater Variety with equal Uniformity.

The greater Uniformity increases the Beauty amidst equal Variety, in these Instances: An Equilateral Triangle, or even an Isosceles, surpasses the Scalenum: A Square surpasses the Rhombus or Lozenge, and this again the Rhomboides, ||¹²which is|| still more beautiful than the Trapezium, or any Figure with irregular curve Sides. So the regular Solids ||¹³vastly|| surpass all other Solids of equal number of plain Surfaces: And the same is observable not only in the Five perfectly regular Solids, but in all those which have any considerable Uniformity, as Cylinders, Prisms, Pyramids, Obelisks; which please every Eye more than any rude Figures, where there is no Unity or Resemblance among the Parts. [19]

Instances of the compound Ratio we have in comparing Circles or Spheres, with Ellipses or Spheroids not very eccentric; and in comparing the compound Solids, the Exoctaedron, and Eicosidodecaedron, with the perfectly regular ones of which they are compounded: and we shall

Variety.

Uniformity.

Compound Ratio.

---

* See Sect. vi. Art. 11, 12, 13.

find, that the Want of that most perfect Uniformity observable in the latter, is compensated by the greater Variety in the ‖[14] others‖, so that the Beauty is nearly equal.

IV. These Observations would probably hold true for the most part, and might be confirm'd by the Judgment of Children in the simpler Figures, where the Variety is not too great for their Comprehension. And however uncertain some of the particular aforesaid Instances may seem, yet this is perpetually to be observ'd, that Children are fond of all regular Figures in their little Diversions, altho they be no more convenient, or useful for them, than the Figures of our common Pebbles: We see how early they discover a Taste or Sense of Beauty, in desiring to see Buildings, regular Gardens, or even Representations of them in Pictures of any kind.

Beauty of Nature. V. ‖[15] It is‖ the same foundation ‖[16] which‖ we have for our Sense of Beauty in the Works of Nature. In every Part of the World [20] which we call Beautiful, there is a ‖[17] vast‖ Uniformity amidst ‖[18] an‖ almost infinite Variety. Many Parts of the Universe seem not at all design'd for the use of Man; nay, it is but a very small Spot with which we have any acquaintance. The Figures and Motions of the great Bodys are not obvious to our Senses, but found out by Reasoning and Reflection, upon many long Observations: and yet as far as we can by Sense discover, or by Reasoning enlarge our Knowledge, and extend our Imagination, we generally find ‖[19] their Structure, Order‖, and Motion, agreeable to our Sense of Beauty. Every particular Object in Nature does not indeed appear beautiful to us; but there is a ‖[20] vast‖ Profusion of Beauty over most of the Objects which occur either to our Senses, or Reasonings upon Observation: For not to mention the apparent Situation of the heavenly Bodys in the Circumference of a great Sphere, which is wholly occasion'd by the Imperfection of our Sight in discerning distances; the Forms of all the great Bodys in the Universe are nearly Spherical; the Orbits of their Revolutions generally Elliptick, and without great Eccentricity, in those which continually occur to our Observation: ‖[21] now‖ these are Figures of great Uniformity, and therefore pleasing to us. [21]

[22] Further, to pass by the less obvious Uniformity in the Proportion

of their Quantitys of Matter, Distances, Times of revolving, to each other; what can exhibit a greater Instance of Uniformity amidst Variety, than the constant Tenour of Revolutions in nearly equal Times, in each Planet, around its Axis, and the central Fire or Sun, thro all the Ages of which we have any Records, and in nearly the same Orbit? ||²³ by which||, after certain Periods, all the same Appearances are again renew'd; the alternate Successions of Light and Shade, or Day and Night, constantly pursuing each other around each Planet, with an agreeable and regular Diversity in the Times they possess the ||²⁴ several|| Hemispheres, in the Summer, Harvest, Winter and Spring; and the various Phases, Aspects, and Situations, of the Planets to each other, their Conjunctions and Oppositions, in which they suddenly darken each other with their Conick Shades in Eclipses, are repeated to us at their fixed Periods with invariable Constancy: These are the Beautys which charm the Astronomer, and make his tedious Calculations pleasant.

Molliter austerum studio fallente laborem.*ⁱ [22]

VI. Again, as to the dry Part of the Surface of our Globe, a great Part   Earth. of which is cover'd with a very pleasant inoffensive Colour, how beautifully is it diversify'd with various Degrees of Light and Shade, according to the different Situations of the Parts of its Surface, in Mountains, Valleys, Hills, and open Plains, which are variously inclin'd toward the great Luminary!

VII. If we descend to the minuter Works of Nature, what ||²⁵ vast|| Uni-   Plants. formity among all the Species of Plants and Vegetables in the manner of their Growth and Propagation! ||²⁶ what exact|| Resemblance among all the Plants of the same Species, whose Numbers surpass our Imagination! And this Uniformity is not only observable in the Form in gross;

---

* Hor. Lib. 2. Sat. 2 v. 12.

i. Translation: "Where the excitement pleasantly beguiles the hard toil." Horace, *Satires, Epistles, and Ars Poetica,* trans. H. Rushton Fairclough, Loeb Classical Library (Cambridge, Mass.: Harvard University Press, 1970), 136.

||²⁷ nay, in this it is not so very exact in all Instances||, but in the Structure of their ||²⁸ minutest Parts,|| which no Eye unassisted with Glasses can discern. In the almost infinite Multitude of Leaves, Fruit, Seed, Flowers of any one Species, we ||²⁹ often|| see ||³⁰ an exact|| Uniformity in the Structure and Situation of the smallest Fibres. This is the Beauty which charms an ingenious Botanist. Nay, what ||³¹ vast|| Uniformity and Regularity of Figure is found in each particular Plant, ||³² Leaf||, or Flower! In all Trees and ||³³ most of the|| smaller Plants, the Stalks or Trunks are either Cylinders nearly, or regular [23] Prisms; the Branches similar to their several Trunks, arising at nearly regular Distances, when no Accidents retard their natural Growth: In one Species the Branches arise in Pairs on the opposite Sides; the perpendicular Plain of Direction of the immediately superior Pair, intersecting the Plain of Direction of the inferior, nearly at right Angles: In another species, the Branches ||³⁴ spring|| singly, and alternately, all around in nearly equal Distances: And the Branches in other Species ||³⁵ sprout|| all in Knots around the Trunk, one for each Year. And in ||³⁶ every|| Species, all the Branches in the first Shoots preserve the same Angles with their Trunk; and they again sprout out into smaller Branches exactly after the Manner of their Trunks. Nor ought we to pass over that great Unity of Colours ||³⁷ which we often see|| in all the Flowers of the same Plant or Tree, and often of a whole Species; and their exact Agreement in many shaded Transitions into opposite Colours, in which all the Flowers of the same Plant generally agree, nay often all the Flowers of a Species.

Animals.   VIII. Again, as to the Beauty of Animals, either in their inward Structure, which we come to the Knowledge of by Experiment and long Observation, or their outward Form, we shall find ||³⁸ vast|| Uniformity among all the Species which are known to [24] us, in the Structure of those Parts, upon which Life depends more immediately. And how amazing is the Unity of Mechanism, when we shall find ||³⁹ an|| almost infinite diversity of Motions, all their Actions in walking, running, flying, swimming; all their serious Efforts for Self-preservation, all their freakish Contortions when they are gay and sportful, in all their various Limbs, perform'd by one simple Contrivance of a contracting Muscle, apply'd with inconceivable Diversitys to answer all these Ends! Various Engines might have obtain'd the same Ends; but then there had been less Uniformity, and the Beauty of our Animal Systems, and of particular Animals, had been much less, when this surprizing Unity of Mechanism had been remov'd from them.

IX. Among Animals of the same Species, the Unity is very obvious, and this Resemblance is the very Ground of our ranking them in such Classes or Species, notwithstanding the great Diversitys in Bulk, Colour, Shape, which are observ'd even in those call'd of the same Species. And then in each Individual, ||⁴⁰what vast Beauty|| arises from the exact Resemblance of all the external double Members to each other, which seems the universal Intention of Nature, when no Accident prevents it! We see the Want of this Resemblance never fails to pass for an [25] Imperfection, and Want of Beauty, tho no other Inconvenience ensues; as when the Eyes are not exactly like, or one Arm or Leg is a little shorter or smaller than its fellow.

||⁴¹ᵃAs to that most powerful Beauty in Countenances, Airs, Gestures, Motion, we shall shew in the second Treatise,* that it arises from some imagin'd Indication of morally good Dispositions of ||⁴²ᵇMind. ᵃᵇ||

X. There is a further Beauty in Animals, arising from a certain Proportion of the various Parts to each other, which still pleases the Sense of Spectators, tho they cannot calculate it with the Accuracy of a Statuary. The Statuary knows what Proportion of each Part of the Face to the whole Face is most agreeable, and can tell us the same of the Proportion of the Face to the Body, or any Parts of it; and between the Diameters and Lengths of each Limb: When this Proportion of the Head to the Body is remarkably alter'd, we shall have a Giant or a Dwarf. And hence it is, that either the one or the other may be represented to us even in Miniature, without Relation to any external Object, by observing how the Body surpasses the Proportion it should have to the Head in Giants, and falls [26] below it in Dwarfs. There is a further Beauty arising from

Proportion.

* Sect. vi. Art. 3.

that Figure, which is a natural Indication of Strength; but this may be pass'd over, because probably it may be alleg'd, that our Approbation of this Shape flows from ||^{43}an|| opinion of Advantage, and not from the Form it self.

The Beauty arising from Mechanism, apparently adapted to the Necessitys and Advantages of any Animal; which pleases us, even tho there be no Advantage to our selves ensuing from it; will be consider'd under the Head of Relative Beauty, or Design.*

Fowls.   XI. The peculiar Beauty of Fowls can scarce be omitted, which arises from the ||^{44}vast|| Variety of Feathers, a curious Sort of Machines adapted to many admirable Uses, which retain a ||^{45}vast|| Resemblance in their Structure among all the Species, ||^{46}and|| a perfect Uniformity in those of the same Species in the corresponding Parts, and in the two Sides of each Individual; besides all the Beauty of lively Colours and gradual Shades, not only in the external Appearance of the Fowl, resulting from an artful Combination of shaded Feathers, but often visible even in one Feather separately. [27]

Fluids.   XII. If our Reasonings about the Nature of Fluids be just, the vast Stores of Water will give us an Instance of Uniformity in Nature above Imagination, when we reflect upon the almost infinite Multitude of small, polish'd, smooth Spheres, which must be suppos'd form'd in all the parts of this Globe. The same Uniformity there is probably among the Parts of other Fluids as well as Water: and the like must be observ'd in several other natural Bodys, as Salts, Sulphurs, and such like; whose uniform Propertys do probably depend upon an Uniformity in the Figures of their Parts.

Harmony.   XIII. Under Original Beauty we may include Harmony, or Beauty of Sound, if that Expression can be allow'd, because Harmony is not usually conceiv'd as an Imitation of any thing else. Harmony often raises Pleasure in those who know not what is the Occasion of it: And yet the

---

* See Sect. iv. Art. 7.

Foundation of this Pleasure is known to be a sort of Uniformity. When the several Vibrations of one Note regularly coincide with the Vibrations of another, they make an agreeable Composition; and such Notes are call'd ‖[47]Concords‖. Thus the Vibrations of any one Note coincide in Time with ‖[48]two Vibrations‖ of its Octave; and two Vibrations of any Note coincide with three of its Fifth; and so on in the rest of the ‖[49a]Con-[28]cords. ‖[50b]Now no Composition can be harmonious, in which the Notes are not, for the most part, dispos'd according to these natural Proportions. Besides which, a due Regard must be had to the Key, which governs the whole, and to the Time and Humour, in which the Composition is begun: ‖[51c]a frequent and inartificial[c]‖ Change of any of which will produce the greatest, and most unnatural Discord.[b]‖ This will appear, by observing the Dissonance which would arise from tacking Parts of different Tunes together as one, altho both were separately agreeable. A like[a]‖ Uniformity is also observable among the Bases, Tenors, Trebles of the same Tune.

‖[52a]There is indeed ‖[53b]observable[b]‖, in the best Compositions, a mysterious Effect of Discords: They often give as great Pleasure as continu'd Harmony; whether by refreshing the Ear with Variety, or by awakening the Attention, and enlivening the Relish for the succeeding Harmony of Concords, as Shades enliven and beautify Pictures, or by some other means not yet known: Certain it is however that they have their place, and some good Effect in our best Compositions.[a]‖ Some other Powers of Musick may be consider'd ‖[54]hereafter‖.* [29]

XIV. But in all these Instances of[55] Beauty let it be observ'd, That the Pleasure is communicated to those who never reflected on this general Foundation; and that all here alledg'd is this, "That the pleasant Sensation arises only from Objects, in which there is Uniformity amidst Variety:" We may have the Sensation without knowing what is the Occasion of it; as a Man's Taste may suggest Ideas of Sweets, Acids, Bitters, tho he be ignorant of the Forms of the small Bodys, or their Motions, which excite ‖[56]these‖ Perceptions in him. [30]

* See Sect. vi. Art. 12.

Of the Beauty of Theorems.

Theorems.   I. The Beauty of Theorems, or universal Truths demonstrated, deserves a distinct Consideration, ‖¹being‖ of a Nature pretty different from the former kinds of Beauty; and yet there is none in which we shall see such an amazing Variety with Uniformity: and hence arises a very great Pleasure distinct from Prospects of any further Advantage.

II. For in one Theorem we may find included, with the most exact Agreement, an infinite Multitude of particular Truths; nay, often ‖²an Infinity‖ of Infinites: so that altho the Necessity of forming abstract Ideas, and universal Theorems, arises perhaps from the Limitation of our Minds, which cannot admit an infinite Multitude of singular Ideas or Judgments at once, yet this Power gives us an Evidence of the Largeness of the human Capacity above our Imagination. Thus for instance, the 47th Proposition of the first Book of Euclid's *Elements* contains an infinite Multitude of Truths, concerning the infinite possible Sizes of right-angled Triangles, as you make the Area greater [31] or less; and in each of these Sizes you may find an infinite Multitude of dissimilar Triangles, as you vary the Proportion of the Base to the Perpendicular; all which ‖³Infinitys of‖ Infinites agree in the general Theorem. ‖⁴ᵃIn Algebraick, and Fluxional Calculations, we shall ‖⁵ᵇstill find a greaterᵇ‖ Variety of particular Truths included in general Theorems; not only in general Equations applicable to all Kinds of Quantity, but in more particular Investigations of Areas and Tangents: In which one Manner of Operation shall discover Theorems applicable to ‖⁶ᶜinfiniteᶜ‖ Orders or

Species of Curves, to the infinite Sizes of each Species, and to the infinite Points of the ||⁷ᵈinfiniteᵈ|| Individuals of each Size.ᵃ||

III. That we may the better discern this Agreement, or Unity of an Infinity of Objects, in the general Theorem, to be the Foundation of the Beauty or Pleasure attending their Discovery, let us compare our Satisfaction in such Discoverys, with the uneasy state of Mind ||⁸in which we are||, when we can only measure Lines, or Surfaces, by a Scale, or are making Experiments which we can reduce to no general Canon, but ||⁹only|| heaping up a Multitude of particular incoherent Observations. Now each of these Trials discovers a new Truth, but with no Pleasure or Beauty, notwithstand-[32]ing the Variety, till we can discover some sort of Unity, or reduce them to some general Canon.

Foundation of their Beauty.

IV. Again, let us ||¹⁰take|| a Metaphysical Axiom, such as this, *Every Whole is greater than its Part;* and we shall find no Beauty in the Contemplation. ||¹¹For tho|| this Proposition ||¹²contains|| many Infinitys of particular Truths; yet the Unity is inconsiderable, since they all agree only in a vague, undetermin'd Conception of Whole and Part, and in an indefinite Excess of the former above the latter, which is sometimes great and sometimes small. So, should we hear that the Cylinder is greater than the inscrib'd Sphere, and this again greater than the Cone of the same Altitude and Diameter ||¹³with|| the Base, we shall find no pleasure in this Knowledge of a general Relation of greater ||¹⁴and|| less, without any precise Difference or Proportion. But when we see the universal exact Agreement of all possible Sizes of such Systems of Solids, that they preserve to each other the constant Ratio of 3, 2, 1; how beautiful is the Theorem, and how are we ravish'd with its first Discovery!

Little Beauty in Axioms.

||¹⁵ᵃWe may likewise observe, that easy or obvious Propositions, even where the Unity is sufficiently distinct, and determinate, do not please us so much as those, which [33] being less obvious, give us some Surprize in the Discovery: Thus we find little Pleasure in discovering that *a Line bisecting the vertical Angle of an Isosceles* ||¹⁶ᵇ *Triangle, bisects*ᵇ|| *the Base,* or the Reverse; or, that *Equilateral Triangles are Equiangular.* These Truths we ||¹⁷ᶜalmostᶜ|| know Intuitively, without Demonstration: They

Easy Theorems.

are like common Goods, or those which Men have long possessed, which do not give such sensible ‖ [18d] Joys [d] ‖ as much smaller new Additions may give us. But let none hence imagine, that the sole Pleasure of Theorems is from Surprize; for the same Novelty of a single Experiment does not please us much: nor ought we to conclude from the greater Pleasure accompanying a new, or unexpected Advantage, that Surprize, or Novelty is the only Pleasure of Life, or the only ground of Delight in ‖ [19e] Truth. [ae] ‖

Corollarys.   V. There is another Beauty in Propositions, ‖ [20] which cannot be omitted; which is‖, When one Theorem ‖ [21] contains‖ a ‖ [22] vast‖ Multitude of Corollarys easily deducible from it. Thus ‖ [23] that Theorem which gives us the Equation of a Curve, whence perhaps most of its Propertys may be deduc'd, does some way please and satisfy our Mind above any other Proposition‖: Such a Theorem ‖ [24] also‖ is the 35th of the 1st Book of Euclid, from which the whole Art of measuring right-lin'd Areas is deduc'd, by [34] Resolution into Triangles, which are the halfs of so many Parallelograms; and these are each respectively equal to so many Rectangles of the Base into the perpendicular Altitude: The 47th of the 1st ‖ [25] Book‖ is another of like Beauty, and so are many ‖ [26] others‖.

[27] In the search of Nature there is the like Beauty in the Knowledge of some great Principles, or universal Forces, from which innumerable Effects do flow. Such is Gravitation, in Sir Isaac Newton's Scheme; ‖ [28] such also is the Knowledge of the Original of Rights, perfect and imperfect, and external; alienable and unalienable, with their manner of Translations; from whence the greatest Part of moral Dutys may be deduc'd in the various Relations of human Life.‖

It is easy to see how Men are charm'd with the Beauty of such Knowledge, besides its Usefulness; and how this sets them upon deducing the Propertys of each Figure from one Genesis, and demonstrating the mechanick Forces from one Theorem of the Composition of Motion; even after they have sufficient Knowledge and Certainty in all these Truths from distinct independent Demonstrations. And this Pleasure we enjoy even when we have no Prospect of obtaining any other ‖ [29] Advantage‖ from such [35] Manner of Deduction, ‖ [30] than‖ the immediate Pleasure of contemplating the Beauty: nor could Love of Fame excite us to such regular Methods of Deduction, were we not conscious that Mankind are pleas'd with them immediately, by this internal Sense of their Beauty.

It is no less easy to see into what absurd ||[31]Attempts|| Men have been led by this Sense of Beauty, and ||[32]a silly Affectation|| of obtaining it in the other Sciences as well as the Mathematicks. 'Twas this probably which set Descartes[i] on that hopeful Project of deducing all human Knowledge from one Proposition, viz. *Cogito, ergo sum;* while others ||[33]with as little Sense contended||, that *Impossibile est idem simul esse & non esse,* had much fairer Pretensions to the Style and Title of *Principium humanae Cognitionis absolutè primum.* Mr. Leibnitz[ii] had an equal Affection for his favourite Principle of a sufficient Reason for every thing in Nature, and ||[34]brags to Dr. Clarke[iii]|| of the Wonders he had wrought in the intellectual World by its Assistance; ||[35]but his learned Antagonist seems to think he had not sufficient Reason for his Boasting.*|| If we look into particular Sciences, we ||[36]may see in the Systems learned Men have given us of them,|| [36] the Inconveniences of this Love of Uniformity. ||[37]How|| aukardly ||[38]is Puffendorf[iv] forc'd to|| deduce the several Dutys of Men to God, themselves, and their Neighbours, from his single fundamental Principle of Sociableness to the whole Race of Man-

Fantastick
Beauty.

i. René Descartes (1596–1650), French philosopher and mathematician, published the cogito-ergo-sum principle first in his *Discours de la méthode* (1637) and in his *Meditationes de prima philosophia* (1641), meditations 2 and 3.

ii. Gottfried Wilhelm von Leibniz (1646–1716), German philosopher, mathematician, historian, and jurist, discovered differential and integral calculus, and developed the first binary arithmetic. Of his numerous writings and extensive correspondence, little was published during his lifetime. The principle of sufficient reason is central to his metaphysics and logic; see his *Monadologie* (1720). In an exchange of letters with Samuel Clarke (see note iii below), he discussed the philosophical principles of Newton's physics, especially space and time. See *The Leibniz-Clarke Correspondence,* ed. H. G. Alexander (New York: Manchester University Press, 1998).

iii. Samuel Clarke (1675–1729), English theologian and philosopher, was a friend of Newton whose philosophical doctrine he defended against Leibniz (see note ii above).

* See the Letters which pass'd between Dr. Clarke and Mr. Leibnitz, Pag. 23.

iv. Samuel Pufendorf (1632–94) was the leading author on natural law in the Enlightenment. See *De Jure Naturae et Gentium* (Lund, 1672; translation: *The Law of Nature and Nations,* London, 1703) and *De officio hominis et civis* (Lund, 1673; translation: *The Whole Duty of Man,* London, 1691).

kind?[39] This Observation ||[40]might easily be extended farther, were it necessary; and|| is a strong Proof that Men ||[41]have a Sense of Beauty in|| Uniformity in the Sciences, ||[42]even from the Contortions of common Sense they are led into by pursuing it||.

VI. This Delight which accompanys Sciences, or universal Theorems, may really be call'd a kind of Sensation; since it necessarily accompanys the Discovery of any Proposition, and is distinct from bare Knowledge it self[43], being most violent at first, whereas the Knowledge is uniformly the same. And however Knowledge enlarges the Mind, and makes us more capable of comprehensive Views and Projects in some kinds of Business, whence Advantage may also arise to us; yet we may leave it in the Breast of every Student to determine, whether he has not often felt this Pleasure without any such prospect of Advantage from the Discovery of his Theorem. All ||[44]which|| can thence be infer'd is only this, that as in our external Senses, so in our internal ones, the pleasant Sensations generally arise from those Objects which calm Reason [37] would have recommended, had we understood their Use, and which might have engag'd our pursuits from Self-interest.

VII. [45]If any alledge, "that this Pleasure in Theorems arises only at first, upon the Novelty of the Discovery, which occasions Surprize:" It must be own'd indeed that* Novelty is generally very agreeable, and heightens the Pleasure in the Contemplation of Beauty; but then the Novelty of a particular Truth, found out by measuring, as above mention'd, gives no considerable Pleasure, nor Surprize. That then which is pleasant and surprizing, is the first Observation of this Unity amidst such a great Variety. There is indeed another kind of Surprize, which adds to the Beauty of some Propositions less universal, and may make them equally pleasant with more universal ones; as when we discover a general Truth which seem'd before, upon some confus'd Opinion, to be a Falshood: as that *Assymptotes always approaching should never meet the Curve.* This is like that Joy, which may be very strong and violent, upon the unex-

---

* See Sect. vi. Art. 13. and the *Spectator* there referr'd to.

pected Arrival of a small Advantage, from that Occasion from which we apprehended great Evil; but still this Unity of many Particulars in the general Theo-[38]rem, is necessary to make it pleasant, in any case.

VIII.[46] As to the Works of Art, were we to run thro the various artificial Contrivances or Structures, we should ‖[47]constantly‖ find the Foundation of the Beauty which appears in them, ‖[48]to be‖ some kind of Uniformity, or Unity of Proportion among the Parts, and of each Part to the Whole. As there is a ‖[49]vast‖ Diversity of Proportions possible, and different Kinds of Uniformity, so there is room enough for that Diversity of Fancys observable in Architecture, Gardening, and such like Arts in different Nations; they all may have Uniformity, tho the Parts in one may differ from those in another. The Chinese or Persian Buildings are not like the Grecian and Roman, and yet the former has its Uniformity of the various Parts to each other, and to the Whole, as well as the latter. In that kind of Architecture which the Europeans call Regular, the Uniformity of Parts is very obvious, the several Parts are regular Figures, and either equal or similar at least in the same Range; the Pedestals are Parallelopipedons or square Prisms; the Pillars, Cylinders nearly; the Arches Circular, and all those in the same Row equal; there is the same Proportion every where observ'd in the same Range between the Diameters of Pillars and their Heights, their Capitals, the Dia-[39]meters of Arches, the Heights of the Pedestals, the Projections of the Cornice, and all ‖[50]the‖ Ornaments in each of our five Orders. And tho other Countrys do not follow the Grecian or Roman Proportions; yet there is even among them a Proportion retain'd, a Uniformity, and Resemblance of corresponding Figures; and every Deviation in one part from ‖[51]that‖ Proportion which is observ'd in the rest of the Building, is displeasing to every Eye, and destroys or diminishes at least the Beauty of the Whole.

[52]IX. The same might be observ'd thro all other Works of Art, even to the meanest Utensil; the Beauty of every one of which we shall always find to have the same Foundation of Uniformity amidst Variety, without which they ‖[53]appear‖ mean, irregular and deform'd. [40]

Works of Art.

Of Relative or Comparative Beauty.

Comparative Beauty.

I. If the preceding Thoughts concerning the Foundation of absolute Beauty be just, we may easily understand wherein relative Beauty consists. All Beauty is relative to the Sense of some Mind perceiving it; but what we call relative is that which is apprehended in any Object, commonly consider'd as an Imitation of some Original: And this Beauty is founded on a Conformity, or a kind of Unity between the Original and the Copy. The Original may be either some Object in Nature, or some establish'd Idea; for if there be any known Idea as a Standard, and Rules to fix this Image or Idea by, we may make a beautiful Imitation. Thus a Statuary, Painter, or Poet, may please us with an Hercules, if his Piece retains that Grandeur, and those marks of Strength, and Courage, which we imagine in that Hero.

[1] And farther, to obtain comparative Beauty alone, it is not necessary that there be any Beauty in the Original; the Imitation of absolute Beauty may indeed in the whole make a more lovely Piece, and yet [41] an exact Imitation shall still be beautiful, tho the Original were intirely void of it: Thus the Deformitys of old Age in a Picture, the rudest Rocks or Mountains in a Landskip, if well represented, shall have abundant Beauty, tho perhaps not so great as if the Original were absolutely beautiful, and as well ||[2] represented.||

Description in Poetry.

II. The same Observation holds true in the Descriptions of the Poets either of natural Objects or Persons; and this relative Beauty is what they should principally endeavour to obtain, as the peculiar Beauty of their

Works. By the *Moratae Fabulae,* or the ἤθη of Aristotle, we are not to understand virtuous Manners ||³in a moral Sense||, but a just Representation of Manners or Characters as they are in Nature; and that the Actions and Sentiments be suited to the Characters of the Persons to whom they are ascrib'd in Epick and Dramatick Poetry. Perhaps very good Reasons may be suggested from the Nature of our Passions, to prove that a Poet should ||⁴not|| draw ||⁵his Characters perfectly Virtuous||; these Characters indeed abstractly consider'd might give more Pleasure, and have more Beauty than the imperfect ones which occur in Life with a mixture of Good and Evil: But it may suffice at present to suggest against this Choice, that we have more lively Ideas of imperfect Men with all their Passions, [42] than of morally perfect Heroes, such as really never occur to our Observation; and of ||⁶which|| consequently we cannot judge exactly as to their Agreement with the Copy. And further, thro Consciousness of our own State, we are more nearly touch'd and affected by the imperfect Characters; since in them we see represented, in the Persons of others, the Contrasts of Inclinations, and the Struggles between the Passions of Self-Love and those of Honour and Virtue, which we often feel in our own Breasts. This is the Perfection of Beauty for which Homer is justly admir'd, as well as for the Variety of his Characters.

III. Many other Beautys of Poetry may be reduc'd under this Class of relative Beauty: The Probability is absolutely necessary to make us imagine Resemblance; it is by Resemblance that the Similitudes, Metaphors and Allegorys are made beautiful, whether either the Subject or the Thing compar'd to it have Beauty or not; the Beauty indeed is greater, when both have some original Beauty or Dignity as well as Resemblance: and this is the foundation of the Rule of studying Decency in Metaphors and ||⁸Similys|| as well as Likeness. The Measures and Cadence are instances of Harmony, and come under the head of absolute Beauty. [43]

Probability, ||⁷Simily||, Metaphor.

IV. We may here observe a strange Proneness in our Minds to make perpetual Comparisons of all things which occur to our Observation, even ||⁹those which would seem very remote||. There are certain Resemblances in the Motions of all Animals upon like Passions, which easily

Proneness to compare.

found a Comparison; but this does not serve to entertain our Fancy: Inanimate Objects have often such Positions as resemble those of the human Body in various Circumstances; these Airs or Gestures of the Body are Indications of ||¹⁰certain|| Dispositions in the Mind, so that our very Passions and Affections as well as other Circumstances obtain a Resemblance to natural inanimate Objects. Thus a Tempest at Sea is often an Emblem of Wrath; a Plant or Tree drooping under the Rain, of a Person in Sorrow; a Poppy bending its Stalk, or a Flower withering when cut by the Plow, resembles the Death of a blooming Hero; an aged Oak in the Mountains shall represent an old Empire, a Flame seizing a Wood shall represent a War. In short, every thing in Nature, by our strange inclination to Resemblance, shall be brought to represent other things, even the most remote, especially the Passions and Circumstances of human Nature in which we are more nearly concern'd; and to confirm this, and furnish Instances of it, one [44] need only look into Homer or Virgil. A fruitful Fancy would find in a Grove, or a Wood, an Emblem ||¹¹for|| every Character in a Commonwealth, and every turn of Temper, or Station in Life.

Intention.   V. Concerning that kind of comparative Beauty which has a necessary relation to some establish'd Idea, we may observe, that some Works of Art acquire a distinct Beauty by their Correspondence to some universally suppos'd Intention in the ||¹²Artificer||, or the Persons who employ'd ||¹³him||: And to obtain this Beauty, sometimes they do not form their Works so as to attain the highest Perfection of original Beauty separately consider'd; because a Composition of this relative Beauty, along with some degree of the original Kind, may give more Pleasure, than a more perfect original Beauty separately. Thus we see, that strict Regularity in laying out of Gardens in Parterres, Vista's, parallel Walks, is often neglected, to obtain an Imitation of Nature even in some of its Wildnesses. And we are more pleas'd with this Imitation, especially when the Scene is large and spacious, than with the more confin'd Exactness of regular ||¹⁴Works||. So likewise in the Monuments erected in honour of deceased Heroes, although a Cylinder, or Prism, or regular Solid, may have more original Beauty than a very acute Pyramid or Obelisk, [45] yet the latter pleases more, by answering better the suppos'd Intentions of Stability, and being conspicuous. For the same reason Cubes, or square Prisms, are generally chosen for the Pedestals of Statues, and not any of the more beautiful Solids, which do not seem so secure from rolling. This may be the reason too, why Columns or Pillars look best when made a little taper from the middle, or a third from the bottom, that they may not seem top-heavy and in danger of falling.

VI. The like reason may influence Artists, in many other Instances, to depart from the Rules of original Beauty, as above laid down. And yet this is no Argument against our Sense of Beauty being founded, as was above explain'd, on Uniformity amidst Variety, but only an Evidence that our Sense of Beauty of the Original Kind may be vary'd and over-ballanc'd by another kind of Beauty.

VII. This Beauty arising from Correspondence to Intention, would open to curious Observers a new Scene of Beauty in the Works of Nature, by considering how the Mechanism of the various Parts known to us, seems adapted to the Perfection of that Part, and yet in Subordination to the Good of some System or Whole. We generally suppose the Good of [46] the greatest Whole, or of all Beings, to have been the Intention of the Author of Nature; and cannot avoid being pleas'd when we see any part of this Design executed in the Systems we are acquainted with. The Observations already made on this Subject are in every one's hand, in the Treatises of our late Improvers of mechanical Philosophy. ||¹⁵We shall only observe here, that every one has a certain Pleasure in|| seeing any Design well executed by curious Mechanism, even when his own Advantage is no way concern'd; ||¹⁶and also|| in discovering the Design to which any complex Machine is adapted, when he has perhaps had a general Knowledge of the Machine before, without seeing its Correspondence or Aptness to execute any Design.¹⁷

The Arguments by which we prove Reason and Design in any Cause from the Beauty of the Effects, are so frequently us'd in some of the highest Subjects, that it may be necessary to enquire a little more particularly into them, to see how far they will hold, and with what degree of Evidence. [47]

*Concerning our Reasonings about Design
and Wisdom in the Cause, from the Beauty
or Regularity of Effects.*

Sense,
Arbitrary in
its Author.

I. There seems to be no necessary Connection of our pleasing Ideas of Beauty with the Uniformity or Regularity of the Objects, from the Nature of things, ||¹antecedent|| to some Constitution of the Author of our Nature, which has made such Forms pleasant to us. Other Minds ||²may|| be so fram'd as to receive no Pleasure from Uniformity; and we actually find that the same regular Forms ||³seem not|| equally to please all the Animals known to us, as shall probably appear ||⁴afterwards||. Therefore let us make what is the most unfavourable Supposition to the present Argument||⁵, viz.|| That the Constitution of our Sense so as to approve Uniformity, is merely arbitrary in the Author of our Nature; and that there are an infinity of Tastes or Relishes of Beauty possible; so that it would be impossible to throw together fifty or a hundred Pebbles, which should not make an agreeable Habitation for some Animal or other, and appear beautiful to it. And then it is [48] plain, that from the Perception of Beauty in any one Effect, we should have no reason to conclude Design in the Cause: for a Sense might be so constituted as to be pleas'd with such Irregularity as may be the effect of an undirected Force.* But

---

* ||⁶ᵃBy undirected Force, or undesigning Force, is to be understood, That Force with which an Agent may put Matter into Motion, without having any Design or Intention to produce any particular Form. ||⁷ᵇThis ᵇ|| *Conatus ad motum,* without an actual Line of Direction, seems such a gross absurdity in the Cartesian Scheme, that it is ||⁸ᶜbelow the Dignity of common Sense to vouchsafe to confute itᶜ||. But Men

then, as there are an Infinity of Forms ||⁹possible|| into which any System may be reduc'd, an Infinity of Places in which Animals may be situated, and an Infinity of Relishes or Senses ||¹⁰in these Animals|| is suppos'd possible; that in the immense Spaces any one Animal should by Chance be plac'd in a System agreeable to its Taste, must be improbable as infinite to one at least: And much more unreasonable is it to expect from Chance, that a multitude of Animals agreeing in their Sense of Beauty should obtain agreeable Places. [49]

II. ||¹¹There is also|| the same Probability, that in any one System of Matter an Undirected Force ||¹²will|| produce a regular Form, as any one given irregular one, of the same degree of Complication: But still the irregular Forms into which any System may be rang'd, surpass in multitude the Regular, as Infinite does Unity; for what holds in one small System will hold in a Thousand, a Million, a Universe, with more Advantage, viz. that the irregular Forms possible infinitely surpass the Regular. For Instance, the Area of an Inch Square is capable of an Infinity of regular Forms, the Equilateral Triangle, the Square, the Pentagon, Hexagon, Heptagon, &c. but for each one regular Form, there are an Infinity of Irregular, as an Infinity of Scalena for the one equilateral Triangle, an Infinity of Trapezia for the one Square, of irregular Pentagons for the one Regular, and so on: and therefore supposing any one System agitated by undesigning Force, it ||¹³is|| infinitely more probable that it ||¹⁴will|| resolve itself into an irregular Form, than a regular. Thus, that a System of six Parts upon Agitation shall not obtain the Form of a regular Hexagon, is at least infinite to Unity; and the more complex

Undirected Force.

------

have so many confus'd Notions of some Nature, or Chance impressing Motions without any Design or Intention of producing any particular Effect, that it may be useful to shew, that even this very absurd Postulatum, tho it were granted them, is insufficient to answer the appearances in the Regularity of the World; and this is what is attempted in the first fourteen Articles of this Section. These Arguments would really be useless, if all Men were persuaded of what to a Man of just Thought will appear pretty Obvious, that there can be no Thought-less Agent; and that Chance and Nature are mere empty Names, as they are us'd on this Occasion, relative only to our Ignorance.ª||

we make the System, the greater is the hazard, from a very obvious Reason. [50]

15 We see this confirm'd by our constant Experience, that Regularity never arises from any undesign'd Force of ours; and from this we conclude, that wherever there is any Regularity in the disposition of a System capable of many other ||16 Dispositions||, there must have been Design in the Cause; and the Force of this Evidence increases, according to the Multiplicity of Parts imploy'd.

But this Conclusion is too rash, unless some further Proof be introduc'd; and what leads us into it is this. Men, who have a Sense of Beauty in Regularity, are led generally in all their Arrangements of Bodys to study some kind of Regularity, and seldom ever design Irregularity; ||17 hence|| we judge the same of other Beings too, ||18 viz.|| that they study Regularity, and presume upon Intention in the Cause wherever we see it, making Irregularity always a Presumption of Want of Design: ||19 Whereas if other Agents have different Senses of Beauty,|| or if they have no Sense of it at all, Irregularity may as well be design'd as Regularity. And then let it be observ'd, that in this Case there is just the same reason to conclude Design in the Cause from any one irregular Effect, as from a regular one; for since there are an Infinity of other Forms possible as well as this irre-[51]gular one produc'd, and since to such a Being* void of a Sense of Beauty, all Forms are as to its own Relish indifferent, and all agitated Matter meeting must make some Form or other, and all

---

* There is a great Difference between such a Being as is here mention'd, and a Being which has no Intention for any reason whatsoever to produce one Form more than another. This latter sort of Being, as to the present Argument, would be the same with Chance, but not the former. For tho a Being has no sense of Beauty, he may notwithstanding be capable of Design, and of Intention to produce regular Forms; and the observation of greater Regularity in any number of Effects, than could be expected from undirected Force, is a presumption of Design and Intention in the Cause, even where the Cause is suppos'd to have no sense of Beauty in such Forms, since perhaps he may have other Reasons moving him to chuse such Forms. Thus supposing the Deity ||20 no way necessarily|| pleas'd with Regularity, Uniformity, or Similarity in Bodys, yet there may be Reasons moving him to produce such Objects, such as the pleasing his Creatures, having given them a sense of Beauty founded on these Qualitys. See the two last Paragraphs of the last Section.

Forms, upon Supposition that the Force is apply'd by an Agent void of a Sense of Beauty, would equally prove Design; it is plain that no one Form proves it more than another, or can prove it at all; except from a general metaphysical Consideration, ||²¹ too subtile to be certain,|| that there is no proper Agent without Design and Intention, and that every Effect flows from the Intention of some Cause.

III. This however follows from the above ||²² mention'd|| Considerations, that supposing a Mass of Matter surpassing a cubick Inch, as [52] infinite of the first Power does Unity, and that this whole Mass were some way determin'd from its own Nature without any Design in a Cause (which perhaps is scarce possible) to resolve itself into ||²³ the solid Content of a cubick Inch||, and into a prismatick Form whose Base should always be $\frac{1}{2}$ of a square Inch; suppose these Conditions determin'd, and all others left to undirected Force; all ||²⁴ which|| we could expect from undirected Force in this Case would be one equilateral Prism, or two perhaps; because there are an Infinity of irregular Prisms possible of the same Base, and solid Content: and when we ||²⁵ met|| with many such Prisms, we must probably conclude ||²⁶ them produc'd by Design,|| since they are more than could have been expected by the Laws of Hazard.

Similar Forms by Chance, impossible.

IV. But if ||²⁷ this|| infinite Mass was ||²⁸ no way|| determin'd to a prismatick Form, we could only expect from its casual Concourse one Prism of any Kind, since there ||²⁹ is an Infinity of other Solids|| into which the Mass might be resolv'd; and if we found any great number of Prisms, we should have ||³⁰ reason to presume|| Design: so that in a Mass of Matter as infinite of the first Power, we could not from any Concourse or Agitation expect with any good ground a Body of any given Dimensions or Size, and of any given [53] Form; since of any Dimension there are infinite Forms possible, and of any Form there are an Infinity of Dimensions; and if we found several Bodys of the same Dimension and Form, we should have so much Presumption for Design.

V. There is one trifling Objection which may perhaps arise from the crystallizing of certain Bodys, when the Fluid is evaporated in which they were swimming; for in this we frequently see regular Forms arising, tho there is nothing ‖³¹ suppos'd in this Affair but an undirected Force of Attraction‖. But to remove this Objection, we need only consider, that we have good Reason to believe, that the smallest Particles of crystalliz'd Bodys have fix'd regular Forms ‖³² given‖ them in the Constitution of Nature; and then it is easy to conceive how their Attractions may produce regular Forms: but unless we suppose some preceding Regularity in the Figures of attracting Bodys, they ‖³³ can‖ never form any regular Body at all. And hence we see how improbable it is, that the whole Mass of Matter, not only in this Globe, but in all the fixed Stars known to us by our Eyes or Glasses, were they a thousand times larger than our Astronomers suppose, could in any Concourse have produc'd any Number of similar Bodys Regular or Irregular. [54]

Combinations by Chance, impossible.

VI. And let it be here observ'd, that there are many Compositions of Bodys which the smallest Degree of Design could easily effect, which yet we would in vain expect from all the Powers of Chance or undesign'd Force, ‖³⁴ after‖ an Infinity of Rencounters; even supposing a Dissolution of every Form except the regular one, that the Parts might be prepar'd for a new Agitation. Thus, supposing we could expect one equilateral Prism of any given Dimensions should be form'd from undirected Force, in an Infinity of Matter some way determin'd to resolve ‖³⁵ itself‖ into Bodys of a given solid Content, (which is all we could expect, since it is infinite to one after the solid Content is obtain'd, that the Body shall not be Prismatical; and allowing it Prismatical, it is infinite to one that it shall not be Equilateral:) And again, supposing another Infinity of Matter determin'd to resolve itself into Tubes, of Orifices exactly equal to the Bases of the former Prisms, it is again at least as the second Power of Infinite to Unity, that not one of these Tubes shall be both Prismatick and Equiangular; and then if the Tube were thus form'd, so as to be exactly capable of receiving one of the Prisms and no more, it is infinite to one that they shall never meet in infinite Space; and should [55] they meet, it is infinite to one that the Axes of the Prism and Tube shall never happen in the same strait Line; and supposing they did, it is again as infinite to three, that Angle shall not meet Angle, so as to enter. We see then how infinitely improbable it is, "that all the Powers of Chance in infinite Matter, agitated thro infinite Ages, could ever effect this small Composition of a Prism entering a Prismatick Bore; and, that all our hazard for it would at most be but as three is to the third Power of Infinite." And yet the smallest Design could easily effect it.

VII. May we not then justly count it altogether absurd, and next to an absolute strict Impossibility, "That all the Powers of undirected Force should ever effect such a complex Machine ||[36]as|| the most imperfect Plant, or the meanest Animal, even in one Instance?" for the Improbability just increases, as the Complication of Mechanism in these natural Bodys surpasses that simple Combination above mention'd.

VIII. Let it be here observ'd, "That the preceding Reasoning from the Frequency of regular Bodys of one Form in the Universe, and from the Combinations of various Bodys, is intirely inde-[56]pendent on any Perception of Beauty; and would equally prove Design in the Cause, altho there were no Being which perceiv'd Beauty in any Form whatsoever:" for it is in short this, "That the recurring of any Effect oftner than the Laws of Hazard ||[37]determine||, gives Presumption of Design; and, That Combinations which no undesign'd Force could give us reason to expect, must necessarily prove the same; and that with superior probability, as the multitude of Cases in which the contrary ||[38]might|| happen, surpass all the Cases in which this could happen:" which appears to be in the simplest Cases at least as Infinite ||[39]does|| Unity. And the frequency of similar irregular Forms, or exact Combinations of them, is an equal Argument of Design in the Cause, since the Similarity, or exact Combinations of irregular Forms, are as little to be expected from all the Powers of undirected Force, as any sort whatsoever.

IX. To bring this nearer to something like a Theorem, altho the Idea of Infinite be troublesome enough to manage in Reasoning. The Powers of Chance, with infinite Matter in infinite Ages, may answer Hazards as the fifth Power of Infinite and no more: thus the Quantity of Matter may be conceiv'd as the third Power of [57] Infinite and no more, the various Degrees of Force may make another Power of Infinite, and the Number of Rencounters may make the fifth. But this last only holds on Supposition, that after every Rencounter there is no Cohesion, but all is dissolv'd again for a new Concourse, except in similar Forms or exact Combinations; which Supposition is entirely groundless, since we see dissimilar Bodys cohering as strongly as any, and rude Masses more than any Combinations. Now to produce any given Body, in a given Place or Situation, and of given Dimensions, or Shape, the Hazards of the contrary are, one Power of Infinite at least to obtain the Place or Situation; when the Situation is obtain'd, the solid Content requires another Power of Infinite to obtain it; the Situation and Solidity obtain'd require, for accomplishing the simplest given Shape, at least the other three Powers of Infinite. For instance, let the Shape be a four-sided Prism or Parallelopiped; that the Surfaces should be Planes requires one Power; that they should be Parallel in this Case, or inclin'd in any given Angle in any other Case, requires another Power of Infinite; and that they should be in any given Ratio to each other, requires at least the third Power: for in each of these Heads there ||[40] is still an Infinity at least|| of other Cases possible beside the one given. So that all [58] the Powers of Chance could only produce perhaps one Body of every simpler Shape or Size at most, and this is all we could expect: we might expect one Pyramid, or Cube, or Prism perhaps; but when we increase the Conditions requir'd, the Prospect must grow more improbable, as in more complex Figures, and in all Combinations of Bodys, and in similar Species, which we never could reasonably hope from Chance; and therefore where we see them, we must certainly ascribe them to Design.

Combinations of irregular Forms, equally impossible. X. The Combinations of regular Forms, or of irregular ones exactly adapted to each other, require such vast Powers of Infinite to effect them, and the Hazards of the contrary Forms are so infinitely numerous, that all Probability or Possibility of their being accomplish'd by Chance seems quite to vanish. Let us apply the Cases in Art. vi. ||[41] of|| this Section about the Prism and Tube, to our simplest Machines, such as a pair of Wheels of our ordinary Carriages; each Circular, Spokes equal in length, thickness, shape; the Wheels set Parallel, the Axle-tree fix'd in the Nave of both, and secur'd from coming out at either End: ||[42] Now|| the Cases in which the contrary might have happen'd from undirected Concourses, were there no more requir'd than what is just now mention'd, must amount in Multitude to a Power of ||[43] Infinite|| [59] equal to every Circumstance requir'd. What shall we say then of a Plant, a Tree, an Animal, a Man, with such multitudes of adapted Vessels, such Articulations, Insertions of Muscles, Diffusion of Veins, Arterys, Nerves? The Improbability that such Machines ||[44] should be the Effect of Chance, must be near the infinitesimal Power of Infinite to Unity.||

XI. Further, were all the former Reasoning from Similarity of Forms and Combinations groundless, and could Chance give us ground to expect such Forms, with exact Combination, yet we could only promise ||[45] ourselves|| one of these Forms among an Infinity of others. When we see then such a multitude of Individuals of a Species, similar to each other in a ||[46] vast|| number of Parts; and when we see in each Individual, the corresponding Members so exactly ||[47] like|| each other, what possible room is there left for questioning Design in the Universe? None but the barest Possibility against an inconceivably great Probability, surpassing every thing which is not strict Demonstration.

XII. This Argument, ||[48] as|| has been already observ'd,* is quite abstracted from any Sense of Beauty in any particular Form; for the exact Similarity of a hundred or a [60] thousand Trapezia, proves Design as well as the Similarity of Squares, since both are equally above all the Powers of undirected Force or Chance||[49], as the hundredth or thousandth Power of Infinite surpasses Unity;|| and what is above the Powers of Chance, must give us proportionable Presumption for Design.

Thus, allowing that a Leg, or Arm, or Eye, might have been the Effect of Chance, (which was shewn to be most absurd, and next to absolutely impossible) that it ||[50] would|| not have a corresponding Leg, Arm, Eye, exactly similar, must be a hazard of a Power of Infinite proportion'd to the Complication of Parts; for in Proportion to this is the multitude of

* See above, Art. viii.

Cases increas'd, in which it would not have a corresponding Member similar: so that allowing twenty or thirty Parts in such a Structure, it would be as the twentieth or thirtieth Power of Infinite to Unity, that the corresponding Part should not be similar. What shall we say then of the similar Forms of a whole Species?

[51]XIII. If it be objected, "That natural Bodys are not exactly similar, but only grosly so to our Senses; as that a Vein, an Artery, a Bone is not perhaps exactly similar to its Correspondent in the same Animal, tho it appears so to [61] our Senses, which ||[52]judge only|| of the Bulk, and do not discern the small constituent Parts; and that in the several Individuals of a Species the Dissimilarity is always sensible, often in the internal Structure, and ||[53]often, nay|| always in the external Appearance." To remove this Objection it will be sufficient to shew, "That the multitude of Cases wherein sensible Dissimilitude cou'd have happen'd, are still infinitely more than all the Cases in which sensible Similitude ||[54]might||;" so that the same Reasoning holds from sensible Similarity, as from the mathematically exact: And again, "That the Cases of gross Dissimilarity do in the same manner surpass the Cases of gross Similarity possible, as infinite does one."

[55]XIV. To prove both these Assertions, let us consider a simple Instance. ||[56]Suppose|| a Trapezium of a foot Square in Area ||[57]should|| appear grosly similar to another, while no one side differs, by $\frac{1}{10}$ of an Inch; or no Angle in one surpasses the corresponding one in the other above ten ||[58]Minutes||: now this tenth of an Inch is infinitely divisible, as ||[59]are also|| the ten Minutes, so that the Cases of insensible Dissimilarity under apparent Similarity are really Infinite. But then it is also plain that there are an Infinity of different sensibly dissimilar Trapezia, even of the same Area, ac-[62]cording as we vary a Side by one Tenth, two Tenths, three Tenths, and so on, and ||[60]vary|| the Angles and another Side so as to keep the Area equal. Now in each of these infinite Degrees of sensible Dissimilitude the several Tenths are infinitely divisible as well as in the first Case; so that the multitude of sensible Dissimilaritys are to the multitude of insensible Dissimilaritys under apparent Resemblance, still as

the second Power of Infinite to the first, or as Infinite to Unity. And then
how vastly greater must the Multitude be, of all possible sensible Dissimilaritys in such complex Bodys as Legs, Arms, Eyes, Arterys, Veins,
Skeletons?

[61]XV. As to the Dissimilaritys of Animals of the same Species, it is in
the same manner plain, that the possible Cases of gross Dissimilarity are
Infinite; and then every Case of gross Dissimilarity contains also all the
Cases of insensible Dissimilarity. Thus, if we would count all Animals
of a Species grosly similar, while there was no Limb which in Length or
Diameter did exceed the ordinary Shape by above a third of the Head;
it is plain that there are an Infinity of ‖[62]gross‖ Dissimilaritys possible,
and then in each of these Cases of gross Dissimilarity, there are an Infinity of Cases of nicer Dissimilarity, since $\frac{1}{3}$ of the Head may be infinitely divided. To take a low [63] but easy Instance; two Cockle-Shells
which fitted each other naturally, may have an Infinity of insensible Differences, but still there are an Infinity of possible sensible Differences;
and then in any one of the sensibly different Forms, there may be the
same Infinity of insensible Differences beside the sensible one: So that
still the hazard for even gross Similarity from Chance is Infinite to one,
and this always increases by a Power of Infinite for every distinct Member of the Animal, in which even gross Similarity is retain'd; since the
Addition of every Member or Part to a complex Machine, makes a new
Infinity of Cases, in which sensible Dissimilarity may happen; and this
Infinity combin'd with the infinite Cases of the former Parts, raises the
Hazard by a Power of Infinite.

   Now this may sufficiently shew us the Absurdity of the Cartesian or
Epicurean Hypothesis, even granting their Postulatum of undirected
Force impress'd on infinite Matter; and seems almost a Demonstration
of Design in the Universe.

[63]XVI. One Objection ‖[64]more‖ remains to be remov'd, viz. "That some
imagine, this Argument may hold better à Priori than à Posteriori; that
is, we have better Reason to believe, when we see a Cause about to act,
without Knowledge, [64] that he will not attain any given, or desir'd

End; than we have on the other hand to believe, when we see ||⁶⁵the|| End actually attain'd, that he acted with Knowledge: Thus, say they, when a ||⁶⁶particular Person|| is about to draw a Ticket in a Lottery, where there is but one Prize to a thousand Blanks, it is highly probable that he shall draw a Blank; but suppose we have seen him actually draw for himself the Prize, we have no ground to conclude that he had Knowledge or Art to accomplish this End." But the Answer is obvious: In such Contrivances we generally have, from the very Circumstances of the Lottery, very strong moral Arguments, which almost demonstrate that Art can have no place; so that a Probability of a ||⁶⁷thousand to one||, ||⁶⁸does|| not surmount those Arguments: But let the Probability be increas'd, and it will soon surmount ||⁶⁹all|| Arguments to the contrary. For instance, If we saw a Man ten times successively draw Prizes, in a Lottery where there were but ten Prizes to ten thousand Blanks, I fancy few would question whether he us'd Art or not: much less would we imagine it were Chance, if we saw a Man draw for his own Gain successively a hundred, or a thousand Prizes, from among a proportionably greater number of Blanks. Now in the Works of Nature the Case is entirely different: we have not the least [65] Argument against Art or Design. An intelligent Cause is surely at least as probable a Notion as Chance, general Force, *Conatus ad Motum,* or the *Clinamen Principiorum,* to account for any Effect whatsoever: And then all the Regularity, Combinations, Similaritys of Species, are so many Demonstrations, that there was Design and Intelligence in the Cause of this Universe: Whereas in fair Lotterys, all ||⁷⁰Art|| in drawing is made, if not actually impossible, at least highly improbable.

⁷¹XVII. Let it be here observ'd also, "That a rational Agent may be capable of impressing Force ||⁷²without|| intending to produce any particular Form, and of designedly producing irregular or dissimilar Forms, as well as regular and similar:" And hence it follows, "That altho all the Regularity, Combination and Similarity in the Universe, are Presumptions of Design, yet Irregularity is no Presumption of the contrary; unless we suppose that the Agent is determin'd from a Sense of Beauty always to act regularly, and delight in Similarity; and that he can have

Irregularity does not prove want of Design.

no other inconsistent Motive of Action:" Which last is plainly absurd. We do not want in the Universe many Effects which seem to have been left to the general Laws of Motion upon some great Impulse, and [66] have many Instances where Similarity has been ‖⁷³plainly design'd‖ in some respects, and probably neglected in others; or even Dissimilarity design'd. Thus we see the general exact Resemblance between the two Eyes of most persons; and yet perhaps no other third Eye in the World ‖⁷⁴is‖ exactly like them. We see a gross Conformity of shape in all Persons in innumerable Parts, and yet no two Individuals of any Species are undistinguishable; which perhaps is intended for valuable Purposes to the whole Species.

⁷⁵XVIII. Hitherto the Proof amounts only to Design or Intention barely, in opposition to blind Force or Chance; and we see the Proof of this is independent on the arbitrary Constitution of our internal Sense of Beauty. Beauty is often suppos'd an Argument of more than Design, to wit, Wisdom and Prudence in the Cause. Let us enquire also into this. *Wisdom, Prudence.*

Wisdom denotes the pursuing of the best Ends by the best Means; and therefore before we can from any Effect prove the Cause to be wise, we must know what is best to the Cause or Agent. Among men who have pleasure in contemplating Uniformity, the Beauty of Effects is an Argument of Wisdom, because this is Good to [67] them; but the same Argument would not hold as to a Being void of this Sense of Beauty. And therefore the Beauty apparent to us in Nature, will not of itself prove Wisdom in the Cause, unless this Cause, or Author of Nature be suppos'd Benevolent; and then indeed the Happiness of Mankind is desirable or Good to the Supreme Cause; and that Form which pleases us, is an Argument of his Wisdom. And the Strength of this Argument is increased always in proportion to the Degree of Beauty produc'd in Nature, and expos'd to the View of any rational ‖⁷⁶Agent‖; since upon supposition of a benevolent Deity, all the apparent Beauty produc'd is an Evidence of the Execution of a Benevolent Design, to give ‖⁷⁷him‖ the Pleasures of Beauty.

⁷⁸But what more immediately proves Wisdom is this; when we see any Machine with a ‖⁷⁹vast‖ Complication of Parts actually obtaining

an End, we justly conclude, "That since this could not have been the Effect of Chance, it must have been intended for that End, which is obtain'd by it;" and then the Ends or Intentions, being in part known, the Complication of Organs, and their nice Disposition adapted to this End, is an Evidence "of a comprehensive large Understanding in the Cause, according to the Multi-[68]plicity of Parts, and the Appositeness of their Structure, even when we do not know the Intention of the Whole."

General Causes. [80]XIX. There is another kind of Beauty ||[81] also which is still pleasing to our Sense, and|| from which we conclude Wisdom in the Cause as well as Design, ||[82] and that is,|| when we see many useful or beautiful Effects flowing from one general Cause. There is a very good Reason for this Conclusion among Men. Interest must lead Beings of limited Powers, who are uncapable of a great diversity of Operations, and distracted by them, to chuse this frugal Oeconomy of their Forces, and to look upon such Management as an Evidence of Wisdom in other Beings like themselves. Nor is this speculative Reason all which influences them, for even beside this Consideration of Interest, they are determin'd by a Sense of Beauty where that Reason does not hold; as when we are judging of the Productions of other Agents about whose Oeconomy we are not sollicitous. Thus, who does not approve of it as a Perfection in Clock-work, that three or four Motions of the Hour, Minute, and second Hands, and monthly Plate, should arise from one Spring or Weight, rather than from three, or four Springs, or Weights, in a very Compound Machine, which should perform the same Effects, and answer all [69] the same Purposes with equal exactness? Now the Foundation of this Beauty plainly appears to be ||[83] Uniformity|| or Unity of Cause amidst Diversity of Effects.

General Laws. [84]XX. We ||[85] shall* hereafter|| offer some Reasons, why the Author of Nature ||[86] may|| chuse to operate in this manner by General Laws and Universal extensive Causes, altho the Reason just now mention'd does

* See the last Section.

not hold with an Almighty Being. This is certain, That we have some of the most delightful Instances of Universal Causes in the Works of Nature, and that the most studious men in these Subjects are so delighted with the Observation of them, that they always look upon them as Evidences of Wisdom in the Administration of Nature, from a Sense of Beauty.

[87] XXI. The wonderfully simple Mechanism which performs all Animal Motions, was mention'd* already; nor is that of the inanimate Parts of Nature less admirable. How innumerable are the Effects of that one Principle of Heat, deriv'd to us from the Sun, which is not only delightful to our Sight and Feeling, and the Means of discerning Objects, but is the Cause of Rains, Springs, Rivers, Winds, [70] and the universal Cause of Vegetation! The uniform Principle of Gravity preserves at once the Planets in their Orbits, gives Cohesion to the Parts of each Globe, and Stability to Mountains, Hills, and artificial Structures; it raises the Sea in Tides, and sinks them again, and restrains them in their Channels; it drains the Earth of its superfluous Moisture, by Rivers; it raises the Vapours by its Influence on the Air, and brings them down again in Rains; it gives an uniform Pressure to our Atmosphere, necessary to our Bodies in general, and more especially to Inspiration in Breathing; and furnishes us with an universal Movement, capable of being apply'd in innumerable Engines. How incomparably more beautiful is this Structure, than if we suppos'd so many distinct Volitions in the Deity, producing every particular Effect, and preventing some of the accidental Evils which casually flow from the general Law! ||[88] We may rashly imagine that|| this latter manner of Operation might have been more useful to us; and ||[89] it|| would have been no distraction to Omnipotence: But then the great Beauty had been lost, and there had been no more Pleasure in the Contemplation of this Scene, which is now so delightful. One would rather chuse to run the hazard of its casual Evils, than part with that harmonious Form which has been ||[90] an|| [71] unexhausted Source of Delight to the successive Spectators in all Ages.

* See above, Sect. ii. Art. 8.

Miracles. [91] XXII. Hence we see, "That however Miracles may prove the Super-intendency of a voluntary Agent, and that the Universe is not guided by Necessity or Fate, yet that Mind must be weak and inadvertent, which needs them to confirm the Belief of a Wise and Good Deity; since the deviation from general Laws, unless upon very extraordinary Occasions, must be a presumption of Inconstancy and Weakness, rather than of steddy Wisdom and Power, and must weaken the best Arguments we can have for the Sagacity and Power of the universal Mind." [72]

Of the Universality of the Sense of Beauty among Men.

I. We before* insinuated, "That all Beauty has a relation to some per-ceiving Power;" and consequently since we know not ||¹how great a|| Variety of Senses ||²there|| may be among Animals, there is no Form in Nature concerning which we can pronounce, "That it has no Beauty;" for it may still please some perceiving Power. But our Inquiry is confin'd to Men; and before we examine the Universality of this Sense of Beauty, or their agreement in approving Uniformity, it may be proper to con-sider, "||³whether||, as the other Senses which give us Pleasure do also give us Pain, so this Sense of Beauty does make some Objects disagree-able to us, and the occasion of Pain."

⁴That many Objects give no pleasure to our Sense is obvious, many are certainly void of Beauty: But then there is no Form which seems necessarily disagreeable of itself, when we dread no other Evil [73] from it, and compare it with nothing better of the Kind. Many Objects are naturally displeasing, and distasteful to our external Senses, as well as others pleasing and agreeable; as Smells, Tastes, and some separate Sounds: ||⁵but as|| to our Sense of Beauty, no Composition of Objects which give not unpleasant simple Ideas, seems positively unpleasant or painful of it self, had we never observ'd any thing better of the Kind. Deformity is only the absence of Beauty, or deficiency in the Beauty

Internal Sense not an immediate Source of Pain.

---

* See above Sect. i. Art. 17. Sect. iv. Art. 1.

expected in any Species: Thus bad Musick pleases Rusticks who never heard any better, and the finest Ear is not offended with tuning of Instruments if it be not too tedious, where no Harmony is expected; and yet much smaller Dissonancy shall offend amidst the Performance, where Harmony is expected. A rude Heap of Stones is no way offensive to one who shall be displeas'd with Irregularity in Architecture, where Beauty was expected. And had there been a Species of that Form which we ||⁶call now|| ugly or deform'd, and had we never seen or expected greater Beauty, we should have receiv'd no disgust from it, altho the Pleasure would not have been so great in this Form as in those we now admire. Our Sense of Beauty seems design'd to give us positive Pleasure, but not ||⁷positive|| Pain or Disgust, any further than what arises from disappointment. [74]

Approbation and Dislike from Association of Ideas.

II. There are indeed many Faces which at first View are apt to raise Dislike; but this is generally not from any ||⁸positive|| Deformity which of it self is positively displeasing, but either from want of expected Beauty, or much more from their carrying some natural indications of morally bad Dispositions, which we all acquire a Faculty of discerning in Countenances, Airs, and Gestures. That this is not occasion'd by any Form positively disgusting, will appear from this, That if upon long acquaintance we are sure of finding sweetness of Temper, Humanity and Cheerfulness, altho the bodily Form continues, it shall give us no Disgust or Displeasure; whereas ||⁹if any thing was|| naturally disagreeable, or the occasion of Pain, or positive Distaste, ||¹⁰it|| would always continue so, even although the Aversion we might have toward it were counterballanc'd by other Considerations. There are Horrors rais'd by some Objects, which are only the Effect of Fear for our selves, or Compassion ||¹¹toward|| others, when either Reason, or some foolish Association of Ideas, makes us apprehend Danger, and not the Effect of any thing in the Form it self: for we find that most of ||¹²those|| Objects which excite Horror at first, when Experience or Reason has remov'd the Fear, may become the occasions of Pleasure; as ||¹³ravenous|| [75] Beasts, a tempestuous Sea, a craggy Precipice, a dark shady Valley.

III. We shall see* ||¹⁴hereafter||, "That Associations of Ideas make Ob-   Associations.
jects pleasant, and delightful, which are not naturally apt to give any such
Pleasures; and the same way, the casual Conjunctions of Ideas may give
a Disgust, where there is nothing disagreeable in the Form it self." And
this is the occasion of many fantastick Aversions to Figures of some Ani-
mals, and to some other Forms: Thus ||¹⁵Swines||, Serpents of all Kinds,
and some Insects really beautiful enough, are beheld with Aversion by
many People, who have got some accidental Ideas associated to them.
And for Distastes of this Kind, ||¹⁶no|| other Account can be given.

IV. But as to the universal Agreement of Mankind in their Sense of   Universality of
Beauty from Uniformity amidst Variety, we must consult Experience: this Sense.
and as we allow all Men Reason, since all Men are capable of understanding simple Arguments, tho few are capable of complex Demonstrations; so in this Case it must be sufficient to prove this Sense of
Beauty universal, "if all Men are better pleas'd with Uniformity in the
[76] simpler Instances than the contrary, even when there is no Advantage observ'd attending it; and likewise if all Men, according as their
Capacity enlarges, so as to receive and compare more complex Ideas,
||¹⁷have a greater|| Delight in Uniformity, and are pleas'd with its more
complex Kinds, both Original and Relative."

Now let us consider if ever any Person was void of this Sense in
||¹⁸the|| simpler Instances. Few Trials have been made in the simplest
Instances of Harmony, because as soon as we find an Ear ||¹⁹incapable||
of relishing complex Compositions, such as our Tunes are, no further
Pains are employ'd about such. But in Figures, did ever any Man make
choice of a Trapezium, or any irregular Curve, for the Ichnography||²⁰or
Plan|| of his House, without Necessity, or some great Motive of ||²¹Con-
venience||? or to make the opposite Walls not parallel, or unequal in
Height? Were ever Trapeziums, irregular Polygons or Curves chosen for
the Forms of Doors or Windows, tho these Figures might have answer'd
the Uses as well, and would have often sav'd a great part of the ||²²Time,
Labour|| and Expence to Workmen, which is now employ'd in suiting

* See below Art. ii, i2. of this Section.

the Stones and Timber to the regular Forms? Among all the fantastick Modes of Dress, [77] none was ever quite void of Uniformity, if it were only in the resemblance of the two Sides of the same Robe, and in some general Aptitude to the human Form. The Pictish Painting had always relative Beauty by resemblance to other Objects, and often those Objects were originally beautiful: however justly we ||²³might|| apply Horace's Censure of impertinent Descriptions in Poetry.

Sed non erat his locus ————*ⁱ

But never were any so extravagant as to affect such Figures as are made by the casual spilling of liquid Colours. Who was ever pleas'd with an inequality of Heights in Windows of the same Range, or dissimilar Shapes of them? with unequal Legs or Arms, ||²⁴Eyes|| or Cheeks in a Mistress? It must ||²⁵however be|| acknowledg'd, "That Interest ||²⁶may often|| counterballance our Sense of Beauty in this Affair as well as in others, and superior good Qualitys may make us overlook such Imperfections."

Real Beauty alone pleases.

V. Nay further, it may perhaps appear, "That Regularity and Uniformity are so copiously diffus'd thro the Universe, and we are so readily determin'd to [78] pursue this as the Foundation of Beauty in Works of Art, that there is scarcely any thing ever fancy'd as Beautiful, where there is not really something of this Uniformity and Regularity." We are indeed often mistaken in imagining that there is the greatest possible Beauty, where it is but very imperfect; but still it is some degree of Beauty which pleases, altho there may be higher Degrees which we do not observe; and our Sense acts with full Regularity when we are pleas'd, altho we are kept by a false Prejudice from pursuing Objects which would please us more.

²⁷A Goth, for instance, is mistaken, when from Education he imagines the Architecture of his country to be the most perfect: and a Conjunction of ||²⁸some|| hostile Ideas, may make him have an Aversion to Roman Buildings, and study to demolish them, as some of our Reformers did the Popish Buildings, not being able to separate the Ideas of the

---

* Hor. de Arte Poet. v. 19.

i. Translation: "But for such things there was no place." Horace, *Satires, Epistles, and Ars Poetica,* trans. H. Rushton Fairclough, Loeb Classical Library (Cambridge, Mass.: Harvard University Press, 1970), 450.

superstitious Worship, from the Forms of the Buildings where it was practised: and yet it is still real Beauty which pleases the Goth, founded upon Uniformity amidst Variety. For the Gothick Pillars are uniform to each other, not only in their Sections, which are Lozenge-form'd; but also in their Heights and Ornaments: Their Arches are not one uniform Curve, but yet [79] they are Segments of similar Curves, and generally equal in the same Ranges. The very Indian Buildings have some kind of Uniformity, and many of the Eastern nations, tho they differ much from us, yet have great ||²⁹ Regularity|| in their Manner, as well as the Romans in theirs. Our Indian Screens, which wonderfully supply ||³⁰ the regular Imaginations of our Ladys|| with Ideas of Deformity, in which Nature is very churlish and sparing, do want indeed all the Beauty arising from Proportion of Parts, and Conformity to Nature; and yet they cannot divest themselves of all Beauty and Uniformity in the separate Parts: And this diversifying the human Body into various Contortions, may give some wild Pleasure from Variety, since some Uniformity to the human Shape is still retain'd.

VI. There is one sort of Beauty which might perhaps have been better mention'd before, but will not be impertinent here, because the Taste or Relish of it is universal in all Nations, and with the Young as well as the Old, and that is the Beauty of History. Every one knows how dull a Study it is to read over a Collection of Gazettes, which shall perhaps relate all the same Events with the Historian: The superior Pleasure then of History must arise, like that of Poetry, from the [80] Manners; ||³¹ as|| when we see a Character well drawn, wherein we find the secret Causes of a great Diversity of seemingly inconsistent Actions; or an Interest of State laid open, or an artful View nicely unfolded, the Execution of which influences very different and opposite Actions, as the Circumstances may alter. Now this reduces the whole to an Unity of Design at least: And this may be observ'd in the very Fables which entertain Children, otherwise we cannot make them relish them.

History pleases in like manner.

VII. What has been said will probably be assented to, if we always remember in our Inquirys into the Universality of the Sense of Beauty, "That there may be real Beauty, where there is not the greatest; and that there are an Infinity of different Forms which ||³²may|| all have some Unity, and yet differ from each other." So that Men may have different Fancys of Beauty, and yet Uniformity be the universal Foundation of our Approbation of any Form whatsoever as Beautiful. And we shall find that it is so in the Architecture, Gardening, Dress, Equipage, and Furniture of Houses, even among the most uncultivated Nations; where Uniformity still pleases, without any other Advantage than the Pleasure of the Contemplation of it. [81]

Diversity of Judgments concerning our Senses. VIII. It will deserve our Consideration on this Subject, how, in like Cases, we form very different Judgments concerning the internal and external Senses. Nothing is more ordinary among those, who after Mr. Locke have ||³³shaken off the groundless Opinions about|| innate Ideas, than to alledge, "That all our Relish for Beauty, and Order, is either from ||³⁴prospect of Advantage,|| Custom, or Education," for no other Reason but the Variety of Fancys in the World: and from this they conclude, "That our Fancys do not arise from any natural Power of Perception, or Sense." And yet all allow our external Senses to be Natural, and that the Pleasures or Pains of their Sensations, however they may be increas'd, or diminish'd, by Custom, or Education, and counterballanc'd by Interest, yet are really antecedent to Custom, Habit, Education, or Prospect of Interest. Now it is certain, "That there is at least as great a variety of Fancys about their Objects, as the Objects of Beauty:" Nay it is much more difficult, and perhaps impossible, to bring the Fancys or Relishes of the external Senses to any general Foundation at all, or to find any Rule for the agreeable or disagreeable: and yet we all allow "that these are natural Powers of Perception." [82]

The Reason of it. IX. The Reason of this different Judgment can be no other than this, That we have got distinct Names for the external Senses, and none, or very few, for the Internal; and by this are led, as in many other Cases, to look upon the former as some way more fix'd, and real and natural, than the latter. The Sense of Harmony has got its Name, ||³⁵viz.|| a good Ear; and we are generally brought to acknowledge this a natural Power of Perception, or a Sense some way distinct from Hearing: now it is certain,

"That there is as necessary a Perception of Beauty upon the presence of regular Objects, as of Harmony upon hearing certain Sounds."

X. But let it be observ'd here once for all, "That an internal Sense no more presupposes an innate Idea, or Principle of Knowledge, than the external." Both are natural Powers of Perception, or Determinations of the Mind to receive necessarily certain Ideas from the presence of Objects. The internal Sense is, a passive Power of receiving Ideas of Beauty from all Objects in which there is Uniformity amidst Variety. Nor does there seem any thing more difficult in this matter, than that the Mind should be always determin'd to receive the Idea of Sweet, when Particles of such a Form enter the Pores of [83] the Tongue; or to have the Idea of Sound upon any quick Undulation of the Air. The one seems to have as little Connection with its Idea, as the other: And the same Power could with equal ease constitute the former the occasion of Ideas as the latter.

An internal Sense does not presuppose innate Ideas.

XI. The Association of Ideas* above hinted at, is one great Cause of the apparent Diversity of Fancys in the Sense of Beauty, as well as in the external Senses; and often makes Men have an aversion to Objects of Beauty, and a liking to others void of it, but under different Conceptions than those of Beauty or Deformity. And here it may not be improper to give some Instances of some of these Associations. The Beauty of Trees, their cool Shades, and their Aptness to conceal from Observation, have made Groves and Woods the usual Retreat to those who love Solitude, especially to the Religious, the Pensive, the Melancholy, and the Amorous. And do not we find that we have so join'd the Ideas of these Dispositions of Mind with those external Objects, that they always recur to us along with them? The Cunning of the Heathen Priests might make such obscure Places the Scene of the fictitious Appearances of their Deitys; and hence we join Ideas of something Divine [84] to them. We know the like Effect in the Ideas of our Churches, from the perpetual use of them only in religious Exercises. The faint Light in Gothick Build-

Associations Cause of Disagreement.

---

* See above Art. 3. of this Section.

ings has had the same Association of a very foreign Idea, which our Poet shews in his Epithet,

———— A Dim religious Light.*ii

In like manner it is known, That often all the Circumstances of Actions, or Places, or Dresses of Persons, or Voice, or Song, which have occur'd at any time together, when we were strongly affected by any Passion, will be so connected that any one of these will make all the rest recur. And this is often the occasion both of great Pleasure and Pain, Delight and Aversion to many Objects, which of themselves might have been perfectly indifferent to us: but these Approbations, or Distastes, are remote from the Ideas of Beauty, being plainly different Ideas.

Musick, how it pleases differently.

XII. There is also another Charm in Musick to various Persons, which is distinct from the Harmony, and is occasion'd by its raising agreeable Passions. The human Voice is obviously vary'd by all the stronger Passions; now when our Ear discerns [85] any resemblance between the Air of a Tune, whether sung or play'd upon an Instrument, either in its Time, or ||³⁶Modulation,|| or any other Circumstance, to the sound of the human Voice in any Passion, we shall be touch'd by it in a very sensible manner, and have Melancholy, Joy, Gravity, Thoughtfulness excited in us by a sort of Sympathy or Contagion. The same Connexion is observable between the very Air of a Tune, and the Words expressing any Passion which we have heard it fitted to, so that they shall both recur to us together, tho but one of them affects our Senses.

³⁷Now in such a diversity of pleasing or displeasing Ideas which may be ||³⁸join'd|| with Forms of Bodys, or Tunes, when Men are of such different Dispositions, and prone to such a variety of Passions, it is no

* Milt. *Il Penseroso.*
ii. John Milton (1608–74), English poet and author. His major poems are *On the Morning of Christ's Nativity, L'Allegro,* and *Il Penseroso* (early works), *Paradise Lost* and *Paradise Regained* (later works). He wrote extensively on theological and political issues as well (for example, *The Doctrine and Discipline of Divorce,* 1643; *The Tenure of Kings and Magistrates,* 1649; *The Ready and Easy Way to Establish a Free Commonwealth,* 1660).

wonder "that they should often disagree in their Fancys of Objects, even altho their Sense of Beauty and Harmony were perfectly uniform;" because many other Ideas may either please or displease, according to Persons Tempers, and past Circumstances. We know how agreeable a very wild Country may be to any Person who has spent the chearful Days of his Youth in it, and how disagreeable very beautiful Places may be, if they were the Scenes of his [86] Misery. And this may help us in many Cases to account for the Diversitys of Fancy, without denying the Uniformity of our internal Sense of Beauty.

XIII. Grandeur and Novelty are two Ideas different from Beauty, which often recommend Objects to us. The Reason of this is foreign to the present Subject. See *Spectator* No. 412. [87]

Of the Power of Custom, Education, and Example, as to our internal Senses.

I. Custom, Education, and Example are so often alledg'd in this Affair, as the occasion of our Relish for beautiful Objects, and for our Approbation of, or Delight in a certain Conduct in Life, in a moral ||¹Sense||, that it is necessary to examine these three particularly, to make it appear "that there is a natural Power of Perception, or Sense of Beauty in Objects, antecedent to all Custom, Education, or Example."

Custom gives no new Sense.

II. Custom, as distinct from the other two, operates in this manner. As to Actions, it only gives a disposition to the Mind or Body more easily to perform those Actions which have been frequently repeated, but never leads us to apprehend them under any other View than what we were capable of apprehending them under at first; nor gives us any new Power of Perception about them. We are naturally capable of Sentiments of Fear, and Dread of any powerful Presence; and [88] so Custom may connect the Ideas of religious Horror to certain Buildings: but ||²Custom could never|| have made a Being naturally incapable of Fear, receive such Ideas. So had we no other Power of perceiving, or forming Ideas of Actions, but as they were advantageous or disadvantageous, Custom could only have made us more ready at perceiving the Advantage or Disadvantage of Actions. But this is not to our present Purpose.

As to our Approbation of, or Delight in external Objects. When the Blood or Spirits of which Anatomists talk are rouz'd, quicken'd, or fermented as they call it, in any agreeable manner by Medicine or Nutriment; or any Glands frequently stimulated to Secretion; it is certain that to preserve the Body easy, we ||³shall|| delight in Objects of Taste which of themselves are not immediately pleasant to ||⁴it||, if they promote that agreeable State which the Body had been accustom'd to. Further, Custom will so alter the State of the Body, that what at first rais'd uneasy Sensations will cease to do so, or perhaps raise another agreeable Idea of the same Sense; but Custom can never give us any Idea of ||⁵a Sense different from those|| we had antecedent to it: It will never make the Blind approve Objects as coloured, or those who have no Taste approve Meats as delicious, however they [89] might ||⁶approve them as|| Strengthning or Exhilarating. Were our Glands and the Parts about them void of Feeling, did we perceive no Pleasure from certain brisker Motions in the Blood, ||⁷Custom could never|| make stimulating or intoxicating Fluids or Medicines agreeable, when they were not so to the Taste: So by like Reasoning, had we no natural Sense of Beauty from Uniformity, Custom could never have made us imagine any Beauty in Objects; if we had had no Ear, Custom could never have given us the Pleasures of Harmony. When we have these natural Senses antecedently, Custom may make us capable of extending our Views further, and of receiving more complex Ideas of Beauty in Bodys, or Harmony in Sounds, by increasing our Attention and quickness of Perception. But however Custom may increase our Power of receiving or comparing complex Ideas, yet it seems rather to weaken than strengthen the Ideas of Beauty, or the Impressions of Pleasure from regular Objects; else how ||⁸is|| it possible that any Person could go into the open Air on a sunny Day, or clear Evening, without the most extravagant Raptures, such as Milton* represents our Ancestor in upon his first Creation? For such any Person would certainly fall into, upon the first Representation of such a Scene. [90]

Custom in like manner ||⁹may|| make it easier for any Person to discern the Use of a complex Machine, and approve it as advantageous; but he would never have imagin'd it Beautiful, had he no natural Sense of Beauty. Custom may make us quicker in apprehending the Truth of

---

* See *Paradise Lost,* Book 8.

complex Theorems, but we all find the Pleasure or Beauty of Theorems as strong at first as ever. Custom makes us more capable of retaining and comparing complex Ideas, so as to discern more complicated Uniformity, which escapes the Observation of Novices in any Art; but all this presupposes a natural Sense of Beauty in Uniformity: for had there been nothing in Forms, which was constituted ||¹⁰the necessary|| occasion of Pleasure to our Senses, no Repetition of indifferent Ideas as to Pleasure or Pain, Beauty or Deformity, could ever have made them grow pleasing or displeasing.

Nor
Education.

III. The Effect of Education is this, that thereby we receive many speculative Opinions, ||¹¹which are|| sometimes true and sometimes false; and are often led to believe that Objects may be naturally apt to give Pleasure or Pain to our external Senses, ||¹²which in reality have|| no such Qualitys. And further, by Education there are some strong Associations of Ideas without any Reason, by mere Accident sometimes, as well as [91] by Design, which it is very hard for us ever after to break asunder. Thus Aversions are rais'd to Darkness, and to many kinds of ||¹³Meat||, and to certain innocent Actions: Approbations without Ground are rais'd in like manner. But in all these Instances, Education never makes us apprehend any Qualitys in Objects, which we have not naturally Senses capable of perceiving. We know what Sickness of the Stomach is, and may without Ground believe that very healthful Meats will raise this; we by our Sight and Smell receive disagreeable Ideas of the Food of Swine, and their Styes, and perhaps cannot prevent the recurring of these Ideas at Table: but never were Men naturally Blind prejudic'd against Objects as of a disagreeable Colour, or in favour of others as of a beautiful Colour; they ||¹⁴perhaps hear|| Men dispraise one Colour, ||¹⁵and may|| imagine this Colour to be some quite different sensible Quality of the other Senses||¹⁶, but that is all||: And the same way, a Man naturally void of Taste could by no Education receive the Ideas of Taste, or be prejudic'd in favour of Meats as delicious: So, had we no natural Sense of Beauty and Harmony, we ||¹⁷could never|| be prejudic'd in favour of Objects or Sounds as Beautiful or Harmonious. Education may make an unattentive Goth imagine that his Countrymen have attain'd the Perfection of Archi-[92]tecture; and an Aversion to their Enemys the Romans, may have join'd some disagreeable Ideas to their very Buildings, and excited them to their Demolition; but he had never form'd these Prejudices, had he been void of a Sense of Beauty. Did ever blind Men debate whether Purple or Scarlet were the finer Colour? or could any Education prejudice them in favour of either as Colours?

Thus Education and Custom may influence our internal Senses, where they are antecedently, by enlarging the Capacity of our Minds to retain and compare the Parts of complex Compositions: And ‖ ^{18} then‖ if the finest Objects are presented to us, we grow conscious of a Pleasure far superior to what common Performances excite. But all this presupposes our Sense of Beauty to be natural. Instruction in Anatomy, Observation of Nature, and of those Airs of the Countenance and Attitudes of Body, which accompany any Sentiment, Action, or Passion, may enable us to know where there is a just Imitation: but why should an exact Imitation please upon Observation, if we had not naturally a Sense of Beauty in it, more than the observing the Situation of fifty or a hundred Pebbles thrown at random? and should we ‖ ^{19} observe‖ them ever so often, we ‖ ^{20} should‖ never dream of their growing Beautiful. [93]

IV. There is something worth our Observation as to the manner of rooting out the Prejudices of Education, not quite foreign to the present purpose. When the Prejudice arises from Associations of Ideas without any natural Connection, we must frequently force our selves to bear Representations of those Objects, or the Use of them when separated from the disagreeable Idea; and this may at last disjoin the unreasonable Association, especially if we can join new agreeable Ideas to them: Thus Opinions of Superstition are best remov'd by pleasant Conversation of Persons we esteem for their Virtue, or ‖ ^{21} by observing that they‖ despise such Opinions. But when the Prejudice arises from an Apprehension or Opinion of natural Evil, as the Attendant, or Consequent of any Object or Action; if the Evil be apprehended to be the constant and immediate Attendant, a few Trials without receiving any Damage will remove the Prejudice, as in that against Meats: But where the Evil is not represented as the perpetual Concomitant, but as what may possibly or probably at

Prejudices how removed.

some time or other accompany the use of the Object, there must be frequent Reasoning with our selves, or a long Series of Trials without any Detriment, to remove the Prejudice; such is the Case of our Fear of Spirits in the dark, and in Church-yards. And [94] when the Evil is represented as the Consequence perhaps a long time after, or in a future State, it is then hardest of all to remove the Prejudice; and this is only to be effected by slow Processes of Reason, because in this Case there can be no Trials made: and this is the Case of superstitious Prejudices against Actions apprehended as offensive to the Deity; and hence it is that they are so hard to be rooted out.

Example not the Cause of internal Sense.

V. Example seems to operate in this manner. We are conscious that we act very much for Pleasure, or private Good; and ||²²are thereby|| led to imagine that others do so too: hence we conclude there must be some Perfection in the Objects which we see others pursue, and Evil in those which we observe them constantly shunning. Or, the Example of others may serve to us as so many Trials to remove the Apprehension of Evil in Objects ||²³to which we had an Aversion||. But all this is done upon an Apprehension of Qualitys perceivable by the Senses which we have; for no Example will induce the Blind or Deaf to pursue Objects as Colour'd or Sonorous; nor could Example any more engage us to pursue Objects as Beautiful or Harmonious, had we no ||²⁴natural Sense of Beauty or Harmony||. [95]

Example may make us ||²⁵conclude without Examination,|| that our Countrymen have obtain'd the Perfection of Beauty in their Works, or that there is less Beauty in the Orders of Architecture or Painting us'd in other Nations, and so content our selves with very imperfect Forms. ||²⁶And|| Fear of Contempt as void of Taste or Genius, ||²⁷often|| makes us join in approving the Performances of the reputed Masters in our Country, and restrains those who have naturally a fine Genius, or the internal Senses very acute, from studying to obtain the greatest Perfection; it makes also those of a bad Taste pretend ||²⁸to|| ||²⁹a|| Perception of ||³⁰Beauty|| ||³¹which in reality they have not||: But all this presupposes some natural Power of receiving Ideas of Beauty

and Harmony. Nor can Example effect any thing further, unless it be
to lead Men to pursue Objects by implicit Faith, for some Perfection
which the Pursuer is conscious he does not know, or which perhaps is
some very different Quality from the Idea perceiv'd by those of a good
Taste in such Affairs. [96]

Of the Importance of the internal Senses in Life, and the final Causes of them.

Importance of the internal Senses.

I. The busy part of Mankind may look upon these things as airy Dreams of an inflam'd Imagination, which a wise Man should despise, who rationally pursues more solid Possessions independent on Fancy: but a little Reflection will convince us, "That the Gratifications of our internal Senses are as natural, real, and satisfying Enjoyments as any sensible Pleasure whatsoever; and that they are the chief Ends for which we commonly pursue Wealth and Power." For how is Wealth or Power advantageous? How do they make us happy, or prove good to us? No otherwise than as they supply Gratifications to our Senses or Facultys of perceiving Pleasure. Now, are these Senses or Facultys only the External ones? No: Every body sees, that a small portion of Wealth or Power will supply more Pleasures of the external Senses than we can enjoy; we know that Scarcity often heightens these Perceptions more than A-[97]bundance, which cloys that Appetite which is necessary to all Pleasure in Enjoyment: and hence the Poet's Advice is perfectly just;

———— Tu pulmentaria quaere Sudando ————*i

---

* Hor. Lib. 2. Sat. 2. v. 20.

i. Translation: "So earn your sauce with hard exercise." Horace, *Satires, Epistles, and Ars Poetica,* trans. H. Rushton Fairclough, Loeb Classical Library (Cambridge, Mass.: Harvard University Press, 1970), 138.

In short, the only use of a great Fortune, above a very small one (except in good Offices and moral Pleasures) must be to supply us with the Pleasures of Beauty, Order, and Harmony.

‖¹ᵃIt is true indeed, that ‖²ᵇthe Enjoyment ofᵇ‖ the ‖³ᶜnoblestᶜ‖ Pleasures of the internal Senses, in the Contemplation of the Works of Nature, ‖⁴ᵈisᵈ‖ expos'd to every one without Expence; the Poor and the Low, may have as free ‖⁵ᵉaᵉ‖ use of these Objects, in this way, as the Wealthy or Powerful. And even in Objects which may be appropriated, the Property is of little Consequence to the Enjoyment of their Beauty, which is often enjoy'd by others beside the Proprietor. But then there are other Objects of these internal Senses, which require Wealth, or Power to procure the use of them as frequently as we desire; as appears in Architecture, Musick, Gardening, Painting, Dress, Equipage, Furniture; of which we cannot [98] have the full Enjoyment without Property. And there are some confus'd Imaginations, which often lead us to pursue Property, even in Objects where it is not necessary to the true Enjoyment of them. These are the ultimate Motives of our pursuing the greater Degrees of Wealth, where there are no generous Intentions of virtuous Actions.ᵃ‖

This is confirm'd by the constant Practice of the very Enemys to these Senses. As soon as they think they are got above the World, or extricated from the Hurrys of Avarice and Ambition; banish'd Nature will return upon them, and set them upon Pursuits of Beauty and Order in their Houses, Gardens, Dress, Table, Equipage. They are never easy without some degree of this; and were their Hearts open to our View, we should see Regularity, Decency, Beauty, as what their Wishes terminate upon, either to themselves or their Posterity; and what their Imagination is always presenting to them as the possible ‖⁶Effects‖ of their Labours. Nor without this, could they ever justify their Pursuits to themselves.

There may perhaps be some Instances of human Nature perverted into a thorow Miser, who loves nothing but Money, and whose Fancy arises no higher than the cold [99] dull Thought of Possession; but such an Instance in an Age, must not be made the Standard of Mankind against the whole Body.

If we examine the Pursuits of the Luxurious, who ‖⁷in the opinion of the World is‖ wholly devoted to his Belly; we shall generally find that the far greater part of his Expence is employ'd to procure other Sensations than those of Taste; such as fine Attendants, regular Apartments, Services of Plate, and the like. ||⁸Besides||, a large share of the Preparation must be suppos'd design'd for some sort of generous friendly Purposes, ||⁹as|| to please Acquaintance, Strangers, Parasites. How few would be contented to enjoy the same Sensations alone, in a Cottage, or out of earthen Pitchers? To conclude this Point, however these internal Sensations may be overlook'd in our Philosophical Inquirys about the human Facultys, we shall find in Fact, "That they employ us more, and are more efficacious in Life, either to our Pleasure, or Uneasiness, than all our external Senses taken together."

Final Cause of the internal Senses. II. As to the final Causes of this internal Sense, we need not enquire, "whether, to an almighty and all-knowing Being, there be any real Excellence in regular Forms, in acting by general Laws, in [100] knowing by Theorems?" We seem scarce capable of answering such Questions any way; nor need we enquire, "whether other Animals may not discern Uniformity and Regularity in Objects which escape our Observation, and may not perhaps have their Senses constituted so as to perceive Beauty, from the same Foundation which we do, in Objects which our Senses are not ||¹⁰fit|| to examine or compare?" We shall confine our selves to a Subject where we have some certain ||¹¹Foundation|| to go upon, and only enquire, "if we can find any Reasons worthy of the great Author of Nature, for making such a Connection between regular Objects, and the Pleasure which accompanys our Perceptions of them; or, what Reasons might possibly influence him to create the World, as it at present is, as far as we can observe, every where full of Regularity and Uniformity?"

¹²Let it be here observ'd, that as far as we know ||¹³concerning|| any of the great Bodys of the Universe, we see Forms and Motions really Beautiful to our Senses; and if we were plac'd in any Planet, the apparent Courses would still be Regular and Uniform, and consequently Beautiful to ||¹⁴our Sense||. Now this gives us no small Ground to imagine, that if the Senses of their Inhabitants are in the same manner [101] adapted to their Habitations, and the Objects occurring to their View, as ours

are here, their Senses must be upon the same general Foundation with ours.

But to return to the Questions: What occurs to resolve them, may be contain'd in the following Propositions.

1. The manner of Knowledge by universal Theorems, and of Operation by universal Causes, as far as we can attain ‖¹⁵it,‖ must be most convenient for Beings of limited Understanding and Power; since this prevents Distraction in their Understandings thro the Multiplicity of Propositions, and Toil and Weariness to their Powers of Action: and consequently their Reason, without any Sense of Beauty, must approve of such Methods when they reflect upon their apparent Advantage.

2. Those Objects of Contemplation in which there is Uniformity amidst Variety, are more distinctly and easily comprehended and retain'd, than irregular Objects; because the accurate Observation of one or two Parts often leads to the Knowledge of the Whole: Thus we can from a Pillar or two, with an intermediate Arch, and Cornice, form a distinct Idea of a whole regular Building, if we know of what Species it is, and have its Length and [102] Breadth: From a Side and solid Angle, we have the whole regular Solid; the measuring one Side, gives the whole Square; one Radius, the whole ‖¹⁶Circle‖; two Diameters, an Oval; one Ordinate and Abscissa, the Parabola; ‖¹⁷and so on in more complex Figures which have any Regularity, which can be entirely determin'd and known in every Part‖ from a few Data: Whereas it must be a long Attention to a vast Multiplicity of Parts, which can ascertain or fix the Idea of any irregular Form, or give any distinct Idea of it, or make us capable of retaining it; as appears in the Forms of rude Rocks, and Pebbles, and confus'd Heaps, even when the Multitude of sensible Parts is not so great as in the regular Forms: for such irregular Objects distract the Mind with Variety, since for every sensible Part we must have a quite different Idea.

3. From ‖¹⁸these‖ two Propositions it follows, "That Beings of limited Understanding and Power, if they act rationally for their own Interest, must chuse to operate by the simplest Means, to invent general Theorems, and to study regular Objects, if they be ‖¹⁹as useful as‖ irregular ones; that they may avoid the endless Toil of producing each Effect by a separate Operation, of searching ‖²⁰out‖ each different Truth by a dif-

ferent [103] Inquiry, and of imprinting the endless Variety of dissimilar Ideas in irregular Objects."

4. But then, beside this Consideration of Interest, there does not appear to be any necessary Connection, ||²¹ antecedent|| to the Constitution of the Author of Nature, ||²² between|| regular Forms, Actions, Theorems, and that sudden sensible Pleasure excited in us upon observation of them, even when we do not reflect upon the Advantage mention'd in the former Proposition. And possibly, the Deity could have form'd us so as to have receiv'd ||²³ no|| Pleasure from such ||²⁴ Objects||, or connected Pleasure to those of a quite contrary Nature. We have a tolerable Presumption of this in the Beautys of various Animals; they give some small Pleasure indeed to every one who views them, but then every ||²⁵ one|| seems ||²⁶ vastly|| more delighted with ||²⁷ the peculiar Beautys of its own Species, than with those of a different one,|| which seldom raise any desire ||²⁸ but among Animals of the same Species with the one admir'd||. This makes it probable, that the Pleasure is not the necessary Result of the Form it self, otherwise it would equally affect all Apprehensions in what Species soever||²⁹; but depends upon a voluntary Constitution,|| adapted to preserve the Regularity of the Universe, and is probably not the Effect of Necessity [104] but Choice in the Supreme Agent, who constituted our Senses.

From the divine Goodness.

5. Now from the whole we may conclude, "That supposing the Deity so kind as to connect sensible Pleasure with certain Actions or Contemplations, beside the rational Advantage perceivable in them; there is a great moral Necessity, from his Goodness, that the internal Sense of Men should be constituted as it is at present, so as to make Uniformity amidst Variety the Occasion of Pleasure." For were it not so, but on the contrary, if irregular Objects, particular Truths, and Operations pleased us, beside the endless Toil this would involve us in, there must arise a perpetual Dissatisfaction in all rational Agents with themselves; since Reason and Interest would lead us to simple general Causes, while a contrary Sense of Beauty would make us disapprove them: Universal Theorems would appear to our Understanding the best Means of increasing our Knowledge of what might be useful; while a contrary Sense would set us on the search after ||³⁰ particular|| Truths: Thought and Reflection would

recommend Objects with Uniformity amidst Variety, and yet this perverse Instinct would involve us in Labyrinths of Confusion and Dissimilitude. And hence we see "how suitable it is to the sagacious [105] Bounty which we suppose in the Deity, to constitute our internal Senses in the manner in which they are; by which Pleasure is join'd to the Contemplation of those Objects which a finite Mind can best imprint and retain the Ideas of with the least Distraction; to those Actions which are most efficacious, and fruitful in useful Effects; and to those Theorems which most enlarge our Minds."

[31] III. As to the other Question, "What Reason might influence the Deity, whom no ||[32]Diversity|| of Operation could distract or weary, to chuse to operate by simplest Means and general Laws, and to diffuse Uniformity, Proportion and Similitude thro all the Parts of Nature which we can observe?" Perhaps there may be some real Excellence in this Manner of Operation, and in these Forms, which we know not: but this we may probably say, that since the divine Goodness, for the Reasons above mention'd, has constituted our Sense of Beauty as it is at present, the same Goodness might ||[33]determine|| the Great Architect to adorn this ||[34]vast|| Theatre in ||[35]a manner|| agreeable to the Spectators, and that part which is expos'd to the Observation of Men, so as to be pleasant to them; especially if we suppose that he design'd to discover himself to them as Wise and Good, [106] as well as Powerful: for thus he has given them greater Evidences, thro the whole Earth, of his Art, Wisdom, Design, and Bounty, than they can possibly have for the Reason, Counsel, and Good-will of their fellow-Creatures, with whom they converse, with full Persuasion of ||[36]these qualities in them, about|| their common Affairs.

Reason of general Laws.

As to the Operations of the Deity by general Laws, there is ||[37]still a further Reason from a Sense|| superior to these already consider'd, even that of Virtue, or the Beauty of Action, which is the Foundation of our greatest Happiness. For were there no general Laws fix'd in the Course of Nature, there could be no Prudence or Design in Men, no rational Expectation of Effects from Causes, no Schemes of Action projected, ||[38]or|| any regular Execution. If then, according to the Frame of our

Nature, our greatest happiness must depend upon our Actions, as it may perhaps be made appear it does, "The Universe must be govern'd, not by particular Wills, but by general Laws, upon which we can found our Expectations, and project our Schemes of Action." ||[39a]Nay further, tho general Laws did ordinarily obtain, yet if the Deity usually stopp'd their ||[40b]Ef-[107]fects[b]|| whenever it was necessary to prevent any particular Evils; this would effectually, ||[41c]and justly[c]|| supersede all human Prudence and Care about Actions; since a superior Mind did thus relieve Men from their Charge.[a]||

||[42]The End of the First Treatise.||

viz.

An Inquiry Concerning the Original of our Ideas of Virtue or Moral Good.

———— Quod magis ad nos
Pertinet, & nescire malum est, agitamus: utrumne
Divitiis homines, an sint Virtute beati:
Quidve ad Amicitias, Usus, Rectumne, trahat nos
Et quae sit natura Boni, summumque quid ejus.[i]

—Hor. *Sat.* 6. Lib. 2. v. 72.‖ [111]

---

i. Translation: "We discuss matters which concern us more, and of which it is harmful to be in ignorance—whether wealth or virtue makes men happy, whether self-interest or uprightness leads us to friendship, what is the nature of the good and what is its highest form." Horace, *Satires, Epistles, and Ars Poetica,* trans. H. Rushton Fairclough, Loeb Classical Library (Cambridge, Mass.: Harvard University Press, 1970), *Satires,* II.vi.72–76, p. 216.

An Inquiry Concerning Moral Good and Evil.

Introduction.

The Word Moral Goodness, ||²in this Treatise,|| denotes our Idea of some Quality apprehended in Actions, which procures Approbation, ||³and Love toward the Actor, from those who receive no Advantage by the Action.|| Moral Evil, denotes our Idea of a contrary Quality, which excites ||⁴Aversion, and Dislike toward the Actor, even from Persons unconcern'd in its natural Tendency.|| We must be contented with these imperfect Descriptions, until we discover ||⁵whether we really have such Ideas, and what general Foundation there is in Nature for|| this Dif-[112]ference of Actions, as morally Good or Evil.

These Descriptions seem to contain an universally acknowledg'd Difference of Moral Good and Evil, from Natural. All Men who speak of moral Good, acknowledge that it procures ||⁶Love|| toward those we apprehend possess'd of it; whereas natural Good does not. In this matter Men must consult their own Breasts. How differently are they affected toward ||⁷those|| they suppose possess'd of Honesty, Faith, Generosity, Kindness||⁸, even when they expect no Benefit from these admir'd Qualitys||; and those who are possess'd of the natural Goods, such as Houses, Lands, Gardens, Vineyards, Health, Strength, Sagacity? We shall find that we necessarily love and approve the Possessors of the former; but the Possession of the latter procures no ||⁹Love|| at all toward the Possessor, but often contrary Affections of Envy and Hatred. In the same manner, whatever Quality we apprehend to be morally Evil, raises our ||¹⁰Hatred|| toward the Person in whom we observe it, such as Treachery, Cruelty, Ingratitude||¹¹, even when they are no way hurtful to our selves||; whereas we heartily love, esteem and pity many who are expos'd to nat-

85

ural Evils, such as Pain, Poverty, Hunger, Sickness, Death‖[12], even when [113] we our selves suffer Inconveniencies, by these natural Evils of others‖.

Now the first Question on this Subject is, "Whence arise these different Ideas of Actions."

Interest.
Advantage.
Because we shall afterwards frequently use the Words Interest, Advantage, natural Good, it is necessary here to fix their Ideas. The Pleasure in our sensible Perceptions of any kind, gives us our first Idea of natural Good, or Happiness; and then all Objects which are apt to excite this Pleasure are call'd immediately Good. Those Objects which may procure others immediately pleasant, are call'd Advantageous: and we pursue both Kinds from a View of Interest, or from Self-Love.

Our Sense of Pleasure is antecedent to Advantage or Interest, and is the Foundation of ‖[13]it‖. We do not perceive Pleasure in Objects, because it is our Interest to do so; but Objects or Actions are Advantageous, and are pursu'd or undertaken from Interest, because we receive Pleasure from them. Our Perception of Pleasure is necessary, and nothing is Advantageous or naturally Good to us, but what is apt to raise Pleasure mediately, or ‖[14]immediately. Such‖ Objects as we know, either from Experience of Sense, or Reason, to be immediately, [114] or mediately Advantageous, or apt to minister Pleasure, we ‖[15]are said to‖ pursue from Self-Interest, when our Intention is only to enjoy this Pleasure, which they have the Power of exciting. Thus Meats, Drink, Harmony, fine Prospects, Painting, Statues, are perceiv'd by our Senses to be immediately Good; and our Reason shews Riches and Power to be mediately so, that is, apt to furnish us with Objects of immediate Pleasure: and both Kinds of these natural Goods are pursu'd from Interest, or Self-Love.

Opinions
about our
Sense of moral
Good and Evil.
Now the greatest part of our latter Moralists[ii] establish it as undeniable, "That all moral Qualitys have necessarily some Relation to the Law of a Superior, of sufficient Power to make us Happy or Miserable;" and since all Laws operate only by Sanctions of Rewards, or Punish-

ii. Cf. Thomas Hobbes, *Leviathan,* London, 1651, pt. 1, chaps. 14, 15; John Locke, *An Essay Concerning Human Understanding,* London, 1690, bk. 4, chap. 28; similar

ments, which determine us to Obedience by Motives of Self-Interest, they suppose, "that it is thus that Laws do constitute some Actions mediately Good, or Advantageous, and others the same way Disadvantageous." They say indeed, "That a benevolent Legislator constitutes no Actions Advantageous to the Agent by Law, but such as in their own Nature tend to the natural Good of the Whole, or, at least, are not inconsistent with it; and that therefore we approve [115] the Virtue of others, because it has some small Tendency to our Happiness, either from its own Nature, or from this general Consideration, That Obedience to a benevolent Legislator, is in general Advantageous to the Whole, and to us in particular; and that for the contrary Reasons alone, we disapprove the Vice of others, that is, the prohibited Action, as tending to our particular Detriment in some degree." ||¹⁶But|| then they maintain, "That we are determin'd to Obedience to Laws, or deterr'd from Disobedience, merely by Motives of Self-Interest, to obtain either the natural Good arising from the commanded Action, or the Rewards promised by the Sanction; or to avoid the natural evil Consequences of Disobedience, or at least the Penaltys of the Law."

Some other Moralists[iii] suppose "an immediate natural Good in the Actions call'd Virtuous; that is, That we are determin'd to perceive some Beauty in the Actions of others, and to love the Agent, even without reflecting upon any Advantage which can any way redound to us from the Action; that we have also a secret Sense of Pleasure ||¹⁷accompanying|| such of our own Actions as we call Virtuous, even when we expect no other Advantage from them." But they [116] alledge at the same time, "That we are excited to perform these Actions, even as we pursue, or purchase Pictures, Statues, Landskips, from Self-Interest, to obtain this Pleasure which ||¹⁸accompanys the very Action, and which we necessarily enjoy in doing it.||" The Design of the following Sections is to enquire into this matter; and perhaps the Reasons to be offer'd may prove,

---

views are in Calvin and Calvinist theology, see John Calvin, *Commentaries on the Bible,* vol. 13, pt. 2.

iii. Here Hutcheson probably thinks of Shaftesbury (*Inquiry Concerning Virtue,* bk. 1, pt. 2, sect. 1).

I. "That some Actions have to Men an immediate Goodness; or, that by a superior Sense, which I call a Moral one, we ‖[19] perceive Pleasure in the Contemplation of such Actions in others, and are determin'd to love the Agent, (and much more do we perceive Pleasure in being conscious of having done such Actions our selves)‖ without any View of further natural Advantage from them."

II. It may perhaps also appear, "‖[20] That what excites us to these Actions which we call Virtuous, is not an Intention to obtain even this sensible Pleasure‖; much less the future Rewards from Sanctions of Laws, or any other natural Good, which may be the Consequence of the virtuous Action; but an entirely different Principle of Action ‖[21] from Interest or Self-Love.‖" [117]

Of the Moral Sense by which we perceive Virtue and Vice, and approve or disapprove them in others.

I. That the Perceptions of moral Good and Evil, are perfectly different from those of natural Good, or Advantage, every one must convince himself, by reflecting upon the different Manner in which he finds himself affected when these Objects occur to him. Had we no Sense of Good distinct from the Advantage or Interest arising from the external Senses, and the Perceptions of Beauty and Harmony; ||¹our Admiration and Love|| toward a fruitful Field, or commodious Habitation, would be much the same with what we have toward a generous Friend, or any noble Character; for both are, or may be advantageous to us: And we should no more admire any Action, or love any Person in a distant Country, or Age, whose Influence could not extend to us, than we love the Mountains of Peru, while we are unconcern'd in the Spanish Trade. We should have the same Sentiments and Affections [118] toward inanimate Beings, which we have toward rational Agents; which yet every one knows to be false. Upon Comparison, we say, "Why should we ||²admire or love with Esteem|| inanimate Beings? They have no Intention of Good to ||³us||; their Nature makes them fit for our Uses, which they neither know nor study to serve. But it is not so with rational Agents: ||⁴they study our Interest, and delight in our Happiness, and are Benevolent toward us.||"

We are all then conscious of the Difference between that ||⁵Love and Esteem||, or Perception of moral Excellence, which Benevolence excites

Different Ideas of Moral and Natural Good.

toward the Person in whom we observe it, and that Opinion of natural Goodness, which only raises Desire of Possession toward the good Object. Now "what should make this Difference, if all Approbation, or Sense of Good be from Prospect of Advantage? Do not inanimate Objects promote our Advantage, as well as Benevolent Persons who do ||⁶us|| Offices of Kindness, and Friendship? Should we not then have the same endearing ||⁷Sentiments|| of both? or only the same cold Opinion of Advantage in both?" The Reason why it is not so, must be this, "That we have a distinct Perception of Beauty, or Excellence in the kind Affec-[119]tions of rational Agents; whence we are determin'd to admire and love such Characters and Persons."

In Actions done to our selves.

Suppose we reap the same Advantage from two Men, one of ||⁸whom|| serves us ||⁹from Delight in our Happiness, and Love toward us;|| the other from Views of Self-Interest, or by Constraint: both are in this Case equally beneficial or advantageous to us, and yet we shall have quite different Sentiments of them. We must then certainly have other Perceptions of moral Actions than those of Advantage: And that Power of receiving these Perceptions may be call'd a Moral Sense, since the Definition agrees to it, viz. a Determination of the Mind, to receive any Idea from the Presence of an Object which occurs to us, ||¹⁰independent|| on our Will.||¹¹*||

Of Evil, Moral and Natural.

This perhaps will be equally evident from our Ideas of Evil, done to us designedly by a rational Agent. Our Senses of natural Good and Evil would make us receive, with equal Serenity and Composure, an Assault, a Buffet, an Affront from a Neighbour, a Cheat from a Partner, or Trustee, as we would an equal Damage from the Fall of a Beam, ||¹²a|| Tile, or a Tempest; and we should have the same Affections and Sentiments ||¹³of both||. Villany, Treachery, [120] Cruelty, would be as meekly resented as a Blast, or Mildew, or an overflowing Stream. But I fancy every one is very differently affected on these Occasions, tho there may be equal natural Evil in both. Nay, Actions no way detrimental, may occasion the strongest Anger, and Indignation, if they evidence only impotent Hatred, or Contempt. And, on the other hand, the Intervention

* See the Preface, Page 6.

of moral Ideas may prevent our ||^{14}Hatred|| of the Agent, or bad moral Apprehension of that Action, which causes to us the greatest natural Evil. Thus the Opinion of Justice in any Sentence, will prevent all Ideas of moral Evil in the Execution, or Hatred toward the Magistrate, who is the immediate Cause of our greatest Sufferings.

II. In our Sentiments of Actions ||^{15}which affect|| our selves, there is indeed a Mixture of the Ideas of natural ||^{16}and moral|| Good, which ||^{17}require|| some Attention to separate ||^{18}them||. But when we reflect upon the Actions ||^{19}which affect other Persons only,|| we may observe the moral Ideas unmix'd with those of natural Good, or Evil. For let it be here observ'd, that those Senses by which we perceive Pleasure in natural Objects, whence they are constituted Advantageous, could never raise in us any Desire of publick Good, but only of what was good to our selves [121] in particular. Nor could they ever make us ||^{20}approve an|| Action ||^{21}because|| of its promoting the Happiness of others. And yet as soon as any Action is represented to us as flowing from Love, Humanity, Gratitude, Compassion, a Study of the good of others, and ||^{22}a Delight in|| their Happiness, altho it were in the most distant Part of the World, or in some past Age, we feel Joy within us, admire the lovely Action, and praise its Author. And on the contrary, every Action represented as flowing ||^{23}from Hatred, Delight in the Misery of others||, or Ingratitude, raises Abhorrence and Aversion.

It is true indeed, that the Actions we approve in others, are generally imagin'd to tend to the natural Good of Mankind, or ||^{24}of|| some Parts of it. But whence this secret Chain between each Person and Mankind? How is my Interest connected with the most distant Parts of it? And yet I must admire ||^{25}Actions which are beneficial to them||, and love the Author. Whence this Love, Compassion, Indignation and Hatred toward even feign'd Characters, in the most distant Ages, and Nations, according as they appear Kind, Faithful, Compassionate, or of the opposite Dispositions, toward their imaginary Contemporaries? If there is no moral Sense, ||^{26}which makes rational Actions appear Beautiful, [122] or Deform'd||; if all Approbation be from the Interest of the Approver,

In Actions toward others.

What's Hecuba to us, or we to Hecuba?*[i]

Moral Ideas not from Interest. III. Some refin'd Explainers of Self-Love may tell us, "That we ||[27] hate, or love|| Characters, according as we apprehend we should have been supported, or injur'd by them, had we liv'd in their Days." But how obvious is the Answer, if we only observe, that had we no Sense of moral Good in Humanity, Mercy, Faithfulness, why should not Self-Love, ||[28] and our Sense of natural Good|| engage us always to the victorious Side, and make us admire and love the successful Tyrant, or Traitor? Why do not we love Sinon, or Pyrrhus, in the *Aeneid*? for had we been Greeks, these two would have been very advantageous Characters. Why are we affected with the Fortunes of Priamus, Polites, Choroebus or Aeneas?[ii] [29] It is plain we have some secret Sense which determines our Approbation without regard to Self-Interest; otherwise we should always favour the fortunate Side without regard to Virtue ||[30], and suppose our selves engaged with that Party||.[31] [123]

Suppose any great Destruction occasion'd by mere Accident, without any Design, or Negligence of the Person who casually was the Author of it: This Action might have been as disadvantageous to us as design'd Cruelty, or Malice; but who will say he has the same Idea of both Actions, or Sentiments of the ||[32] Agents?|| "Whence then this Difference?"

And further, Let us make a Supposition, which perhaps is not far from Matter of Fact, to try if we cannot approve even disadvantageous Actions, and perceive moral Good in them. A few ingenious Artisans, per-

* Tragedy of *Hamlet.*
    i. Shakespeare, *Hamlet, Prince of Denmark,* act 2, scene 2, verse 562: "What's Hecuba to him, or he to Hecuba . . . ?"
    ii. According to Virgil (*Aeneid* 2, 57) Sinon used deceit to make the Trojans take the wooden horse into the city. Pyrrhos I, king of Epirus, 306–302 and 297–277 B.C., defeated the Romans in 280/279 but lost most of his own troops, hence the phrase *Pyrrhic victory.* Priam, king of Troy and grieving father of Hector, who was slain by Achilles in the Trojan War. Choroebos (Greek: Korroibos) liberated Argos from a disaster sent by Apollo; as punishment Choroebos had to carry a holy tripod and to found a city where he dropped it (see Pausanias, *Description of Greece,* 4.17.4). According to legend, Aeneas escaped the conquered Troy and, after a long odyssey, founded Rome.

secuted in their own Country, flee to ours for Protection; they instruct us in Manufactures which support Millions of Poor, ||^{33}increase|| the Wealth of almost every Person in the State, and make us formidable to our Neighbours. In a Nation not far distant from us, some resolute Burgomasters, full of Love to their Country, and Compassion toward their Fellow-Citizens, opprest in Body and Soul by a Tyrant, and Inquisition, with indefatigable Diligence, public Spirit, and Courage, support a tedious perilous War against the Tyrant and form an industrious Republick, which rivals us in Trade, and almost in Power.[iii] All the World sees whether the former or the latter have been more ad-[124]vantageous to us: and yet let every Man consult his own Breast, which of the two Characters he has the most agreeable Idea of? whether of the useful Refugee, or the public-spirited Burgomaster, by whose Love to his own Country, we have often suffer'd in our Interests? And I am confident he will find some other Foundation of Esteem than Advantage, and will see a just Reason, why the Memory of our Artisans is so obscure among us, and yet that of our Rivals is immortal.

IV. Some Moralists,[iv] who will rather twist Self-Love into a thousand Shapes, than allow any other Principle of Approbation than Interest, may tell us, "That whatever profits one Part without detriment to another, profits the Whole, and then some small Share will redound to each Individual; that those Actions which tend to the Good of the Whole, if universally perform'd, would most effectually secure to each Individual his own Happiness; and that consequently, we may approve such Actions, from the Opinion of their tending ultimately to our own Advantage."

Self-Love not the Ground of Approbation.

^{34}We need not trouble these Gentlemen to shew by their nice Train of Consequences, and Influences of Actions by way of Precedent in particular Instances, that [125] we in this Age reap any Advantage from

iii. Hutcheson refers to the Dutch struggle for freedom from Spain.

iv. For example, Thomas Hobbes, *De Cive,* chap. 1, and Bernard Mandeville, *Enquiry into the Origin of Moral Virtue* (in the second edition of *The Fable of the Bees,* 1723).

Orestes's killing the treacherous Aegysthus, or from the Actions of Codrus or Decius.ᵛ Allow their Reasonings to be perfectly good, they only
prove, that after long Reflection, and Reasoning, we may find out some
ground, ‖³⁵ even from Views of Interest, to approve the same Actions‖
which every Man admires as soon as he hears of them; and that too under
a quite different Conception.

³⁶ Should any of our Travellers find some old Grecian Treasure, the
Miser who hid it, ‖³⁷ certainly perform'd‖ an Action more to the Traveller's Advantage than Codrus or Orestes; for he must have but a small
Share of Benefit from their Actions, whose Influence is so dispers'd, and
lost in various Ages, and Nations: Surely then this Miser must appear to
the Traveller a prodigious Hero in Virtue! For Self-Interest will ‖³⁸ make
us only esteem Men‖ according to the Good they do to our Selves, and
not give us high Ideas of public Good, but in proportion to our Share
of it. But must a Man have the Reflection of Cumberland,ᵛⁱ or Puffendorf, to admire Generosity, Faith, Humanity, Gratitude? Or reason so
nicely to apprehend the Evil in Cruelty, Treachery, Ingratitude? Do not
the former excite our Admiration, and Love, [126] and Study of Imitation, wherever we see them, almost at first View, without any such
Reflection; and the latter, our ‖³⁹ Hatred,‖ Contempt and Abhorrence?
Unhappy would it be for Mankind, if a Sense of Virtue was of as narrow
an Extent, as a Capacity for such Metaphysicks.

Our Moral
Sense cannot
be brib'd.

V. This moral Sense, either of our own Actions, or of those of others,
has this in common with our other Senses, that however our Desire of
Virtue may be counterballanc'd by Interest, our Sentiment or Perception

v. Orestes, according to legend, son of Agamemnon and Clytemnestra, killed his
mother and her lover Aegisthus to avenge their assassination of Agamemnon (Aes-
chylus, *Oresteia,* especially *The Libation Bearers;* Euripides, *Electra;* Sophocles, *Electra*). Codrus, the last king of Athens, gave his life fighting against Sparta in order to
free Athens (Cicero, *De finibus bonorum et malorum,* V, 62). Publius Decius Mus
(Roman consul, 340 B.C.) supposedly was killed in the war against the Latins (340–
338 B.C.) near Capua (see Cicero, *De Finibus,* II, 61; see note viii below).

vi. Richard Cumberland (1632–1718) criticized Hobbes in the work *De legibus
naturae disquisitio philosophica* (London, 1672); translation: *A Treatise of the Law of
Nature,* London, 1727.

of its Beauty cannot; as it certainly might be, if the only Ground of our Approbation were Views of Advantage. Let us consider this both as to our own Actions and those of others.

A Covetous Man shall dislike any Branch of Trade, how useful soever it may be to the Publick, if there is no Gain for himself in it; here is an Aversion from Interest. Propose a sufficient Premium, and he shall be the first who sets about it, with full Satisfaction in his own Conduct. Now is it the same way with our Sense of moral Actions? Should any one advise us to wrong a Minor, or Orphan, or to do an ungrateful Action toward a Benefactor; we at first View abhor it: Assure us that it will be very advantageous to us, propose even a Reward; [127] our Sense of the Action is not alter'd. It is true, these Motives may make us undertake it; but they have no more Influence upon us to make us approve it, than a Physician's Advice has to make a nauseous Potion pleasant to the Taste, when we perhaps force our selves to take it for the Recovery of Health.

In judging of our own Actions.

[40]Had we no Notion of Actions, beside our Opinion of their Advantage, or Disadvantage, could we ever chuse an Action as Advantageous, which we are conscious is still Evil? as it too often happens in human Affairs. Where would be the need of such high Bribes to prevail with Men to abandon the Interests of a ruin'd Party, or of Tortures to force out the Secrets of their Friends? Is it so hard to convince Mens Understandings, if that be the only Faculty we have to do with, that it is ||[41]probably more|| advantageous to secure present Gain, and avoid present Evils, by joining with the prevalent Party, than to wait for the remote Possibility of future Good, upon a Revolution often improbable, and sometimes unexpected? And when Men are overpersuaded by Advantage, do they always approve their own Conduct? Nay, how often is their remaining Life odious, and shameful, in their own Sense of it, as well as in that of others, to whom the base Action was profitable? [128]

If any one becomes satisfy'd with his own Conduct in such a Case, upon what Ground is it? How does he please himself, or vindicate his Actions to others? Never by reflecting upon his private Advantage, or alledging this to others as a Vindication; but by gradually warping into the moral Principles of his new Party; for no Party is without them. And thus Men become pleas'd with their Actions under some Appearance of moral Good, distinct from Advantage.

Our Moral Sense not founded on Religion.

It may perhaps be alledg'd, "That in those Actions of our own which we call Good, there is this constant Advantage, superior to all others, which is the Ground of our Approbation, and the Motive to them from Self-love, viz. That we suppose the Deity will reward them." This will be more fully consider'd* ||⁴²afterwards||: At present it is enough to observe, that many have high Notions of Honour, Faith, Generosity, Justice, who have scarce ||⁴³any Opinions about the Deity, or any Thoughts of future Rewards||; and abhor any thing which is Treacherous, Cruel, or Unjust, without any regard to future Punishments. [129]

⁴⁴But further, tho these Rewards, and Punishments, may make my own Actions appear advantageous to me, ||⁴⁵and make me approve them from Self-Love,|| yet they would never make me approve, and love another Person for the like Actions, whose Merit would not be imputed to me. Those Actions are advantageous indeed to the Agent; but his Advantage is not my Advantage: and Self-Love could never ||⁴⁶influence me to approve|| Actions as advantageous to others, or ||⁴⁷to love|| the Authors of them on that account.

Our Moral Sense of the Actions of others, not to be brib'd.

||⁴⁸This is|| the second thing to be consider'd, ||⁴⁹"Whether|| our Sense of the moral Good or Evil, in the Actions of others, can be over-ballanc'd, or brib'd by Views of Interest." ||⁵⁰Now I may indeed|| easily be capable of wishing, that another would do an Action I abhor as morally Evil, if it were very Advantageous to me: Interest in that Case may overballance my Desire of Virtue in another. But no Interest ||⁵¹to my self|| will make me approve an Action as ||⁵²morally|| Good, which, without that Interest to my self, would have appear'd morally Evil||⁵³; if, upon computing its whole Effects, it appears to produce as great a Moment of Good in the Whole, when it is not beneficial to me, as it did before when it was. In our Sense of moral Good or [130] Evil, our own private Advantage or Loss is of no more moment, than the Advantage or Loss of a third Person, to make an Action appear Good or Evil. This Sense therefore cannot be over-ballanc'd by Interest.|| How ridiculous an At-

* See Sect. ii. Art. 7.

tempt wou'd it be, to engage a Man by Rewards, or ‖⁵⁴to threaten him‖ into a good Opinion of an Action, which was contrary to his moral Notions? We may procure Dissimulation by such means, and that is all.

VI. A late witty Author* says, "That the Leaders of Mankind do not really admire ‖⁵⁵such Actions‖ as those of Regulus, or Decius, but only observe, that Men of such Dispositions are very useful for the Defence of any State; and therefore by Panegyricks, and Statues, they encourage such Tempers in others, as the most tractable, and useful."[vii] Here first let us consider, If a Traitor, who would sell his own Country to us, may not often be as advantageous to us, as ‖⁵⁶a‖ Hero who defends us: And yet we can love the Treason, and hate the Traitor. We can at the same time praise a gallant Enemy, who is very pernicious to us. Is there nothing in all this but an Opinion of Advantage? [131]

⁵⁷Again, upon this Scheme what could a Statue or Panegyrick effect?—Men love Praise—They will do the Actions which they observe to be praised—Praise, with Men who have no other Idea of Good but Self-Interest, is the Opinion which a Nation or Party have of a Man as useful to them—Regulus, or Cato, or Decius,[viii] had no Advantage by the Actions which profited their Country, and therefore they themselves could not admire them, however the Persons who reap'd the Advantage might praise such Actions.—Regulus or Cato could not possibly praise or love another Hero for a virtuous Action; for this would not gain them the Advantage of Honour; and their own Actions they must have look'd

Marginal note: Not occasion'd by Praise.

---

* See the *Fable of the Bees,* Page 34, 36. 3d Edition.

vii. Hutcheson used the third edition of Mandeville's *Fable of the Bees,* London, 1724 (ed. F. B. Kaye, 2 vols., Oxford, 1924, vol. 2, p. 393); the text is not a quotation but a paraphrase of Mandeville.

viii. Marcus Atilius Regulus (consul 267 and 256 B.C.) was a prisoner of the Carthagenians during the First Punic War and was later (?249 B.C.) sent back to Rome in order to negotiate an exchange of prisoners; he advised against it, went back to Carthage, and was murdered cruelly. M. Porcius Cato Uticensis (95–46 B.C.) was an educated Stoic and politician. As a republican he was a firm adversary of Caesar; he committed suicide after the battle near Thapsus in Utica (see Cicero's *Cato*). According to Livy (8, 6–11) P. Decius Mus sacrificed himself in the war against the Latins in 340 B.C. near Capua; see note v above.

upon as the hard Terms on which Honour was to be purchas'd, without any thing amiable in them, ||⁵⁸ᵃwhich they could contemplate or reflect upon with ||⁵⁹ᵇPleasure. ᵃᵇ||—Now how unlike is this to what the least Observation would teach a Man concerning such Characters?

But says* he, "These wondrous cunning Governours made Men believe, by their Statues and Panegyricks, that there was publick Spirit, and that this was in [132] it self Excellent; and hence Men are led to admire it in others, and to imitate it in themselves, forgetting the Pursuit of their own Advantage." So easy a matter it seems to him, to quit judging of others by what we feel in our selves!—for a Person who is wholly selfish, to imagine others to be publick-spirited!—for one who has no Ideas of Good but in his own Advantage, to be led, by the Persuasions of others, into a Conception of Goodness in what is avowedly detrimental to himself, and profitable to others; nay so entirely, as not to approve the Action thorowly, ||⁶⁰but so|| far as he was conscious that it proceeded from a disinterested Study of the Good of others!—Yet this it seems Statues and Panegyricks can accomplish!

Nil intra est oleam, nil extra est in nuce duri!†ⁱˣ

It is an easy matter for Men to assert any thing in Words; but our own Hearts must decide the Matter, "Whether some moral Actions do not at first View appear amiable, even to those who are unconcern'd in their Influence? ||⁶¹ᵃWhether we do not ||⁶²ᵇsincerelyᵇ|| love a generous kind Friend, or Patriot, whose [133] Actions procure Honour to him only without any Advantage to our selves?ᵃ||" It is true, that the Actions which we approve, are useful to Mankind; but not always to the Approver. It would perhaps be useful to the Whole, that all Men agreed in performing such Actions; and then every one would have his Share of the Advantage: But this only proves, that Reason and calm Reflection may recommend

---

* See the same Author in the Same Place.

† Hor. Ep. 1. Lib. 2. v. 31.

ix. Translation: "The olive has no hardness within, the nut has none without." Horace, *Satires, Epistles, and Ars Poetica,* trans. H. Rushton Fairclough, Loeb Classical Library (Cambridge, Mass.: Harvard University Press, 1970), p. 398. The correct location of the text is not Ep. 1. Lib. 2, but Ep. 2. Lib. 1. v. 31.

to us, from Self-Interest, those Actions, which at first View our moral
Sense determines us to admire, without considering this Interest. Nay,
our Sense shall operate even where the Advantage to our selves does not
hold. We can approve the Justice of a Sentence against our selves: A
condemn'd Traitor may approve the Vigilance of a Cicero in discovering
conspiracies, tho it had been for the Traitor's Advantage, that there never
had been in the World any Men of such Sagacity. To say that he may
still approve such Conduct as tending to the publick Good, is a Jest from
one whose only Idea of Good is Self-Interest. Such a Person has no
‖⁶³Desire‖ of publick Good further than it tends to his own Advantage,
which it does not at all in the present Case.

VII. If what is said makes it appear, that we have some other amiable **Nor Custom,**
Idea of Actions than that of Advantageous to our selves, we may con- **Education,**
clude, "That this [134] Perception of moral Good is not deriv'd from **&c.**
Custom, Education, Example, or Study." These give us no new Ideas:
They might make us see ‖⁶⁴Advantage to our selves‖ in Actions whose
Usefulness did not at first appear; or give us Opinions of some Tendency
of Actions to our Detriment, by some nice Deductions of Reason, or
by a rash Prejudice, when upon the first View of the Action we should
have observ'd no such thing: but they never could have made us apprehend Actions as amiable or odious, ‖⁶⁵without‖ any Consideration of
our own Advantage.

VIII. It remains then, "That as the Author of Nature has determin'd us
to receive, by our external Senses, pleasant or disagreeable Ideas of Objects, according as they are useful or hurtful to our Bodys; and to receive
from uniform Objects the Pleasures of Beauty and Harmony, to excite
us to the Pursuit of Knowledge, and to reward us for it; or to be an
Argument to us of his Goodness, as the Uniformity it self proves his
Existence, whether we had a Sense of Beauty in Uniformity or not: ‖⁶⁶in
the same manner‖ he has given us a Moral Sense, to direct our Actions,
and to give us still nobler Pleasures; so that while we are only intending
the Good of others, we [135] undesignedly promote our own greatest
private Good."

This Moral
Sense does not
infer innate
Ideas or
Propositions.

We are not to imagine, that this moral Sense, more than the other Senses, supposes any innate ||[67]Ideas,|| Knowledge, or practical Proposition: We mean by it only a Determination of our Minds to receive ||[68a]amiable or disagreeable Ideas of Actions, when ||[69b]they[b]|| occur to our Observation[a]||, ||[70]antecedent|| to any Opinions of Advantage or Loss to redound to our selves from them; even as we are pleas'd with a regular Form, or an harmonious Composition, without having any Knowledge of Mathematicks, or seeing any Advantage in that Form, or Composition, different from the immediate ||[71]Pleasure.|| [136]

Concerning the immediate
Motive to virtuous Actions.

The Motives of human Actions, or their immediate Causes, would be ‖¹‖
best understood after considering the Passions and Affections; but here
we shall only consider the Springs of the Actions which we call virtuous,
as far as it is necessary to settle the general Foundation of the Moral Sense.

I. Every Action, which we apprehend as either morally good or evil, is **Affections, the**
always suppos'd to flow from some Affection toward ‖² rational Agents‖; **Motives to**
Actions.
and whatever we call Virtue or Vice, is either some such Affection, or
some Action consequent upon it. Or it may perhaps be enough to make
an Action, or Omission, appear vitious, if it argues the Want of such
Affection toward rational Agents, as we expect in Characters counted
morally good. All the Actions counted religious in any Country, are suppos'd, by those who count them ‖³so‖, to flow from some Affections
toward the Deity; and whatever we call social Virtue, we still suppose to
flow from [137] Affections toward our Fellow-Creatures: for in this all
seem to agree, "That external Motions, when accompany'd with no Affections toward God or Man, or evidencing no Want of the expected
Affections toward either, can have no moral Good or Evil in them."

⁴Ask‖⁵, for instance,‖ the most abstemious Hermit, if Temperance
of it self would be morally good, supposing it shew'd no Obedience
toward the Deity, made us no fitter for Devotion, or the Service of Mankind, or the Search after Truth, than Luxury; and he will easily grant,
that it would be no moral Good, tho still it might be naturally good or

advantageous to Health: And mere Courage, or Contempt of Danger, if we conceive it to have no regard to the Defence of the Innocent, or repairing of Wrongs, ||⁶or Self-Interest,|| wou'd only entitle its Possessor to Bedlam. When such sort of Courage is sometimes admir'd, it is upon some secret Apprehension of a good Intention in the use of it||⁷, or as a natural Ability capable of an useful Application||. Prudence, if it ||⁸was|| only employ'd in promoting private Interest, is never imagin'd to be a Virtue: and Justice, or observing a strict Equality, if it ||⁹has|| no regard to the Good of Mankind, the Preservation of Rights, and securing Peace, is a Quality properer [138] for its ordinary Gestamen, a Beam and Scales, than for a rational Agent. So that these four Qualitys, commonly call'd Cardinal Virtues, obtain that Name, because they are Dispositions universally necessary to promote publick Good, and denote Affections toward rational Agents; otherwise there would appear no Virtue in them.

Affections, disinterested. II. Now if it can be made appear, that none of these Affections which we ||¹⁰call virtuous, spring from|| Self-love, or Desire of private Interest; since all Virtue is either some such Affections, or Actions consequent upon them; it must necessarily follow, "||¹¹That Virtue is not pursued from the Interest or Self-love of the Pursuer, or any Motives of his own Advantage.||"

Love of Complacence, and Hatred of Displicence. The Affections which are of most Importance in Morals, ||¹²are Love and Hatred: All the rest seem but different Modifications of these two original Affections||. Now in discoursing of Love ||¹³toward rational Agents||, we need not be caution'd not to include that Love between the Sexes, which, when no other Affections accompany it, is only Desire of Pleasure, and is never counted a Virtue. Love toward rational Agents, is subdivided into Love of Complacence or Esteem, and Love of Be-[139]nevolence: And Hatred is subdivided into Hatred of Displicence or Contempt, and Hatred of ||¹⁴Malice.|| Concerning each of these separately we shall consider, "Whether they can be influenc'd by Motives of Self-Interest."

Are entirely disinterested. ||¹⁵Love of|| Complacence, Esteem, or Good-liking, at first view appears to be disinterested, and so ||¹⁶the Hatred of|| Displicence or Dislike; and are entirely excited by some moral Qualitys, Good or Evil, appre-

hended to be in the Objects; which Qualitys the very Frame of our Na-
ture determines us ||[17] to love or hate,|| to approve or disapprove, ac-
cording to the moral Sense* above explain'd. Propose to a Man all the
Rewards in the World, or threaten all the Punishments, to engage him
to ||[18] love with|| Esteem, and Complacence, ||[19] a third|| Person entirely
unknown, or if known, apprehended to be cruel, treacherous, ungrateful; you may procure external Obsequiousness, or good Offices, or Dis-
simulation ||[20] of Love||; but real ||[21] Love of|| Esteem no Price can pur-
chase. And the same is obvious as to ||[22] Hatred of|| Contempt, which no
Motive of Advantage can prevent. On the contrary, represent a Character as generous, kind, faithful, humane, tho in the most distant Parts
of the World, and we cannot avoid ||[23] loving it with|| Es-[140] teem, and
Complacence. A Bribe may ||[24] possibly|| make us attempt to ruin such
a Man, or some strong Motive of Advantage may excite us to oppose
his Interest; but it can never make us ||[25] hate|| him, while we ||[26] appre-
hend him as morally excellent||. Nay, when we consult our own Hearts,
we shall find, that we can scarce ever persuade our selves to attempt any
Mischief against such Persons, from any Motive of Advantage, nor exe-
cute it, without the strongest Reluctance, and Remorse, until we have
blinded our selves into a ||[27] bad Opinion of the Person in a moral Sense||.

III. As to the Love of Benevolence, the very Name excludes Self-Interest.
We never call that Man benevolent, who is in fact useful to others, but
at the same time only intends his own Interest, without any ||[28] desire of,
or delight in,|| the Good of others. If there be any ||[29] Benevolence|| at
all, it must be disinterested; for the most useful Action imaginable, loses
all appearance of Benevolence, as soon as we discern that it only flowed
from Self-Love or Interest. Thus, never were any human Actions more
advantageous, than the Inventions of Fire, and Iron; but if these were
casual, or if the Inventor only intended his own Interest in them, there
is nothing which can be call'd Benevolent in them. Wherever then Benevolence is suppos'd, there it is [141] imagin'd disinterested, and de-
sign'd for the Good of ||[30] others.||

*Benevolence
and Malice,
disinterested.*

* See Sect. i.

Self-Love
join'd with
Benevolence.

But it must be here observ'd, That as all Men have Self-Love, as well as Benevolence, these two Principles may jointly excite a Man to the same Action; and then they are to be consider'd as two Forces impelling the same Body to Motion; sometimes they conspire, sometimes are indifferent to each other, and sometimes are in some degree opposite. Thus, if a Man have such strong Benevolence, as would have produc'd an Action without any Views of Self-Interest; that such a Man has also in View private Advantage, along with publick Good, as the Effect of his Action, does no way diminish the Benevolence of the Action. When he would not have produc'd so much publick Good, had it not been for Prospect of Self-Interest, then the Effect of Self-Love is to be deducted, and his Benevolence is proportion'd to the remainder of Good, which pure Benevolence would have produc'd. When a Man's Benevolence is hurtful to himself, then Self-Love is opposite to Benevolence, and the Benevolence is proportion'd to the Sum of the Good produc'd, ||³¹ added to|| the Resistance of Self-Love surmounted by it. In most Cases it is impossible for Men to know how far their Fellows are influenc'd by the one or other of these Principles; but yet the [142] general Truth is sufficiently certain, That this is the way in which the Benevolence of Actions is to be computed. ||³² Since then, no Love to rational Agents can proceed from Self-Interest, every Action must be disinterested, as far as it flows from Love to rational Agents.||

Cause of
Benevolence.

||³³ If any enquire, "Whence arises this Love of Esteem, or Benevolence, to good Men, or to Mankind in general, if not from some nice Views of Self-Interest? Or, how we can be mov'd to desire the Happiness of others, without any View to our own?" It may be answer'd, "That the same Cause which determines us to pursue Happiness for our selves, determines us both to Esteem and Benevolence on their proper Occasions; even the very Frame of our Nature, or a generous Instinct, which shall be afterwards explain'd."

Benevolence
presupposes
Esteem.

IV. Here we may observe, That as Love of Esteem and Complacence is always join'd with Benevolence, where there is no strong Opposition of Interest; so Benevolence seems to presuppose some small degree of Esteem, not indeed of actual good Qualitys; for there may be strong Benevolence, where there is the Hatred of Contempt for actual Vices; as a Parent may have great Benevolence to a most abandon'd [143] Child, whose Manners he hates with the greatest Displicence: but Benevolence supposes a Being capable of Virtue. We judge of other rational Agents by our selves. The human Nature is a lovely Form; we are all conscious of some morally good Qualitys and Inclinations in our selves, how partial and imperfect soever they may be: we presume the same of every thing in human Form, nay almost of every living Creature: so that by this suppos'd remote Capacity of Virtue, there may be some small degree of Esteem along with our Benevolence, even when they incur our greatest Displeasure by their Conduct.‖

‖³⁴As to Malice,‖ Human Nature seems scarce capable of malicious disinterested Hatred, or a sedate ‖³⁵Delight in‖ the Misery of others, when we imagine them no way pernicious to us, or opposite to our ‖³⁶Interest‖: And for that Hatred which makes us oppose those whose Interests are opposite to ours, it is only the Effect of Self-Love, and not of disinterested Malice. A sudden Passion may give us wrong Representations of our Fellow-Creatures, and for a little time represent them as absolutely Evil; and during this Imagination perhaps we may give some Evidences of disinterested Malice: but as soon as we reflect upon human Nature, and [144] form just Conceptions, this unnatural Passion is allay'd, and only Self-Love remains, which may make us, from Self-Interest, oppose our Adversarys.

Human Nature incapable of sedate Malice.

Every one at present rejoices in the Destruction of our Pirates; and yet let us suppose a Band of such Villains cast in upon some desolate Island, and that we were assur'd some Fate would confine them there perpetually, so that they should disturb Mankind no more. Now let us calmly reflect that these Persons are capable of Knowledge and Counsel, may be happy, and joyful, or may be involv'd in Misery, Sorrow, and Pain; that they may return to a State of Love, Humanity, Kindness, and become Friends, Citizens, Husbands, Parents, with all the sweet Sentiments which accompany these Relations: then let us ask our selves, when Self-Love ‖³⁷or regard to the Safety of better Men,‖ no longer makes us desire their Destruction, and when we cease to look upon them, under the Ideas suggested by fresh Resentment of Injurys done to us or

our Friends, as utterly incapable of any good moral Quality; whether
we ||^{38}would|| wish them the Fate of Cadmus's Army,^{i} by plunging their
Swords in each others Breast, or a worse Fate by the most exquisite Tortures; or rather that they should recover the ordinary Affections of Men,
[145] become Kind, Compassionate, and Friendly; contrive Laws, Con-
stitutions, Governments, Propertys; and form an honest happy Society,
with Marriages, and

> Relations dear, and all the Charities
> Of Father, Son, and Brother ———*

I fancy the latter would be the Wish of every Mortal, notwithstanding
our present just Abhorrence ||^{39}of them|| from Self-Interest, or publick
Love and Desire of promoting the Interest of our Friends who are expos'd to their Fury. Now this plainly evidences, that we scarce ever have
any sedate Malice against any Person, or ||^{40}delight in|| his Misery. Our
||^{41}Hatred|| is only from Opposition of Interest; or if we can entertain
sedate Malice, it must be toward a Character apprehended necessarily
and unalterably Evil in a moral Sense; such as a sudden Passion some-
times represents our Enemies to us: ||^{42}and|| perhaps no such Being oc-
curs to us among the Works of a good Deity.

Other Affections disinterested. V. ||^{43}Having|| offer'd what may perhaps prove, That ||^{44}our Love either
of Esteem, or Benevolence, is not founded on Self-Love||, or views of
Interest; let us see "if some other Affections, in which Virtue may be
plac'd, do arise from Self-[146]Love;" such as Fear, or Reverence, arising
from an Apprehension of Goodness, Power, and Justice. For no body
apprehends any Virtue in base Dread and Servitude toward a powerful
Evil Being: This is indeed the meanest Selfishness. Now the same Ar-
guments which prove ||^{45}Love of|| Esteem to be disinterested, will prove
this honourable Reverence to be so too; for it plainly arises from an Ap-

---

i. On Athene's advice Cadmus sowed the teeth of a dragon he had killed. Out of
these teeth grew an army, most of which killed each other (except for the five Spartoi,
the progenitors of the Thebans).

* Milt. Par. Lost, B. iv. v. 756.

prehension of amiable Qualitys in the Person, and Love toward him, which raises an Abhorrence of offending him. Could we reverence a Being because it ||⁴⁶was|| our Interest to do so, a third Person might bribe us into Reverence toward a Being neither Good, nor Powerful, which every one sees to be a Jest. And this we might shew to be common to all other Passions, which have ||⁴⁷rational Agents for their Objects||.

⁴⁸VI. There is one Objection against disinterested ||⁴⁹Love||, which oc- Objections.
curs from considering, "That nothing so effectually ||⁵⁰excites|| our Love toward rational Agents, as their Beneficence ||⁵¹to us||; whence we are led to imagine, that our Love of Persons, as well as irrational Objects, flows intirely from Self-Interest." But let us here examine our selves more narrowly. Do we only ||⁵²love|| the Beneficent, because it is our Interest to ||⁵³love them||? Or do we chuse to love them, because our love is the [147] means of procuring their Bounty? If it be so, then we could indifferently love any Character, even to obtain the Bounty of a third Person; or we could be brib'd by a third Person to love the greatest Villain heartily, as we may be brib'd to external Offices: Now this is plainly impossible.

||⁵⁴But further||, is not our ||⁵⁵Love always|| the Consequent of Bounty, and not the Means of procuring it? External Shew, Obsequiousness, and Dissimulation may precede an Opinion of Beneficence; but real Love always presupposes it, and ||⁵⁶shall|| necessarily arise even when we expect no more, from consideration of past Benefits. ⁵⁷Or can any one say he only loves the Beneficent, as he does a Field or Garden, because of its Advantage? His Love then must cease toward one who has ruin'd himself in kind Offices to him, when he can do him no more; as we cease to love an inanimate Object which ceases to be useful, unless a Poetical Prosopopoeia animate it, and raise an imaginary Gratitude, which is indeed pretty common. ||⁵⁸And then again, our Love would be the same towards the worst Characters that 'tis towards the best, if they were equally bountiful to us, which is also false. Beneficence then must raise our Love as it is an amiable moral Quality||: and ||⁵⁹hence we|| love even those who are beneficent to others. [148]

||⁶⁰ᵃIt may be further alledg'd, "That Bounty toward our selves is ||⁶¹ᵇa

stronger Incitement to^b|| Love, than equal Bounty toward others." This is true for a Reason to be offer'd below:* but it does not prove, that in this Case our Love of Persons is from Views of Interest; since this Love is not prior to the Bounty, as the means to procure it, but subsequent upon it, even when we expect no more.^a|| In the Benefits which we receive our selves, we are more fully sensible of their Value, and of the Circumstances of the Action, which are Evidences of a generous Temper in the Donor; and ||⁶²from|| the good Opinion we have of our selves, ||⁶³we are apt to|| look upon the Kindness ||⁶⁴as|| better employ'd, than when it is bestow'd on others, of whom perhaps we have less favourable Sentiments. It is however sufficient to remove the Objection, that Bounty from a Donor apprehended as morally Evil, or extorted by Force, or conferr'd with some View of Self-Interest, will not procure real ||⁶⁵Love||; nay, it may raise Indignation, if we suspect Dissimulation of Love, or a Design to allure us into any thing Dishonourable: whereas wisely employ'd Bounty is always approv'd, and gains love to the Author from all who hear of it. [149]

Virtue disinterested. If then no ||⁶⁶Love|| toward Persons ||⁶⁷be influenc'd by|| Self-Love, or Views of Interest, and all Virtue flows from ||⁶⁸Love|| ||⁶⁹toward Persons||, or some other Affection equally disinterested; it remains, "That there must be some other ||⁷⁰Motive|| than Self-Love, or Interest, which excites us to the Actions we call Virtuous."

Objection from Religion. ||^{71a}VII. There may perhaps still remain another Suspicion of Self-Interest in our Prosecution of Virtue, ||^{72b}arising^b|| from this, "That the whole Race of Mankind seems persuaded of the Existence of an Almighty Being, who will certainly secure Happiness either now, or hereafter, to those who are Virtuous, according to their several Notions of Virtue in various Places: and upon this Persuasion, Virtue may in all Cases be pursu'd from Views† of Interest." Here again we might appeal to all Mankind, whether there be no Benevolence but what flows from a View of Reward from the Deity? Nay, do we not see a great deal of it

---

* See Sect. v. Art. 2.
† See above Sect. i. Art. 5. Par. ||⁷³4||.

among those who entertain few ||^{74c}if any^c|| Thoughts of Devotion at all? Not to say that this Benevolence ||^{75d}scarce deserves^d|| the Name, when we desire not, nor delight in the Good of others, ||^{76e}further^e||than it serves our own Ends.^{a}|| [150]

||^{77a}But if we have no other Idea of Good, ||^{78b}than^b|| Advantage to our selves^a||, we must imagine that every rational Being ||^{79}acts only|| for its own Advantage; and however we may call a beneficent Being, a good Being, because it acts for our Advantage, yet upon this Scheme ||^{80}we should not be apt to think|| there is any beneficent Being in Nature, or a Being who acts for the Good of others. Particularly, if there is no Sense of Excellence in publick Love, and promoting the Happiness of others, whence should this Persuasion arise, "That the Deity will make the Virtuous happy?" Can we prove that it is for the Advantage of the Deity to do so? This I fancy will be look'd upon as very absurd, ||^{81a}unless we suppose some beneficent Dispositions essential to the Deity, which determine him to consult the publick Good of his Creatures, and reward such as co-operate with ||^{82b}his^b|| kind Intention^a||. And if there be such Dispositions in the Deity, where is the impossibility of some small degree of this publick Love in ||^{83}his|| Creatures? And why must they be suppos'd incapable of acting but from Self-Love?

^{84}In short, without acknowledging some other Principle of Action in rational Agents than Self-Love, I see no Foundation to expect Beneficence, or Rewards [151] from God, or Man, further than it is the Interest of the Benefactor; and all Expectation of Benefits from a Being whose Interests are independent on us, must be perfectly ridiculous. What should engage the Deity to reward Virtue? Virtue is commonly suppos'd, upon this Scheme, to be only a consulting our own Happiness in the most artful way, consistently with the Good of the Whole; and in Vice the same thing is foolishly pursu'd, in a manner which will not so probably succeed, and which is contrary to the Good of the Whole. But how is the Deity concern'd in this Whole, if every Agent always acts from Self-Love? And what Ground have we, from the Idea of ||^{85}a God it self||, to believe the Deity is good in the Christian Sense, that is, studious of the Good of his Creatures? Perhaps the Misery of ||^{86}his|| Creatures may ||^{87}give him as much|| Pleasure, as their Happiness: And who can find fault, or blame such a Being to study their Misery; for what else should we expect? A Manichean[ii] Evil God, is a Notion which Men would as readily run into, as that of a Good one, if there is no Excellence in disinterested Love, and no Being acts but for its own Advantage; unless we prov'd that the Happiness of Creatures was advantageous to the Deity. [152]

From
Concomitant
Pleasure.

‖ [88a] VIII. The last, and only remaining Objection against what has been said, is this, "That ‖ [89b] Virtue perhaps[b] ‖ is pursu'd because of the concomitant Pleasure." To which we may answer, first, by observing, that this plainly supposes a Sense of Virtue antecedent to Ideas of Advantage, upon which this Advantage is founded; and that from the very Frame of our Nature we are determin'd to perceive Pleasure in the practice of Virtue, and to approve it when practis'd by our selves, or others.

[90c] But further, may we not justly question, whether all Virtue is pleasant? Or, whether we are not determin'd to some amiable Actions in which we find no Pleasure? 'Tis true, all the Passions, and Affections justify themselves; or, we approve our being affected in ‖ [91d] a certain[d] ‖ manner on ‖ [92e] certain Occasions[e] ‖, and condemn a Person who is otherwise affected. So the Sorrowful, the Angry, the Jealous, the Compassionate, think it reasonable they should be so upon the several Occasions which move these Passions; but we should not therefore say that Sorrow, Anger, Jealousy, or Pity are pleasant, and that we chuse to be in these Passions because of the concomitant Pleasure. The matter is plainly this. The Frame of our Nature, on such Occasions as move these Passions, determines us to be thus [153] affected, and to approve our being so: Nay, we dislike any Person who is not thus affected upon such occasions, not-

---

ii. Manicheanism, named after its Persian founder Mani (209–76?), was a religion of later antiquity, whose syncretic system contained Zoroastrian and Gnostic doctrines. Hutcheson refers to the Manichean dualism: evil and the demons of matter (hyle) control the present material world and constantly struggle against the powers of light; the human soul, imprisoned in the body, is part of the good god. Mandeville gives a favorable description of Manicheanism in *Free Thoughts on Religion, the Church and National Happiness,* 2nd ed. (London, 1729); 1st ed. 1720, 103ff.

withstanding the uneasiness of these Passions. ‖⁹³ᶠThisᶠ‖ uneasiness determines us to endeavour an Alteration in the state of the Object; but
not otherwise to remove the painful Affection, while the occasion is un-
alter'd: which shews that these ‖⁹⁴ᵍAffections are neither chosen for their
concomitant Pleasure, nor voluntarily brought ‖⁹⁵ʰupon our selvesʰ‖
with a view to private Goodᵍ‖. The Actions which these Passions move
us to, ‖⁹⁶ⁱtend generallyⁱ‖ to remove the uneasy Passion by altering the
state of the Object; but the ‖⁹⁷ʲRemoval of our Pain is seldom directly
intended in the uneasy Benevolent Passions: nor is the Alteration intended in the State of the Objects by such Passions, imagin'd to be a
private Good to the Agent, as it always is in the selfish Passions. If our
sole Intention, in Compassion or Pity, ‖⁹⁸ᵏwasᵏ‖ the Removal of our
Pain,ʲ‖ we should run away, shut our Eyes, divert our Thoughts from
the miserable Object, to avoid the Pain of Compassion, which we seldom do: nay, we croud about such Objects, and voluntarily ‖⁹⁹ˡexpose
our selves toˡ‖ Pain, unless Reason, and Reflection upon our Inability to
relieve the Miserable, countermand our Inclination; or some selfish Affection, as fear of Danger, overballances it. [154]

Now there are several morally amiable Actions, which flow from these
Passions which are so uneasy; such as Attempts of relieving the Distress'd, of defending the Injur'd, of repairing of Wrongs done by our
selves. These Actions are often accompany'd with no Pleasure in the
mean time, nor have they any subsequent Pleasure, except as they are
successful; unless it be that which may arise from calm Reflection, when
the Passion is over, upon our having been in a Disposition, which to our
moral Sense appears lovely and good: but this Pleasure is never intended
in the Heat of Action, nor is it any Motive exciting to it.

Besides, In the pleasant Passions, we do not love, because it is pleasant
to love; we do not chuse this State, because it is an advantageous, or
pleasant State: This Passion necessarily arises from seeing its proper Object, a morally good Character. And if we could love, whenever we see
it would be our Interest to love, Love could be brib'd by a third Person;
and we could never love Persons in Distress, for then our Love gives us
Pain. The same Observation may be extended to all the other Affections
from which Virtue is suppos'd to flow: And from the whole we may

conclude, "That the virtuous Agent [155] is never apprehended by us as acting only from Views of his own Interest, but as principally influenc'd by some other Motive."ᵃ‖

The true
Spring of
Virtue.

¹⁰⁰ IX. Having remov'd these ‖¹⁰¹ false‖ Springs of ‖¹⁰² virtuous Actions‖, let us next establish the true one, viz. some Determination of our Nature to study the Good of others; or some Instinct, antecedent to all Reason from Interest, which influences us to the Love of others; even as the moral Sense,* above ‖¹⁰³ explain'd‖, determines us to approve the Actions which flow from this Love in our selves or others. This disinterested Affection, may appear strange to Men impress'd with Notions of Self-Love, as the sole ‖¹⁰⁴ Motive‖ of Action, from the Pulpit, the Schools, the Systems, and Conversations regulated by them: but let us consider it in its strongest, and simplest Kinds; and when we see the Possibility of it in these Instances, we may easily discover its universal Extent.

Natural
Affection.

An honest Farmer will tell you, that he studies the Preservation and Happiness of his Children, and loves them without any design of Good to himself. But say some of our Philosophers, ⁱⁱⁱ "The Happiness of [156] their Children gives Parents Pleasure, and their Misery ‖¹⁰⁵ gives them‖ Pain; and therefore to obtain the former, and avoid the latter, they study, from Self-Love, the Good of their Children." Suppose several Merchants join'd in Partnership of their whole Effects; one of them ‖¹⁰⁶ is employ'd‖ abroad in managing the Stock of the Company; his Prosperity occasions Gain to all, and his Losses give them Pain ‖¹⁰⁷ from‖ their Share in the Loss: is this then the same Kind of Affection with that of Parents to their Children? Is there the same tender, personal Regard? I fancy no Parent will say so. In this Case of Merchants there is a plain Conjunction of Interest; but whence the Conjunction of Interest between the Parent and Child? Do the Child's Sensations give Pleasure or Pain to the Parent? Is the Parent hungry, thirsty, sick, when ‖¹⁰⁸ the Child is so‖? ‖¹⁰⁹ "No, but his Love to the Child makes him affected with his Pleasures or Pains." This Love‖ then is antecedent to the Conjunction

---

* See Sect. i.

iii. For example, Bernard Mandeville, *The Fable of the Bees,* ed. F. B. Kaye, 2 vols. (Indianapolis: Liberty Fund, 1988), vol. 1, p. 75.

of Interest, and the Cause of it, not the Effect: ||[110] this Love|| then must be disinterested. "No, ||[111] says another Sophist||, Children are Parts of our selves, and in loving them we but love our selves in them." A very good Answer! Let us carry it as far as it will go. How are they Parts of our selves? Not as a Leg or an Arm: We are not conscious of their Sensations. "But their [157] Bodys were form'd from Parts of ours." So is a Fly, or a Maggot which may breed in any discharg'd Blood or Humour: Very dear Insects surely! There must be something else then which makes Children Parts of our selves; and what is this but that Affection which Nature determines us to have toward them? This Love makes them Parts of our selves, and therefore does not flow from their being so before. This is indeed a good Metaphor; and wherever we find a Determination among several rational Agents to mutual Love, let each Individual be look'd upon as a Part of a great Whole, or System, and concern himself in the publick Good of ||[112] it.||

[113] But a later Author observes,* [iv] "That natural Affection in Parents is weak, till the Children begin to give Evidences of Knowledge and Affections." Mothers say they feel it strong from the very first: and yet I could wish for the Destruction of his Hypothesis, that what he alledges ||[114] was|| true; as I fancy it is ||[115] in some measure, tho we may find in some Parents an Affection toward Idiots||. The observing of Understanding and Affections in Children, which make them ||[116] appear moral|| Agents, can increase Love toward them without prospect of Interest; for I hope this [158] Increase of Love, is not from Prospect of Advantage from the Knowledge or Affections of Children, for whom Parents are still toiling, and never intend to be refunded their Expences, or recompens'd for their Labour, but in Cases of extreme Necessity. If then the observing a moral Capacity can be the occasion of increasing Love without Self-Interest, even from the Frame of our Nature; pray, may not this be a Foundation of weaker degrees of Love where there is no preceding tie of Parentage, and extend it to all Mankind?

---

* See the *Fable of the Bees,* Page 68, 3d Ed.
iv. Mandeville, *Fable of the Bees,* ed. Kaye, vol. 1, p. 75.

[117]X. And that this is so in fact, will appear by considering some more distant Attachments. If we observe any Neighbours, from whom perhaps we have receiv'd no good Offices, form'd into Friendships, Familys, Partnerships, and with Honesty and Kindness assisting each other; pray ask any Mortal if he would not ‖[118]be better pleas'd with‖ their Prosperity, when their Interests are no way inconsistent with his own, than with their Misery, and Ruin; and you shall find a Bond of Benevolence further extended than a Family and Children, altho the Ties are not so strong. Again, suppose a Person, for Trade, had left his native Country, and with all his Kindred had settled his Fortunes abroad, without any View of returning; and only [159] imagine he had receiv'd no Injurys from his Country: ask such a Man, ‖[119]would it give him no Pleasure to hear of the Prosperity of his Country‖? Or could he, now that his Interests are separated from that of his Nation, as ‖[120]gladly hear‖ that it was laid waste by Tyranny or a foreign Power? I fancy his Answer would shew us a Benevolence extended beyond Neighbourhoods or Acquaintances. Let a Man of a compos'd Temper, out of the hurry of his private Affairs, ‖[121]only‖ read of the Constitution of a foreign Country, even in the most distant parts of the Earth, and observe Art, ‖[122]Design, and a Study‖ of publick Good in the Laws of this Association; and he shall find his Mind mov'd in their favour; he shall be contriving Rectifications and Amendments in their Constitution, and regret any unlucky part of it which may be pernicious to their Interest; he shall bewail any Disaster which befalls them, and accompany all their Fortunes with the Affections of a Friend. Now this ‖[123]proves Benevolence to be in‖ some degree extended to all Mankind, where there is no interfering Interest, which from Self-Love may obstruct it. And had we any Notions of rational Agents, capable of moral Affections, in the most distant Planets,[v] our

v. Travels to moons and planets were a popular literary subject during the seventeenth and eighteenth centuries. The most famous writer of such travels was Cyrano de Bergerac, *Histoire comique des états et empires de la lune,* Paris, 1657, translated as *Selenarhia, or the Government of the World in the Moon, a Comical History,* by Sir Thomas St. Serfe, London, 1659. Other writers include David Russen, *Iter Lunare: or, a Voyage to the Moon,* London, 1705, and Daniel Defoe, *The Consolidator, or, Memoirs of Sundry Transactions from the World in the Moon,* London, 1705. Of

good Wishes would still attend them, and we should ∥¹²⁴delight in∥ their ∥¹²⁵Happiness.∥ [160]

¹²⁶XI. Here we may transiently remark the Foundation of what we call national Love, or Love of one's native Country. Whatever place we have liv'd in for any considerable time, there we have most distinctly remark'd the various Affections of human Nature; we have known many lovely Characters; we remember the Associations, Friendships, Familys, natural Affections, and other human Sentiments: our moral Sense determines us to approve these lovely Dispositions where we have most distinctly observ'd them; and our Benevolence concerns us in the Interests of ∥¹²⁷the∥ Persons possess'd of them. When we come to observe the like as distinctly in another Country, we begin to acquire a national Love toward it also; nor has our own Country any other preference in our Idea, unless it be by an Association of the pleasant Ideas of our Youth, with the Buildings, Fields, and Woods where we receiv'd them. This may let us see, how Tyranny, ∥¹²⁸Faction∥, a Neglect of Justice, a Corruption of Manners, ∥¹²⁹and∥ any thing which occasions the Misery of the Subjects, destroys this national Love, and the dear Idea of a Country.

National Love.

We ought here to observe, That the only Reason of that apparent want of natural Affection among collateral Rela-[161]tions, is, that these natural Inclinations, in many Cases, are overpower'd by Self-Love, where there happens any Opposition of Interests; but where this does not happen, we shall find all Mankind under its Influence, ∥¹³⁰tho∥ with different degrees of Strength, according to the nearer or more remote Relations they stand in to each other; and according as the natural Affection of Benevolence ∥¹³¹is∥ join'd with and strengthen'd by Esteem, Gratitude, Compassion, or other kind Affections; or on the contrary, weaken'd by Displicence, Anger, or Envy. [162]

The Reason why natural Affections do not always appear.

major importance for scientific speculation was Bernard de Bouvier de Fontenelle, *Entretiens sur la pluralité des mondes,* Paris, 1686; there were several contemporary English translations.

The Sense of Virtue, and the various
Opinions about it, reducible to one general
Foundation. The Manner of computing the
Morality of Actions.

All Virtue Benevolent. I. If we examine all the Actions which are counted amiable any where, and enquire into the Grounds upon which they are approv'd, we shall find, that in the Opinion of the Person who approves them, they ||¹always|| appear as Benevolent, or flowing from ||²Love of others||, and ||³a|| Study of their Happiness, whether the Approver be one of the Persons belov'd, or profited, or not; so that all those kind Affections which incline us to make others happy, and all Actions suppos'd to flow from such Affections, appear morally Good, if while they are benevolent toward some Persons, they be not pernicious to others. Nor shall we find any thing amiable in any Action whatsoever, where there is no Benevolence imagin'd; nor in any Disposition, or Capacity, which is not suppos'd applicable to, and design'd for benevolent Purposes. Nay, as was before observ'd,* [163] the Actions which in fact are exceedingly useful, shall appear void of moral Beauty, if we ||⁵know|| they proceeded from no kind Intentions ||⁶toward|| others; and yet an unsuccessful Attempt of Kindness, or of promoting publick Good, shall appear as amiable as the most successful, if it flow'd from as strong Benevolence.

---

* See Sect. ii. Art. 3. Par. 1. Art. ||⁴6. Par. 2||.

II. ‖[7]Hence those‖ Affections which would lead us to do good to our   Religion.
Benefactor, shall appear amiable, and the contrary Affections odious,
even when our Actions cannot possibly be of any advantage or hurt to
him. Thus a sincere Love and Gratitude toward our Benefactor, a chearful Readiness to do whatever he shall require, how burdensom soever, a
hearty Inclination to comply with his Intentions, and Contentment with
the State he has plac'd us in, are the strongest Evidences of Benevolence
we can shew to such a Person; and therefore they must appear exceedingly amiable. And under these is included all the rational Devotion, or
Religion toward a Deity apprehended as Good, which we can possibly
perform.

We may here transiently observe one Circumstance in the Frame of   ‖[8]Gratitude.‖
our Nature, which is wonderfully adapted to promote Benevolence, viz.
that as a Benefit conferr'd necessarily raises Gratitude in the [164] ‖[9]Per-
son who receives it‖, so the Expressions of this Gratitude, even from the
meanest of Mankind, are wonderfully delightful to the Benefactor.
Never were there any Mortals so poor, so inconsiderable, whose grateful
Praise would not be some way delightful; and by whom we would not
rather chuse to be ‖[10]lov'd‖, than hated, if their Love no way evidenc'd
us to be Partners in their Vices, or concern'd in their Meanness. And
thus the most abject ‖[11]Person oblig'd‖ is capable, and inclin'd to make
no small addition to our Happiness by his Love, and Gratitude, when
he is utterly incapable of any other Return, and when we expect none
from him: Thus,

> ———— A grateful Mind
> By owing owes not, ‖[12]and‖ still pays, at once
> Indebted and discharg'd ————*

As to external Performances of Religion, they are no doubt very various in different Nations, and Ages; and Education may give Men Opinions, that certain Actions are pleasing, and others displeasing to the Deity: but then wherever any external Rite of Worship is approv'd, there
also it is look'd upon to proceed from Love toward the Deity, or some

* Par. Lost, B. iv. l. 55.

other Affec-[165]tion necessarily join'd with Love, as Reverence, Repen-tance, or Sorrow to have offended. So that the general Principle of Love, is the Foundation of all the apparent moral Excellence, even in the most fantastick Rites of Worship which were ever approv'd. For as to Rites design'd only to appease a furious Being, no Mortal, I fancy, apprehends there is any Virtue, or Excellence in them; but that they are chosen only as the dishonourable Means of avoiding a greater Evil. Now as there are various ‖ ^{13} speculative‖ Opinions about what is acceptable to the Deity, it necessarily follows, "That, accordingly, Practices, and Approbation, must be various; tho all the moral Goodness of Actions is still presum'd to flow from Love."

Social Virtues.   III. Again, that we may see how ‖ ^{14} Love, or‖ Benevolence, is the Foun-dation of all apprehended Excellence in social Virtues, let us only ob-serve, That amidst the diversity of Sentiments on this Head among vari-ous Sects, this is still allow'd to be the way of deciding the Controversy about any disputed Practice, ‖ ^{15} viz.‖ to enquire whether this Conduct, or the contrary, will most effectually promote the publick Good. The Morality is immediately adjusted, when the natural Tendency, or Influ-ence of the Action upon the universal natural Good of Mankind is agreed upon. That which pro-[166]duces more Good than Evil in the Whole, is acknowledg'd Good; and what does not, is counted Evil. In this Case, we no other way regard the good of the Actor, or that of those who are thus enquiring, than as they make a Part of the great System.

In our late Debates about Passive Obedience, and the Right of Re-sistance in Defence of Privileges, [i] the Point disputed among Men of Sense was, "whether universal Submission would probably be attended with greater natural Evils, than temporary Insurrections, when Privileges are invaded; and not whether what tended in the Whole to the publick natural Good, was also morally Good?" And if a divine Command was alledg'd in favour of the Doctrine of Passive Obedience, this would, no

---

i. George Berkeley's *Passive Obedience* (1712) was criticized by the Molesworth circle. See *The Works of George Berkeley,* ed. A. A. Luce and T. E. Jessop (London, 1953), vol. 4, pp. 17–46, and the editors' introduction, pp. 3–11.

doubt, by its eternal Sanctions cast the ballance of natural Good to its own side, and determine our Election from Interest; and yet our Sense of the moral Good in Passive Obedience, would still be founded upon some Species of Benevolence, such as Gratitude toward the Deity, and Submission to his Will to whom we are so much oblig'd. But I fancy those, who believe the Deity to be Good, would not rashly alledge such a Command, unless they also asserted, that the thing commanded did tend more to the universal Good, than the contrary, either by prevent-[167]ing the external Evils of Civil War, or by enuring Men to Patience, or some other Quality which they apprehended necessary to their ever-lasting Happiness. And were it not so, Passive Obedience might be rec-ommended as an inglorious Method of escaping a greater Mischief, but could never have any thing morally amiable in it.

But let us quit the Disputes of the Learned, on whom, it may be alledg'd, Custom and Education have a powerful Influence; and con-sider upon what Grounds, in common Life, Actions are approv'd or con-demn'd, vindicated or excus'd. We are universally asham'd to say an Ac-tion is Just, because it ‖ ^{16} tends‖ to my Advantage, or to the Advantage of the Actor: And we as seldom condemn a beneficent kind Action, be-cause it ‖ ^{17} is‖ not advantageous to us, or to the Actor. Blame, and Cen-sure, are founded on a Tendency to publick Evil, or a Principle of private Malice in the Agent, or Neglect at least of the Good of others; on In-humanity of Temper, or at least such strong Selfishness as makes the Agent careless of the Sufferings of others: and thus we blame and censure when the Action no way affects our selves. All the moving and persuasive Vindications of Actions, which may, from some partial evil Tendency, appear evil, are taken from this, that they were necessary to some [168] greater Good which counterballanc'd the Evil: "Severity toward a few, is Compassion toward multitudes.—Transitory Punishments are nec-essary for avoiding more durable Evils.—Did not some suffer on such Occasions, there would be no living for honest Men."—and such like. And even when an Action cannot be entirely justify'd, yet how greatly is the Guilt extenuated, if we can alledge; "That it was only the Effect of Inadvertence without Malice, or of partial good Nature, Friendship, Compassion, natural Affection, or Love of a Party?" All these Considerations shew what is the universal Foundation of our Sense of moral Good, or Evil, viz. Benevolence toward others on ‖ ^{18} one‖ hand, and Malice, or even Indolence, and Unconcernedness about the ‖ ^{19} apparent‖ publick Evil on the other. And let it be here observ'd, that we are so far from imagining all Men to ‖ ^{20} act‖ only ‖ ^{21} from‖ Self-Love, that we universally expect in others a Regard for the Publick; and do not look upon the want of this, as barely the absence of moral Good, or Virtue, but even as positively evil and hateful.

Moral Evil not always Malice. IV. Contrarys may illustrate each other; let us therefore observe the general Foundation of our Sense of moral Evil more particularly. Disinterested Malice, or ‖ ^{22} Delight in‖ the Misery of others, is the [169] highest pitch of what we count vitious; and every Action appears evil, which is imagin'd to flow from any degree of this Affection. Perhaps a violent Passion may hurry Men into it for a few Moments, and our rash angry Sentiments of our Enemys, may represent them as having such odious Dispositions; but it is very probable, from the Reasons offer'd above,* that there is no such degree of Wickedness in human Nature, as in cold blood, to ‖ ^{23} be pleas'd with‖ the Misery of others, when it is ‖ ^{24} conceiv'd no‖ way useful to our Interests.

‖ ^{25a} The Story of Nero and Paetus[ii] may be alledg'd against this, but perhaps unjustly, even allowing the Fact to be true. Nero was ‖ ^{26b} conscious he[b]‖ was hated by those whom the World call'd good Men, and that they were dangerous to him; he fancy'd his best Security lay in being terrible, and appearing such on all Occasions, by making others miserable when he pleas'd, to let his Enemys see, that they should have no Security from that Compassion which a Nero would imagine argu'd Weakness. This unfortunate Gentleman's Happiness might by some foolish Courtier be so related, as to carry a Reproof of the Tyrant's unnatural Pursuits, whereby his Passion might be excited to cut off the

---

* See Sect. ii. Art. 4.

ii. Thrasea Paetus, a Stoic of republican attitude, who had written a biography of Cato with a clear bias against Caesar, was accused of high treason by Nero and committed suicide after his conviction in A.D. 66.

Per-[170]son admir'd, and prefer'd before him. Any of these Motives of apparent Interest seem more probably to have influenc'd him, than that we should in him, and a few others, suppose^a‖ a Principle of calm Malice without Interest, of which the rest of Mankind seem entirely incapable.

The Temper of a Tyrant seems ‖²⁷probably to be‖ a continu'd state of Anger, Hatred, and Fear. To form our Judgment then of his Motives of Action, and those of Men of like Tempers in lower Stations, let us reflect upon the Apprehensions we form of Mankind, when we are under any of those Passions which to the Tyrant are habitual. When we are under the fresh Impressions of an Injury, we ‖²⁸plainly‖ find, that our Minds are wholly fill'd with Apprehensions of the Person who injur'd us, as if he ‖²⁹was‖ absolutely Evil, and delighted in doing Mischief: We overlook the Virtues, which, when calm, we could have observ'd in him: we forget ‖³⁰that‖ perhaps ‖³¹only Self-Love, and not Malice, was his Motive; or‖ it may be some generous or kind Intention toward others. These, probably, are the Opinions which a Tyrant constantly forms concerning Mankind; and having very much weaken'd all kind Affections in himself, however he may pretend to them, he judges of the Tempers of others by his own. And were [171] ‖³²Men‖ really such as he apprehends them, his Treatment of them would not be very unreasonable. We shall generally find our Passions arising suitably to the Apprehensions we form of others: if ‖³³these be‖ rashly form'd upon some sudden slight Views, it is no wonder if we find Dispositions following upon them, very little suited to the real State of human Nature.

The ordinary ‖³⁴Springs‖ of Vice ‖³⁵then‖ among Men, ‖³⁶must be‖ a mistaken Self-Love, made ‖³⁷so‖ violent, ‖³⁸as‖ to overcome Benevolence;³⁹ or Affections arising from false, and rashly form'd Opinions of Mankind, which we run into thro the weakness of our Benevolence. When Men, who ‖⁴⁰had‖ good Opinions of each other, happen to have contrary Interests, they are apt to have their good Opinions of each other abated, by imagining a design'd Opposition from Malice; without this, they can scarcely hate one another. ‖⁴¹Thus‖ two Candidates for the same Office wish each other dead, because that is an ordinary way by which Men make room for each other; but if there remains any Reflection on each other's Virtue, as there sometimes may in benevolent Tem-

Temper of a Tyrant.

Ordinary Springs of Vice.

pers, then their Opposition may be without Hatred; and if another better Post, where there is no Competition, were [172] bestow'd on one of
them, the other shall rejoice at it.

Self-Love
indifferent.

V. ||⁴²The|| Actions which flow solely from Self-Love, and yet evidence
no Want of Benevolence, having no hurtful Effects upon others, ||⁴³seem
perfectly indifferent in a moral Sense||, and neither raise the Love or
Hatred of the Observer. Our Reason can ||⁴⁴indeed discover|| certain
Bounds, within which we may not only act from Self-Love, consistently
with the Good of the Whole, but every Mortal's acting thus within these
Bounds for his own Good, is absolutely necessary for the Good of the
Whole; and the Want of such Self-Love would be universally pernicious.
||⁴⁵Hence||, he who pursues his own private Good, with an Intention
also to concur with that Constitution which tends to the Good of the
Whole; and much more he who promotes his own Good, with a direct
View of making himself more capable of serving God, or doing good
to Mankind; acts not only innocently, but also honourably, and virtu-
ously: for in both these Cases, ||⁴⁶a Motive of|| Benevolence concurs with
Self-Love to excite him to the Action. And thus a Neglect of our own
Good, may be morally evil, and argue a Want of Benevolence toward
the Whole. But when Self-Love breaks over the Bounds above-mention'd,
and leads us into Actions detrimen-[173]tal to others, and to the whole;
or makes us insensible of the generous kind Affections; then it appears
vitious, and is disapprov'd. So also, when upon any small Injurys, or
sudden Resentment, or any weak superstitious Suggestions, our Benev-
olence ||⁴⁷becomes|| so faint, as to let us ||⁴⁸entertain|| odious Concep-
tions of ||⁴⁹Men||, or any Part of them, without just Ground, as if they
were wholly Evil, or Malicious, or as if they were a worse Sort of Beings
than they really are; these Conceptions must lead us into malevolent
Affections, or at least weaken our good ones, and make us really Vitious.

Self-Love not
excluded by
Benevolence.

VI.⁵⁰ Here we must also observe, that every moral Agent justly considers
himself as a Part of this rational System, which may be useful to the
Whole; so that he may be, in part, an Object of his own Benevolence.
Nay further, as was hinted above, he may see, that the Preservation of

the System ||⁵¹requires every one to be|| innocently sollicitous about himself. Hence he may conclude, that an Action which brings greater Evil to the Agent, than Good to others, however it may evidence ||⁵²strong Benevolence or|| a virtuous Disposition in the Agent, yet it ||⁵³must be founded upon a mistaken Opinion of its Tendency to publick Good, when it has no such Tendency: so that a|| Man who reason'd [174] justly, and consider'd the whole, would not be led into it, ||⁵⁴were his Benevolence ever so strong||; nor would he recommend it to the Practice of others; however he might acknowledge, that the Detriment arising to the Agent from a kind Action, did evidence a ||⁵⁵strong Disposition to Virtue||. Nay ||⁵⁶further, if any Good was|| propos'd to the Pursuit of an Agent, and he had a Competitor in every respect only equal to himself; the highest Benevolence possible would not lead a wise Man to prefer another to himself, were there no Ties of Gratitude, or some other external Circumstance to move him to yield to his Competitor. A Man surely of the strongest Benevolence, may just treat himself as he would do a third Person, who was a Competitor of equal Merit with the other; and as his preferring one to another, in such a Case, would argue no Weakness of Benevolence; so, no more would he evidence it by preferring himself to a Man of only equal Abilitys.

||⁵⁷ᵃWherever a Regard to my self, tends as much to the good of the Whole, as Regard to another; or where the Evil to my self, is equal to the Good obtain'd for another; tho by acting, in such Cases, for the good of another, I really shew a very amiable Disposition; yet by acting in the contrary manner, from Regard to [175] my self, I evidence no evil Disposition, nor any want of the most extensive Benevolence; since the Moment of good to the Whole is, in both Cases, exactly equal. And let it be here observ'd, that this does not supersede the necessity of Liberality, or gratuitous Gifts, altho in such Actions the Giver loses ||⁵⁸ᵇas much asᵇ|| the other receives; since the Moment of Good to any Person, in any given Case, is in a compound ||⁵⁹ᶜRatioᶜ|| of the Quantity of the Good it self, and the Indigence of the Person. Hence it appears, that a Gift may make a much greater Addition to the happiness of the Receiver, than the Diminution it occasions in the happiness of the Giver: And that the most useful and important Gifts are those from the Wealthy to

the Indigent. $\|$ [60d] Gifts [d] $\|$ from Equals are not useless $\|$ [61e] neither [e] $\|$, since they often increase the Happiness of both, as they are strong Evidences of mutual Love: but Gifts from the Poor to the Wealthy are really foolish, unless they be only little Expressions of Gratitude, which are also fruitful of Joy on both Sides: for these Expressions of Gratitude are really delightful and acceptable to the Wealthy, if they have any Humanity; and their Acceptance of them is matter of Joy to the poor Giver.

In like manner, when an Action does more Harm to the Agent, than Good to [176] the Publick; the doing it evidences an amiable and truly virtuous Disposition in the Agent, tho 'tis plain he acts upon a mistaken View of his Duty. But if the private Evil to the Agent be so great, as to make him incapable at another time, of promoting a publick Good of greater moment than what is attain'd by this Action; the Action may really be Evil, so far as it evidences a prior Neglect of a greater $\|$ [62f] attainable [f] $\|$ publick Good for a smaller one; tho at present this Action also flows from a virtuous Disposition. [a] $\|$

Benevolence, how affected by the Qualitys of its Object.

[63] VII. The moral Beauty, or Deformity of Actions, is not alter'd by the moral Qualitys of the Objects, any further $\|$ [64] than $\|$ the Qualitys of the Objects increase or diminish the Benevolence of the Action, or the publick Good intended by it. Thus Benevolence toward the worst Characters, or the Study of their Good, may be as amiable as any whatsoever; yea often more so than that toward the Good, since it argues such a strong Degree of Benevolence as can surmount the greatest Obstacle, the moral Evil in the Object. Hence the Love of unjust Enemys, is counted among the highest Virtues. Yet when our Benevolence to the Evil, encourages them in their bad Intentions, or makes them more capable of Mischief; this diminishes or destroys the Beauty of the Action, or even makes [177] it evil, as it betrays a Neglect of the Good of others more valuable; Beneficence toward whom, would have tended more to the publick Good, than that toward our [65] Favourites: But Benevolence toward evil Characters, which neither encourages $\|$ [66] them $\|$, nor enables them to do Mischief, nor diverts our Benevolence from Persons more useful, has as much moral Beauty as any whatsoever.

[67] VIII. In comparing the moral Qualitys of Actions, in order to regulate our Election among various Actions propos'd, or to find which of them has the greatest moral Excellency, we are led by our moral Sense of Virtue ‖[68] to judge thus‖; that in equal Degrees of Happiness, expected to proceed from the Action, the Virtue is in proportion to the Number of Persons to whom the Happiness shall extend; (and here the Dignity, or moral Importance of Persons, may compensate Numbers) and in equal Numbers, the Virtue is as the Quantity of the Happiness, or natural Good; or that the Virtue is in a compound Ratio of the Quantity of Good, and Number of Enjoyers. ‖[69] In‖ the same manner, the moral Evil, or Vice, is as the Degree of Misery, and Number of Sufferers; so that, that Action is best, which ‖[70] procures‖ the greatest Happiness for the greatest Numbers; and that, [178] worst, which, in like manner, occasions Misery. [iii]

Qualitys
determining
our Election.

[71] IX. Again, when the Consequences of Actions are of a mix'd Nature, partly Advantageous, ‖[72] and‖ partly Pernicious; that Action is good, whose good Effects preponderate the evil, by being useful to many, and pernicious to few; and that, evil, which is otherwise. Here also the moral Importance of Characters, or Dignity of Persons may compensate Numbers; as may also the Degrees of Happiness or Misery: for to procure an inconsiderable Good to many, but an immense Evil to few, may be Evil; and an immense Good to few, may preponderate a small Evil to many.

Consequences,
how they
affect the
Morality of
Actions.

‖[73a] But the Consequences which affect the Morality of Actions, are not only the direct and natural Effects of the Actions themselves; but also all those Events which otherwise would not have happen'd. ‖[74b] For[b]‖ many Actions which have no immediate or natural evil Effects, nay

---

iii. This maxim became the central phrase of utilitarianism. Also used by Cesare Beccaria (1738–94) in the introduction to his work *Dei dilitti e delle pene* (Livorno, 1764). Jeremy Bentham calls it the "principle of utility"; compare with the title of chapter I of *An Introduction to the Principles of Morals and Legislation* (London, 1789), ed. H. L. A. Hart (London: Athlone, 1970), p. II.

which actually produce good Effects, may be evil; if a man foresees that ||^{75c}the evil^c|| Consequences, which will probably flow from the Folly of others, upon his doing of such Actions, are so great as to overballance all the ||^{76d}Good produc'd by those Actions^d||, or all the Evils which would flow from the Omission of ||^{77e}them^e||: And in such Cases the [179] Probability is to be computed on both sides. Thus if an Action of mine will probably, thro the ||^{78f}Mistakes^f|| or Corruption of others, be made a Precedent in unlike Cases, to very evil Actions; or when my Action, tho good in it self, will probably provoke Men to very evil Actions, upon some mistaken Notion of their Right; any of these Considerations foreseen by me, may make such an Action of mine evil, whenever the Evils ||^{79g}which will probably^g|| be occasion'd by the Action, ||^{80h}are greater^h|| than the Evils occasion'd by the Omission.

And this is the Reason that many Laws prohibit Actions in general, even when some particular Instances of ||^{81i}those^i|| Actions would be very useful; because an universal Allowance of them, considering the Mistakes Men would probably fall into, would be more pernicious than an universal Prohibition; nor could there be any more special Boundarys fix'd between the right and wrong Cases. In such Cases, it is the Duty of Persons to comply with the generally useful Constitution; or if in some very important Instances, the Violation of the Law would be of less evil Consequence than Obedience to it, they must patiently resolve to undergo those Penalties, which the State has, for valuable Ends to the Whole, appointed: and this Disobedience will have nothing criminal in ||^{82j}it. ^{aj}|| [180]

Partial Benevolence, how virtuous. ||^{83}X||. From ||^{84}the two last|| Observations, we may see what Actions our moral Sense would most recommend to our Election, as the most perfectly Virtuous: viz. such as appear to have the most universal unlimited Tendency to the greatest and most extensive Happiness of all the rational Agents, to whom our Influence can ||^{85}reach||. All ||^{86}Benevolence||, even toward a Part, is amiable, ||^{87}when|| not inconsistent with the Good of the Whole: But this is a smaller Degree of Virtue, unless our Beneficence be restrain'd by want of Power, and not want of Love to the Whole. All strict Attachments to Partys, Sects, Factions, have but an imperfect Species of Beauty, ‖ 88 unless‖ when the Good of the Whole requires a stricter Attachment to a Part, as in natural Affection, or virtuous Friendships; ‖ 89 or‖ when some Parts are so eminently useful to the Whole, that even universal Benevolence ‖ 90 would‖ determine us with special Care and Affection to study their Interests. Thus universal Benevolence would incline us to a more strong Concern for the Interests of great and generous Characters in a high Station, or make us more earnestly study the Interests of any generous Society, whose whole Constitution ‖ 91 was‖ contriv'd to promote universal Good. Thus a good Fancy in Architecture, would lead a Man, who was not able to bear the Expence [181] of a compleatly regular Building, to chuse such a Degree of Ornament as he could keep uniformly thro the Whole, and not move him to make a vain unfinish'd Attempt in one Part, of what he foresaw he could not succeed in as to the Whole. And ‖ 92 the most perfect Rules of Architecture condemn an excessive‖ Profusion of Ornament on one Part, above the Proportion of the Whole, unless that Part be some eminent Place of the Edifice, such as the chief Front, or publick Entrance; the adorning of which, would beautify the Whole more than an equal Expence of Ornament on any other Part.

‖ 93a This Increase of the moral Beauty of Actions, or Dispositions, according to the Number of Persons to whom the good Effects of them extend, may shew us the Reason why Actions which flow from the nearer Attachments of Nature, such as that between the Sexes, and the Love of our Offspring, are not so amiable, nor do they appear so virtuous as Actions of equal Moment of Good towards Persons less attach'd to us. The Reason is plainly this. These strong Instincts are by Nature limited to small Numbers of Mankind, such as our Wives or Children; whereas a Disposition, which would produce a like Moment of Good to others, upon no special Attachment, ‖ 94b if it was b‖ accompany'd with [182] natural Power to accomplish its Intention, would be incredibly more fruitful of great and good Effects to the Whole. a‖

95 From this primary Idea of moral Good in Actions, ‖ 96 arises the Idea of‖ Good in those Dispositions, whether natural or acquir'd, which enable us to do good to others; or which are presum'd to be design'd, and acquir'd or cultivated for that purpose 97. And hence those Abilitys,

Moral
Dispositions
and Abilitys.

while nothing appears contrary to our Presumption, may increase our
||^{98}Love to|| the Possessor of them; but when they are imagin'd to be
intended for publick Mischief, they make us hate him the more: Such
are a penetrating Judgment, a tenacious Memory, a quick Invention;
Patience of Labour, Pain, Hunger, Watching; a Contempt of Wealth,
Rumour, Death. These may be rather call'd natural Abilitys, than moral
||^{99}Qualitys. Now, a Veneration for these Qualitys, any further than they
are employ'd for the publick Good, is foolish, and flows from our moral
Sense, grounded upon a false Opinion; for if|| we plainly see them ma-
liciously employ'd, they make the Agent more detestable.

How we
compute the
Morality of
Actions in our
Sense of them.

XI. To find a universal ||^{100}Canon|| to compute the Morality of any Ac-
tions, with all their Circumstances, when we judge of the Actions done
by our selves, or by others, [183] we must observe the following Propositions, or Axioms.

||^{101a}1. The moral Importance of any ||^{102b}Agent^{b}||, or the Quantity
of publick Good produc'd by him, is in a compound Ratio of his
Benevolence and Abilitys: or (by substituting the initial Letters for
the Words, as M = Moment of Good, and μ = Moment of Evil)
M = B × A.

2. ||^{103c}In like manner, the Moment of private Good, or Interest
produc'd by any Person ||^{104d}to himself^{d}||, is in a compound Ratio
of his Self-Love, and Abilitys: or (substituting the initial Letters)
I = S × A.^{c}||

3. When in comparing the Virtue of two ||^{105e}Actions, the Abilitys of
the Agents are^{e}|| equal; the ||^{106f}Moment of publick Good produc'd by
them in like Circumstances, is as the Benevolence: or M = B × 1^{f}.||

4. When Benevolence in two Agents is equal, and other Circumstances alike; the Moment of publick Good is as the Abilitys: or
M = ||^{107g}A^{g}|| × 1.

5. The Virtue then of Agents, or their Benevolence, is always directly
as the Moment of Good produc'd in like Circumstances, and inversly as
their Abilitys: or B = $\frac{M}{A}$. [184]

6. But as the natural Consequences of our Actions are various, some
good to our selves, and evil to the Publick; and others evil to our selves,

and good to the Publick; or either useful both to our selves and others, or pernicious to both; the entire ‖[108h]Motive to[h]‖ good Actions is not always Benevolence alone; ‖[109i]or Motive to Evil[i]‖, Malice alone; (nay, ‖[110j]this last is seldom any Motive at all[j]‖) but in most Actions we must look upon Self-Love as another Force, sometimes conspiring with Benevolence, and assisting it, when we are excited by Views of private Interest, as well as publick Good; and sometimes opposing Benevolence, when the good Action is any way difficult or painful in the Performance, or detrimental in its Consequences to the Agent. ‖[111k]In the former Case, $M = (B + S) \times A = BA + SA$; and therefore $BA = M - SA = M - I$, and $B = \frac{M - I}{A}$. In the latter Case, $M = (B - S) \times A = BA - SA$; therefore $BA = M + SA = M + I$, and $B = \frac{M + I}{A}$.[ak]‖

These selfish Motives shall be* ‖[112hereafter]‖ more ‖[113fully]‖ explain'd; here we may in general denote them by the Word In-[185]terest: which when it concurs with Benevolence, in any Action capable of Increase, or Diminution, must produce a greater Quantity of Good, than Benevolence alone in the same Abilitys; and therefore when the Moment ‖[114]of Good, in an‖ Action partly intended for the Good of the Agent, is but equal to the Moment ‖[115]of Good‖ in the Action of another Agent, influenc'd only by Benevolence, the former is less virtuous; and in this Case the Interest must be deducted to find the true Effect of the Benevolence, or Virtue. ‖[116]In‖ the same manner, when Interest is opposite to Benevolence, and yet is surmounted by it; this Interest must be added to the Moment, to increase the Virtue of the Action, or the Strength of the Benevolence‖[117]: Or thus, in advantageous Virtue, $B = \frac{M - I}{A}$. And in laborious, painful, dangerous or expensive Virtue, $B = \frac{M + I}{A}$‖. By Interest, in this last Case, is understood all the Advantage which the Agent might have obtain'd by omitting the Action, which is a negative Motive to it; and this, when subtracted, becomes positive.

But here we must observe, that no Advantage, not intended, altho casually, or naturally redounding to us from the Action, [186] does at all affect its Morality to make it less amiable; nor does any Difficulty or Evil unforeseen, or not resolved upon, [118] make a kind Action more virtuous;

Intention, and Foresight, affect Actions.

* Vide Sect. v.

since in such Cases Self-Love neither assists nor opposes Benevolence. Nay, Self-Interest ||[119] then only|| diminishes the Benevolence, when without this View of Interest the Action would not have been undertaken, or so much Good would not have been produc'd by the Agent; and it extenuates the Vice of an evil Action, ||[120] only|| when without this Interest the Action would not have been ||[121] pleasing to|| the Agent, ||[122] or|| so much Evil have been produc'd by him.

The ||[123] sixth|| Axiom only explains the external Marks by which Men must judge, who do not see into each others Hearts; for it may really happen in many Cases, that Men may have Benevolence sufficient to ||[124] surmount|| any Difficulty, and yet they may meet with none at all: And in that Case, it is certain there is as much Virtue in the Agent, tho he does not give such Proof of it to his Fellow-Creatures, as if he had surmounted Difficultys in his kind Actions. And this too must be the Case with the Deity, to whom nothing is difficult. [187]

Perfect Virtue. Since then ||[125] Benevolence, or Virtue in any Agent, is as $\frac{M}{A}$, or as $\frac{M \pm I}{A}$, and no Being can act above his natural Ability||; that must be the Perfection of Virtue where ||[126] $M = A$||, or when the Being acts to the utmost of ||[127] his|| Power for the publick Good; and hence the Perfection of Virtue in this Case, ||[128] or $\frac{M}{A}$,|| is as Unity. And this may shew us the only Foundation for the boasting of the Stoicks, "That a Creature suppos'd Innocent, by pursuing Virtue with ||[129] his|| utmost Power, may in Virtue equal the Gods." For in their Case, if ||[130] [A] or|| the Ability be Infinite, unless ||[131] [M] or|| the Good to be produc'd in the whole, be so too, the Virtue is not absolutely perfect; and the Quotient can never surmount Unity.

Moral Evil, how computed. ||[132a] XII. The same Axioms may be apply'd to compute the moral Evil in Actions; that is, calling the Disposition which leads us to Evil, Hatred, tho it is oftner only Self-Love, with Inadvertence to its Consequences: then,

1st. The Moment of Evil produc'd by any Agent, is as the Product of his Hatred into his Ability, or $\mu = H \times A$. And, [188]

2dly. In equal Abilitys, ||[133b] $H = \mu \times 1$ b||.

merely indifferent, ||[158]to be ingag'd in Actions only as they appear to tend to their own private Good.||" Surely, the Supposition of a benevolent universal Instinct, would recommend human Nature, and its Author, more to the Love of a good Man, and leave room enough for the Exercise of our Reason, in contriving and settling Rights, Laws, Constitutions; in inventing Arts, and practising them so as to gratify, in the most effectual manner, that generous Inclination. And if we must bring in Self-Love to make Virtue Rational, a [194] little Reflection will discover, as ||[159]shall appear hereafter||, that this Benevolence is our greatest Happiness; and thence we may ||[160]resolve to cultivate, as much as possible,|| this sweet Disposition, and to despise every opposite Interest. Not that we can be truly Virtuous, if we intend only to obtain the Pleasure which ||[161]accompanies|| Beneficence, without the Love of others: Nay, this very Pleasure is founded on our being conscious of disinterested Love to others, as the Spring of our Actions. But Self-Interest may be our Motive, ||[162]in chusing to|| continue in this agreeable State, tho it cannot be the sole, or principal Motive of any Action, which to our moral Sense appears Virtuous. [163]

Heroism, in all stations. ||[164a]The applying a mathematical Calculation to moral Subjects, ||[165b]will[b]|| appear perhaps at first extravagant and wild; but some Corollarys, which are easily and certainly deduc'd below,* may shew the Conveniency of this Attempt, if it could be further pursu'd. At present, we ||[167c]shall only draw[c]|| this one[a]||, which seems the most joyful imaginable, even to the lowest rank of Mankind, viz. "That no external Circumstances of Fortune, no involuntary Disadvantages, can exclude any Mortal from the most heroick Virtue." For how small soever the Moment of publick Good be, [195] which any one can accomplish, yet if his Abilitys ||[168]are|| proportionably small, the ||[169]Quotient, which expresses the Degree of|| Virtue, may be as great as any whatsoever. Thus, not only the Prince, the Statesman, the General, are capable of true Heroism, tho these are the chief Characters, whose Fame is diffus'd thro various Nations and Ages; but when we find in an honest Trader, the kind Friend, the faithful prudent Adviser, the charitable and hospitable

* See Sect. vii. Art. ||[166]8, 9||.

3dly. When Hatred is equal; $\mu = A \times 1$: And,

4thly. The Degree of moral Evil, ||[134c]or Vice[c]||, which is equal to the Hatred or Neglect of publick Good, is thus express'd, $H = \frac{\mu}{A}$.

5thly. The Motives of Interest may ||[135d]co-operate with Hatred, or oppose[d]|| it the same way as with Benevolence; and then according as Self-Interest may partly excite to the Action, and so diminish the Evil; or dissuade from it, and so increase it, the Malice which surmounts it, or $H = \frac{\mu \pm I}{A}$, in like manner as in the Case of moral Good.[a]||

Intention, Foresight. But we must observe, that not only Innocence is expected from all Mortals, but they are presum'd from their Nature, in some measure inclin'd to publick Good;[136] so that a bare Absence of this Desire is enough to make an Agent be reputed Evil: Nor is a direct Intention of publick Evil necessary to make an Action evil, it is enough that it flows from Self-Love, with a plain Neglect of the Good of others||[137a], or an Insensi-[189]bility of their Misery, which we either actually foresee, or have a probable Presumption of.

It is true indeed, that that publick Evil which I neither certainly foresee, nor have actual Presumptions of, as the Consequence of my Action, does not make my present Action Criminal, or Odious; even altho I might have foreseen this Evil by a serious Examination of my own Actions; because such Actions do not, at present, evidence either Malice, or want of Benevolence. But then it is also certain, that my prior Negligence, in not examining the Tendency of my Actions, is a plain Evidence of the want of that Degree of good Affections which is necessary to a virtuous Character; and consequently the Guilt properly lies in this Neglect, rather than in an Action which really flows from a good Intention. Human Laws however, which cannot examine the Intentions, ||[138b]or secret[b]|| Knowledge of the Agent, must judge in gross of the Action itself; presupposing all that Knowledge as actually attain'd, which we are oblig'd to attain.

In like manner, no good Effect which I did not actually foresee and intend, makes my Action morally Good; however Human ||[139c]Laws or Governours[c]||, who cannot search into Mens Intentions, or know their [190] secret Designs, justly reward Actions ||[140d]which tend[d]|| to the publick Good, altho the Agent was engag'd to those Actions only by selfish Views; and consequently had no virtuous Disposition influencing him to them.

The difference in degree of Guilt between Crimes of Ignorance, when the Ignorance is Vincible, and Faulty, as to the natural Tendency of the Action; and Crimes of Malice, or direct evil Intention, consists in this; that the former, by a prior Neglect, argues ||^{141e}a^e|| want of the due degree of Benevolence, or right Affection; the latter, evidences direct evil Affections, which are vastly more odious^a||.

Morality distinct from Interest. XIII. ||¹⁴²From Axiom the 5th||, we may form almost a demonstrative Conclusion, "that we have a Sense of Goodness and moral Beauty in Actions, distinct from Advantage;" for had we no other Foundation of Approbation of Actions, but the Advantage which might arise to us from them, if they were done toward our selves, we ||¹⁴³should|| make no Account of the Abilitys of the Agent, but would barely esteem them according to their Moment. The Abilitys come in only to shew the Degree of Benevolence, which supposes Benevolence necessarily amiable. Who was ever the better pleas'd with a barren rocky [191] Farm, or an inconvenient House, by being told that the poor Farm gave as great Increase as it could; or that the House accommodated its Possessor as well as it could? And yet in our Sentiments of Actions, whose Moment is very inconsiderable, it shall wonderfully increase the Beauty to alledge, "That it was all the poor Agent could do for the Publick, or his Friend."

Morality of Characters. XIV. The moral Beauty of Characters arises from their Actions, or sincere Intentions of the publick Good, according to their Power. We form our Judgment of them according to what appears to be their fix'd Disposition, and not according to any particular Sallys of unkind Passions; altho ||¹⁴⁴these|| abate the Beauty of good Characters, as the Motions of the kind ||¹⁴⁵Affections|| diminish the Deformity of the bad ones. What then properly constitutes a virtuous Character, is not some few accidental Motions of Compassion, natural Affection, or Gratitude; but such a fix'd Humanity, or Desire of the publick Good of all, to whom our Influence can extend, as uniformly excites us to all Acts of ||¹⁴⁶Benefi-

cence, according to our utmost Prudence and Knowledge of the Interests of others: and a strong Benevolence will not fail to make us|| careful of informing our selves right, concerning the truest Methods [192] of serving ||¹⁴⁷the Interests of Mankind||. Every Motion indeed of the kind Affections appears in some degree amiable; but we denominate the Character from the prevailing Principle.

Instinct be the sp of Virtu XV. ||¹⁴⁸I Know not for what Reason some will not allow that to be Virtue, which flows from Instincts, or Passions; but how do they help themselves? They say, "Virtue arises from Reason." What is Reason but that Sagacity we have in prosecuting any End? The ultimate End propos'd by the common Moralists is the Happiness of the Agent himself, and this certainly he is determin'd to pursue from Instinct.|| Now may not another Instinct toward the Publick, or the Good of others, be as proper a Principle of Virtue, as the Instinct toward private Happiness? ||¹⁴⁹And is there not the same Occasion for the Exercise of our Reason in pursuing the former, as the latter?|| This is certain, that whereas we behold the selfish Actions of others, with Indifference at best, we see something amiable in every Action which flows from kind Affections or Passions ||¹⁵⁰toward|| others; if they be conducted by Prudence, so as any way to attain their ||^{151a}End. ||^{152b}Our passionate Actions, as we shew'd* above, are not ||^{153c}always^c|| Self-interested; since our In-[193]tention is not to free our selves from the Uneasiness of the Passion, but to alter the State of the Object.^{ab}||

¹⁵⁴If it be said, "That Actions from Instinct, are ||¹⁵⁵not the|| Effect of Prudence and Choice;" this Objection holds full as strongly against ||¹⁵⁶the|| Actions which flow from ||¹⁵⁷Self-Love; since the use of our Reason is as requisite, to find the proper Means of promoting publick Good, as private Good. And as it must be an Instinct, or a Determination previous to Reason, which makes us pursue private Good, as well as publick Good, as our End; there is the same occasion for Prudence and Choice, in the Election of proper Means for promoting of either. I see|| no harm in supposing, "that Men are naturally dispos'd to Virtue, and not left

* See Sect. ii. Art. 8.

Neighbour, the tender Husband and affectionate Parent, the sedate yet chearful Companion, the generous Assistant of Merit, the cautious Allayer of Contention and Debate, the Promoter of Love and good Understanding among Acquaintances; if we consider, that these were all the good Offices which his Station in the World gave him an Opportunity of performing to Mankind, we must judge this Character really as amiable, as those, whose external Splendor dazzles an injudicious World into an Opinion, "that they are the only Heroes in Virtue." [196]

All Mankind agree in this general
Foundation of their Approbation of moral
Actions. The Grounds of the different
Opinions about Morals.

This Moral
Sense
universal.

I. To ‖¹shew‖ how far Mankind agree in that which we have made the universal Foundation of this moral Sense, viz. Benevolence, we have observ'd already,‖²*‖ that when we are ask'd the Reason of our Approbation of any Action, we ‖³perpetually‖ alledge its Usefulness to the Publick, and not to the Actor himself. If we are vindicating a censur'd Action, and maintaining it lawful, we ‖⁴always‖ make this one Article of our Defence, "That it injur'd no body, or did more Good than Harm." On the other hand, when we blame any piece of Conduct, we shew it to be prejudicial to others, besides the Actor; or to evidence at least a Neglect of their Interest, when it was in our power to serve them; or when Gratitude, natural Affection, or some other disinterested Tye [197] should have rais'd in us a Study of their Interest. ‖⁵ªIf we sometimes blame foolish Conduct in others, without any reflection upon its Tendency to publick Evil, it is ‖⁶ᵇstill occasion'dᵇ‖ by our Benevolence, which makes us concern'd for the Evils befalling ‖⁷ᶜthe Agent, whom we must always look upon as a part of the System. ᵃᶜ‖ We all know how great an Extenuation of Crimes ‖⁸it‖ is, to alledge, "That the poor Man does harm to no body but himself;" and how often this turns Hatred into Pity. And yet ‖⁹if we examine the Matter well,‖ we shall find, that the

* See above, Sect. iii, Art. 3. Par. 3.

greatest part of the Actions which are immediately prejudicial to our selves, and are often look'd upon as innocent toward others, do really tend to the publick Detriment, by making us incapable of performing the good Offices we could otherwise have done, and perhaps would have ||¹⁰been|| inclin'd to do. This is the Case of Intemperance and extravagant Luxury.

II. And further, we may observe, that no Action of any other Person was ever approv'd by us, but upon some Apprehension, well or ill grounded, of some really good moral Quality. If we observe the Sentiments of Men concerning Actions, we shall find, that it is ||¹¹always|| some really amiable and benevolent Appearance which engages their Approbation. We may perhaps commit Mistakes, in judging ||¹²that Actions tend|| [198] to the publick Good, which do not; or be so ||¹³stupidly|| inadvertent, that while our Attention is fix'd on some partial good Effects, we may quite over-look many evil Consequences which counter-ballance the Good. Our Reason may be very deficient in its Office, by giving us partial Representations of the tendency of Actions; but it is still some apparent Species of Benevolence which commands our Approbation. And this Sense, like our other Senses, tho counter-acted ||¹⁴from Motives of external Advantage, which are stronger than it||, ||¹⁵ceases not|| to operate, but ||¹⁶has Strength enough to make|| us uneasy and dissatisfy'd with our selves; even as the Sense of Tasting ||¹⁷makes|| us loath, and dislike the nauseous Potion which we may ||¹⁸force|| our selves, from Interest, to swallow.

> **Benevolence the sole ground of Approbation.**

It is therefore to no purpose to alledge here, "That many Actions are really done, and approv'd, which tend to the universal Detriment." For the same way, Actions are often perform'd, and in the mean time approv'd, ||¹⁹which tend|| to the Hurt of the Actor. But as we do not from the latter, infer the Actor to be void of Self-Love, or a Sense of Interest; no more should we infer from the former, that such Men are void of a Sense of Morals, or a desire of publick [199] Good. The matter is plainly this. Men are often mistaken in the Tendency of Actions either to publick, or private Good: Nay, sometimes violent Passions, while they last, will make ||²⁰them|| approve very bad Actions ||²¹in a moral|| Sense,

> **False Approbations.**

||²²or|| very pernicious ones to the Agent, ||²³as|| advantageous: But this proves only, "That sometimes there may be some more violent Motive to Action, than a Sense of moral Good; or that ||²⁴Men, by Passion, may become blind|| even to their own Interest."

||²⁵But to prove that Men|| are void of a moral Sense, we should find some Instances of cruel, malicious Actions, done, ||²⁶and approv'd in others, when there is no Motive of Interest, real or apparent, save gratifying that very Desire of Mischief to others||: We must find a Country where Murder in cold blood, Tortures, and every thing malicious, without any Advantage, is, if not approv'd, at least look'd upon with indifference, and raises no Aversion toward the Actors, in the unconcern'd Spectators: We must find Men with whom the Treacherous, Ungrateful, Cruel, are in the same account with the Generous, Friendly, Faithful, and Humane; and who approve the latter, no more than the former, in all Cases where they are not affected by the Influence of these Dispositions, or when the natural Good or Evil befals other [200] Persons. And it may be question'd, whether the Universe, tho large enough, and stor'd with no inconsiderable variety of Characters, will yield us any Instance, not only of a Nation, but even of a Club, or a single ||²⁷Person, who|| will think all Actions indifferent, but those which ||²⁸regard|| his own Concerns.

Diversity of Manners accounted for. III. From what has been said, we may easily account for the vast Diversity of moral Principles, in various Nations, and Ages; ||²⁹ᵃwhich is indeed a good Argument against innate Ideas, or Principles, but will not evidence Mankind to be void of a moral Sense to perceive Virtue or Vice ||³⁰ᵇin Actions, when theyᵇ|| occur to their Observation.

Theᵃ|| Grounds of this Diversity are principally these:

From various Notions of Happiness. 1st. Different Opinions of Happiness, or natural Good, and of the most effectual Means to advance it. Thus in one Country, where there prevails a courageous Disposition, where Liberty is counted a great Good, and War an inconsiderable Evil, all Insurrections in Defence of Privileges, will have the Appearance of moral Good to our Sense, because of their appearing benevolent; and yet the same Sense of moral Good in Benevolence, shall [201] in another Country, where the Spirits of Men are more abject and timorous, where Civil War appears the greatest natural Evil, and Liberty no great Purchase, make the same Actions appear odious. So in Sparta, where, thro Contempt of Wealth, the Security of Possessions was not much regarded, but the thing chiefly desir'd, as naturally good to the State, was to abound in a hardy shifting Youth; Theft, if dexterously perform'd, was so little odious, that it receiv'd the Countenance of a Law to give it Impunity.

[31] But in these, and all other Instances of the like nature, the Approbation is founded on Benevolence, because of some real, or apparent Tendency to the publick Good. For we are not to imagine, that this Sense should give us, ||[32]without|| Observation, Ideas of complex Actions, or of their natural Tendencys to Good or Evil: It only determines us to approve Benevolence, whenever it appears in any Action, and to hate the contrary. So our Sense of Beauty does not, without Reflection, Instruction, or Observation, give us Ideas of the regular Solids, Temples, Cirques, and Theatres; but determines us to approve and delight in Uniformity amidst Variety, wherever we observe it. Let us read the Preambles of any Laws we count unjust, or the Vindications of any dispu-[202]ted Practice by the Moralists, and we shall find no doubt, that Men are often mistaken in computing the Excess of the natural Good, or evil Consequences of certain Actions; but the Ground on which any Action is approv'd, is still some Tendency to the greater natural Good of others, apprehended by those who approve it.

The same Reason may ||[33]remove|| also the Objections against the Universality of this Sense, from some Storys of Travellers, concerning strange Crueltys practis'd toward the Aged, or Children, in certain Countrys. If such Actions be done in ||[34]sudden|| angry Passions, they only prove, that other Motives, or Springs of Action, may overpower Benevolence in its strongest Ties; and if they really be universally allow'd, look'd upon as innocent, and vindicated; it ||[35]is certainly|| under some Appearance of Benevolence; such as to secure them from Insults of Enemys, to avoid the Infirmitys of Age, which perhaps appear greater Evils than Death, or to free the vigorous and useful Citizens from the

Travellers accounts of barbarous Customs.

Charge of maintaining them, or the Troubles of Attendance upon them. A love of Pleasure and Ease, may, in the immediate Agents, be stronger in some Instances, than Gratitude toward Parents, or natural Affection to Children. But that such Nations are continu'd, notwithstanding all the [203] Toil in educating their Young, is still a sufficient Proof of natural Affection: For I fancy we are not to imagine any nice Laws in such Places, compelling Parents to a proper Education of some certain number of their Offspring. We know very well that an Appearance of publick Good, was the Ground of Laws, equally barbarous, enacted by Lycurgus and Solon, of killing the deform'd, or weak, to prevent a burdensome Croud of useless Citizens.[i]

‖[36a]A late ingenious Author* has justly observ'd the Absurdity of the monstrous Taste, which has possess'd both the Readers and Writers of Travels. ‖[37b]They scarce give us any Account[b]‖ of the natural Affections, the Familys, Associations, Friendships, Clans, of the Indians; and as ‖[38c]rarely[c]‖ do they mention their Abhorrence of Treachery among themselves; their Proneness to mutual Aid, and to the Defence of their several States; their Contempt of Death in defence of their Country, or upon points of Honour. "These are but common Storys.—No need to travel to the Indies for what we see in Europe every Day." The Entertainment therefore in these ingenious Studys consists chiefly in exciting Horror, and making Men Stare. The ordinary Employment of [204] the Bulk of the Indians in support of their Wives and Offspring, or Relations, has nothing of the Prodigious. But a Human Sacrifice, a Feast upon Enemys Carcases, can raise an Horror and Admiration of the wondrous Barbarity of Indians, in Nations no strangers to the Massacre at Paris, the Irish Rebellion, or the Journals of the Inquisition. These they

i. Concerning Solon, Hutcheson refers to a passage in Sextus Empiricus, *Pyrrhoneion Hypotypóseon,* Book III, 211, in *Sextus Empiricus,* ed. R. G. Bury, Loeb Classical Library (Cambridge, Mass.: Harvard University Press, 1961), vol. 1, p. 267, reporting that the father had been allowed to kill his son. Lycurgus's law on killing of the weak and malformed is mentioned in *Plutarch's Lives,* ed. B. Perrin, Loeb Classical Library (Cambridge, Mass.: Harvard University Press, 1967), vol. 1, p. 255.

* Ld. Shaftesbury, Vol. i. p. 346, 7, 8, 9, &c.

behold with religious Veneration; but the Indian Sacrifices, flowing from a like Perversion of Humanity by Superstition, raise the highest Abhorrence and Amazement. What is most surprizing in these Studys, is the wondrous Credulity of some Gentlemen, of great Pretensions ‖^{39d} in other matters to Caution of Assent^d‖, for these marvellous Memoirs of Monks, Fryars, Sea-Captains, Pyrates; and for the Historys, Annals, Chronologys, receiv'd by Oral Tradition, or Hieroglyphicks.^a‖

Men have Reason given them, to ‖⁴⁰ judge of the Tendencys of their‖ Actions, that they may not stupidly follow the first Appearance of public Good; but it is still some Appearance of Good which they pursue. And it is strange, that Reason is universally allow'd to Men, notwithstanding all the stupid, ridiculous Opinions receiv'd in many Places, and yet absurd Practices, founded upon those very Opinions, shall seem an Argument against any moral Sense; [205] altho the bad Conduct is not ‖⁴¹ owing to‖ any Irregularity in the moral Sense, but ‖⁴² to a wrong‖ Judgment or Opinion. If putting the Aged to death, with all ‖⁴³ its‖ Consequences, really tends to the publick Good, and ‖⁴⁴ to‖ the lesser Misery of the Aged, it is no doubt justifiable; nay, perhaps the Aged chuse it, in hopes of a future State. If a deform'd, or weak Race, could never, by Ingenuity and Art, make themselves useful to Mankind, but should grow an absolutely unsupportable Burden, so as to involve a whole State in Misery, it is just to put them to death. This all allow to be just, in the Case of an over-loaded Boat in a Storm. And as for killing of their Children, when Parents are sufficiently stock'd, it is perhaps practis'd, and allow'd from Self-love; but I can scarce think it passes for a good Action any where. If Wood, or Stone, or Metal be ‖⁴⁵ a Deity‖, have Government, and Power, and have been the Authors of Benefits to us; it is morally ‖⁴⁶ amiable‖ to praise and worship them. Or if the true Deity be pleas'd with Worship before Statues, or any other Symbol of some more immediate Presence, or Influence; Image-Worship is virtuous. If he delights in Sacrifices, Penances, Ceremonys, Cringings; they are all laudable. Our Sense of Virtue, generally leads us exactly enough according to our Opinions; and therefore the absurd [206] Practices which prevail in the World, are much better Arguments that Men have no Reason, than that they have no moral Sense of Beauty in Actions.

Use of Reason in Morals.

Narrow Systems pervert the moral Sense.

IV. The next Ground of Diversity in Sentiments, is the Diversity of Systems, to which Men, from foolish Opinions, confine their Benevolence. We ||⁴⁷insinuated|| above,* that it is regular and beautiful to have stronger Benevolence, toward the morally good Parts of Mankind, who are useful to the Whole, than toward the useless or pernicious. Now if Men receive a low, or base Opinion of any Body, or Sect of Men; if they imagine them bent upon the Destruction of the more valuable Parts, or but useless Burdens of the Earth; Benevolence itself will lead ||⁴⁸them|| to neglect the Interests of such, and to suppress them. This is the Reason, why, among Nations who have high Notions of Virtue, every Action toward an Enemy may pass for just; why Romans, and Greeks, could approve of making those they call'd Barbarians, Slaves.

Sects pernicious to Virtue.

||⁴⁹ᵃA late ingenious Author||⁵⁰ᵇ†ᵇ|| justly observes, "That the various Sects, Partys, ||⁵¹ᶜFactions, Cabalsᶜ|| of Mankind in larger [207] Societys, are all influenc'd by a publick Spirit: That some generous Notions of publick Good, some strong friendly Dispositions, raise them at first, and excite Men of the same Faction or Cabal to the most disinterested mutual Succour and Aid: That all the Contentions of the different Factions, and even the fiercest Wars against each other, are influenc'd by a sociable publick Spirit in a limited ||⁵²ᵈSystem."ᵈ|| But certain it is, that Men are little oblig'd to those, who often artfully raise and foment this Party Spirit; or cantonize them into several Sects for the Defence of very trifling Causes. Associations for innocent Commerce, or Manufactures; Cabals for Defence of Liberty against a Tyrant; or even lower Clubs for Pleasantry, or Improvement by Conversation, are very amiable and good. But when Mens heads are filled with some trifling Opinions; when designing Men raise in their Minds some unaccountable ||⁵³ᵉnotionᵉ|| of Sanctity, and Religion, in Tenets or Practices, which neither increase our Love to God, or our own Species; when the several Factions are taught to look upon each other as Odious, Contemptible, Profane, because of their different Tenets, or Opinions; even when these Tenets, whether true or false, are perhaps perfectly useless to the publick Good; when the

---

* See Sect. iii. Art. 10. Par. 1.
† Ld. Shaftesbury's *Essay on Wit and Humour,* Part iii. Sect. ii. Vol. 1. p. 110.

keenest Passions are rais'd about such Trifles, and [208] Men begin to
hate each other for what, of it self, has no Evil in it; and to love the
Zealots of their own Sect for what is no way valuable; nay, even for their
Fury, Rage, and Malice against opposite Sects; (which is what all Partys
commonly call Zeal) 'tis then no wonder if our moral Sense ||⁵⁴ᶠbe
much ᶠ|| impair'd, and our natural Notions of Good and Evil almost lost;
when our Admiration, and Love, or Contempt, and Hatred, are thus
perverted from their natural Objects.

If any Mortals are so happy as never to have heard of the Party-Tenets
of most of our Sects; or if they have heard of them, have either never
espous'd any Sect, or all equally; they bid fairest for a truly natural and
good Disposition, because their Tempers have never been soured about
vain Trifles; nor have they contracted any Sullenness, or Rancour against
any Part of their own Kind. If any Opinions deserve to be contended
for, they are those which give us lovely Ideas of the Deity, and of our
Fellow-Creatures: If any Opinions deserve Opposition, they are such as
raise Scruples in our Minds about the Goodness of Providence, or represent our Fellow-Creatures as base and selfish, by instilling into us some
ill-natur'd, cunning, shreud Insinuations, "that our most generous Actions proceed wholly from [209] selfish Views." This wise Philosophy
of some Moderns, after Epicurus, must be fruitful of nothing but Discontent, Suspicion, and Jealousy; a State infinitely worse than any little
transitory Injurys to which we might be expos'd by a good-natur'd Credulity. But thanks be to the kind Author of our Nature, that, in spite of
such Opinions, our Nature it self leads us into Friendship, Trust, and
mutual Confidence. ᵃ||

Were we freely conversant with Robbers, who shew a moral Sense in
the equal or proportionable Division of their Prey, and in Faith to each
other, we should find they have their own sublime moral Ideas of their
Party, as Generous, Courageous, Trusty, nay Honest too; and that those
we call Honest and Industrious, are imagin'd by them ||⁵⁵ to be|| Mean-
spirited, Selfish, Churlish, or Luxurious; on whom that Wealth is ill bestow'd, which therefore they would apply to better Uses, to maintain
gallanter Men, who have a Right to a Living as well as their Neighbours,
who are their profess'd Enemys. Nay, if we observe the Discourse of our

profess'd Debauchees, our most dissolute Rakes, we shall find their Vices cloth'd, in their Imaginations, with some amiable Dress of Liberty, Generosity, just Resentment against the Contrivers of artful Rules to [210] enslave Men, and rob them of their Pleasures.

[56] Perhaps never any Men pursu'd ||[57] Vice long with Peace of Mind||, without some such deluding Imagination of moral Good,* while they may be still inadvertent to the barbarous and inhuman Consequences of their Actions. The Idea of an ill-natur'd Villain, is too frightful ever to become familiar to any Mortal. ||[59] Hence|| we shall find, that the basest Actions are dress'd in some tolerable Mask. What others call Avarice, appears to the Agent a prudent Care of a Family, or Friends; Fraud, artful Conduct; Malice and Revenge, a just Sense of Honour, and a Vindication of our Right in Possessions, or Fame; Fire and Sword, and Desolation among Enemys, a just thorow Defence of our Country; Persecution, a Zeal for the Truth, and for the eternal Happiness of Men, which Hereticks oppose. In all these Instances, Men generally act from a Sense of Virtue upon false Opinions, and mistaken Benevolence; upon wrong or partial Views of publick Good, and the means to promote it; or upon very narrow Systems form'd by like foolish Opinions. It is not a Delight in the Misery of others, or Malice, which occasions the horrid Crimes which fill our [211] Historys; but generally an injudicious unreasonable Enthusiasm for some kind of limited Virtue.

> Insani sapiens nomen ferat, aequus iniqui,
> Ultra, quam satis est, Virtutem si petat ipsam.†[ii]

False Opinions of the divine Laws.

V. The last Ground of Diversity which occurs, are the false Opinions of the Will or Laws of the Deity. To obey these we are determin'd from Gratitude, and a Sense of Right imagin'd in the Deity, to dispose at

---

* See below, Sect. vi. Art. 2. Par. ||[58] 2||.

† Hor. Ep. 6. Lib. I. v. 15.

ii. Translation: "Let the wise bear the name of madman, the just of unjust, should he pursue Virtue herself beyond due bounds." Horace, *Satires, Epistles, and Ars Poetica,* trans. H. Rushton Fairclough, Loeb Classical Library (Cambridge, Mass.: Harvard University Press, 1970), pp. 286–87.

pleasure the Fortunes of his Creatures. This is so abundantly known to have produc'd Follys, Superstitions, Murders, Devastations of Kingdoms, from a Sense of Virtue and Duty, that it is needless to mention particular Instances. Only we may observe, "That all those Follys, or Barbaritys, rather confirm than destroy the Opinion of a moral Sense;" since the Deity is believ'd to have a Right to dispose of his Creatures; and Gratitude to him, if he be conceiv'd good, must move us to Obedience to his Will: if he be not ‖⁶⁰conceiv'd good‖, Self-love may overcome our moral Sense of the Action which we undertake to avoid his Fury. [212]

As for the Vices which ‖⁶¹commonly‖ proceed from Love of Pleasure, or any violent Passion, since generally the Agent is soon sensible of their Evil, and ‖⁶²that sometimes‖ amidst the heat of the Action, they only prove, "That this moral Sense, and Benevolence, may be overcome by the more importunate Sollicitations of other Desires."

VI. Before we leave this Subject, it is necessary to remove one of the strongest Objections against what has been said so often, viz. "That this Sense is natural, and independent on Custom and Education." The Objection is this, "That we shall find some Actions always attended with the strongest Abhorrence, even at first View, in some whole Nations, ‖⁶³in which there appears nothing contrary to Benevolence‖; and that the same Actions shall in another Nation be counted innocent, or honourable.⁶⁴ Thus Incest, among Christians, is abhorr'd at first appearance as much as Murder; ‖⁶⁵even by those who do not know or reflect upon any necessary tendency of it to the detriment of Mankind. Now we generally allow, that what is from Nature in one Nation, would be so in all. This‖ Abhorrence ‖⁶⁶therefore‖ cannot be from Nature, since in Greece, the [213] marrying half Sisters was counted honourable; and among the Persian Magi,ⁱⁱⁱ the marrying of Mothers. Say they then, may not all our Approbation or Dislike of Actions arise the same way from Custom and Education?"

Objection
from Incest.

iii. The Magi were the priestly caste of the ancient Persian Zoroastrian or Mazdean religion.

The Answer to this may be easily found from what is already said. Had we no moral Sense natural to us, we should only look upon Incest as hurtful to our selves, and shun it, and never ||⁶⁷hate|| other incestuous Persons, more than we do a broken Merchant; so that still this Abhorrence supposes a Sense of moral Good. And further, it is true, that ||⁶⁸many who abhor Incest do not know, or reflect upon the|| natural tendency of some sorts of Incest to the publick Detriment; but wherever it is hated, it is apprehended as offensive to the Deity, and that it exposes the ||⁶⁹Person|| concern'd to his just Vengeance. Now it is universally acknowledg'd to be the grossest Ingratitude and Baseness, in any Creature, to counteract the Will of the Deity, to whom it is under such ||⁷⁰Obligations. This then|| is plainly a moral evil Quality apprehended in Incest, and reducible to the general Foundation of ||⁷¹Malice, or rather Want of Benevolence||. Nay further, where this Opinion, "that Incest is offensive to the Deity," prevails, Incest must have another direct Contrariety to Benevolence; since [214] we must apprehend the Incestuous, as exposing an Associate, who should be dear to him by the Ties of Nature, to the lowest State of Misery, and Baseness, Infamy and Punishment. But in those Countrys where no such Opinion prevails of the Deity's abhorring ||⁷²or prohibiting Incest; if no obvious natural Evils attend it||, it may be look'd upon as innocent. And further, as Men who have the Sense of Tasting, may, by Company and Education, have Prejudices against Meats they never tasted, as unsavoury; so may Men, who have a moral Sense, acquire an Opinion by implicit Faith, of the moral Evil of Actions, altho they do not themselves discern in them any tendency to natural Evil; imagining that others ||⁷³do: or, by Education, they may have some Ideas associated, which raise an abhorrence without Reason. But|| without a moral Sense, we could receive no Prejudice against Actions, under any other View than as naturally disadvantageous to our selves.

Moral Sense not from Education.

VII. The Universality of this moral Sense, and that it is antecedent to Instruction, may appear from observing the Sentiments of Children, upon hearing the Storys with which they are commonly entertain'd as soon as they understand Language. They always passionately interest themselves on that side where Kindness and Humanity are found; and detest the Cruel, the Covetous, [215] the Selfish, or the Treacherous. How strongly do we see their Passions of Joy, Sorrow, Love, and Indignation, mov'd by these moral Representations, even tho there has been no pains taken to give them Ideas of a Deity, of Laws, of a future State, or of the more intricate Tendency of the universal Good to that of each Individual! [216]

A further Confirmation that we have practical Dispositions to Virtue implanted in our Nature; with a further Explication ||¹ of our Instinct to Benevolence in its various Degrees||; with the additional Motives of Interest, viz. Honour, Shame and Pity.

Degrees of Benevolence. I. We have already endeavour'd to prove, "That there is ||²a|| universal Determination to Benevolence in Mankind, even toward the most distant parts of the Species:" But we are not to imagine that ||³this Benevolence is equal, or in the same degree toward all.|| There are ||⁴some|| nearer and stronger ||⁵Degrees|| of Benevolence, when the Objects stand in some nearer relations to our selves, which have obtain'd distinct Names; such as natural Affection, ||⁶and|| Gratitude, ||⁷ᵃor when Benevolence is increas'd by greater ||⁸ᵇLove of ᵃᵇ|| Esteem.

Natural Affection. One Species of natural Affection, viz. That in Parents towards ||⁹their|| Children, has [217] been consider'd already;* we ||¹¹shall only observe further||, That there is the same kind of Affection among collateral Relations, tho in a weaker degree; which is universally observable where no Opposition of Interest produces contrary Actions, or counterballances the Power of this natural Affection.

Not founded on Merit, or Acquaintance. ¹²We may also observe, that as to the Affection of Parents, it cannot be entirely founded on Merit ||¹³or|| Acquaintance; not only because it is antecedent to all Acquaintance, which might occasion the ||¹⁴Love of||

* See above, Sect. ii. Art. 9. Par. 2||¹⁰, 3||.

Esteem; but because it operates where Acquaintance would produce Hatred, even toward Children apprehended to be vitious. And this Affection is further confirm'd to be from Nature, because it is always observ'd to descend‖[15], and not ascend‖ from Children to Parents mutually. Nature, who seems sometimes frugal in her Operations, has strongly determin'd Parents to the Care of their Children, because they universally stand in absolute need of Support from them; but has left it‖[16]‖ to Reflection, and a Sense of Gratitude, to produce Returns of Love in Children, toward such tender kind Benefactors, who very seldom stand in such absolute need of Support from their Posterity, as their Chil-[218]dren did from them. Now did Acquaintance, or Merit produce natural Affection, we surely should find it strongest in Children, on whom all the Obligations are laid by a thousand good Offices; which yet is quite contrary to Observation. Nay, this Principle seems not confin'd to Mankind, but extends to other Animals, where yet we scarcely ever suppose any Ideas of Merit; and is observ'd to continue in them no longer than the Necessitys of their Young require. Nor could it be of any service to the Young that it should, since when they are grown up, they can receive little Benefit from the Love of their Dams. But as it is otherwise with rational Agents, so their Affections are of longer continuance, even during their whole lives.

II. ‖[17]But‖ nothing will give us a juster Idea of the wise Order in which   Gratitude. human Nature is form'd for universal Love, and mutual good Offices, than considering that strong attraction of Benevolence, which we call Gratitude. Every one knows that Beneficence toward our selves makes a much deeper Impression upon us, and raises Gratitude, or a stronger Love toward the Benefactor, than equal Beneficence toward a third Person.* Now because of the ‖[19]vast‖ Numbers of Mankind, their distant Habi-[219]tations, and the Incapacity of any one to be remarkably useful to ‖[20]vast‖ Multitudes; that our Benevolence might not be quite distracted with ‖[21]a multiplicity‖ of Objects, whose equal Virtues would equally recommend them to our regard; or ‖[22a]become useless, by being

* See above, Sect. ii. Art. 6. ‖[18]Par. 3‖.

equally extended to Multitudes ||[23b]at vast distances[b]||, whose Interest we could not understand[a]||, nor be capable of promoting, having no Intercourse of Offices with them; Nature has ||[24a]more powerfully determin'd us to admire, and love the moral Qualitys of others which affect our selves, and has given us more powerful Impressions of Good-will ||[25b]toward[b]|| those who are beneficent to our ||[26c]selves[a]||. This we call Gratitude. And thus a Foundation is laid[c]|| for joyful Associations in all kinds of Business, and virtuous Friendships.

By this Constitution also the Benefactor is more encourag'd in his Beneficence, and better secur'd of an increase of Happiness by grateful Returns,* than if his Virtue were only to be honour'd by the colder general Sentiments of Persons unconcern'd, who could not know his Necessitys, nor how to be profitable to him; especially, when they would all be equally determin'd to love innumerable Multitudes, whose equal Virtues would have the same Pretensions to their Love||[28a], were there not [220] an increase of Love, according as the Object is more nearly attach'd to us, or our Friends, by ||[29b]good[b]|| Offices which affect our selves, or them[a]||.

||[30]This|| universal Benevolence toward all Men, we may compare to that Principle of Gravitation, which perhaps extends to all Bodys in the Universe; but||[31], like the Love of Benevolence,|| increases as the Distance is diminish'd, and is strongest when Bodys come to touch each other. Now this increase ||[32]of Attraction|| upon nearer Approach, is as necessary ||[33]to the Frame of the Universe,|| as that there should be any Attraction at all. For a general Attraction, equal in all Distances, would by the Contrariety of such multitudes of equal Forces, put an end to all Regularity of Motion, and perhaps stop it ||[34]altogether.||

||[35]This increase of Love toward the Benevolent,|| according to their nearer Approaches to our selves by their Benefits, is observable in the high degree of Love, which Heroes and Law-givers universally obtain in their own Countrys, above what they find abroad, even among those who are not insensible of their Virtues; and in all the strong Ties of Friendship, Acquaintance, Neighbourhood, Partnership; which are ex-

---

* See above, Sect. iii. Art. 2. ||[27]Par.|| 2.

ceedingly necessary to the Order ||³⁶and Happiness|| of human Society.
[221]

III. From considering that ||³⁷strong Determination in our Nature to|| Love of
Gratitude, and Love toward our Benefactors, which was already shewn   Honour.
to be disinterested;* we are easily led to consider another Determination
of our Minds, equally natural with the former, which is to ||³⁸delight||
in the good Opinion and Love of others, even when we expect no other
Advantage from them, except what flows from this Constitution, whereby
Honour is made an immediate Good. This Desire of Honour I would
call Ambition, had not Custom join'd some evil Ideas to that Word,
making it denote such a violent desire of Honour, and of Power also,
as will make us stop at no base Means to obtain them. On the other
hand, we are by Nature subjected to a grievous Sensation of Misery, from
the unfavourable Opinions of others concerning us, even when we dread
no other Evil from them. This we call Shame; which in the same manner
||³⁹is constituted an immediate Evil, as we said Honour was an imme-
diate Good.||

Now were there no moral Sense, or had we no other Idea of Actions
but as advantageous or hurtful, I see no reason why we should be delighted with Honour, or sub-[222]jected to the uneasiness of Shame; or
how it could ever happen, that a Man, who is secure from Punishment
for any Action, should ever be uneasy at its being known to all the World.
The World may have ||⁴⁰the worse Opinion of him for it; but what sub-
jects my Ease to the Opinion of the World? Why, perhaps, we|| shall not
be so much trusted henceforward in Business, and so suffer Loss. If this
be the only reason of Shame, and it has no immediate Evil, or Pain in
it, distinct from Fear of Loss; then wherever we expose our selves to Loss,
we should be asham'd, and endeavour to conceal the Action: and yet it
is quite otherwise.

A Merchant, for instance, ||⁴¹lest it should impair his Credit||, con-
ceals a Shipwrack, or a very bad Market, which he has sent his Goods
to. But is this the same with the Passion of Shame? Has he that Anguish,

* See above, Sect. ii. Art. 6.

that Dejection of Mind, and Self-condemnation, which one shall have whose Treachery is detected? Nay, how will Men sometimes glory in their Losses, when in a Cause imagin'd morally good, tho they really weaken their Credit in the Merchant's Sense; that is, the Opinion of their Wealth, or fitness for Business? Was any Man ever asham'd of impoverishing himself to serve his Country, or his Friend? [223]

The Foundation of Morals not the Opinions of our Country.

IV. The Opinions of our Country are by some made the first Standard of Virtue. They alledge, "That by comparing Actions to them, we first distinguish between moral Good, and Evil: And then, say they, Ambition, or the Love of Honour, is our chief Motive." But what is Honour? It is not ‖[42] the being‖ universally known, no matter how. A covetous Man is not honour'd by being universally known as covetous; nor a weak, selfish, or luxurious Man, when he is known to be so: Much less can a treacherous, cruel, or ungrateful Man, be said to be honour'd for his being known as such. A Posture-master, a Fire-eater, or Practiser of Leger-de-main, is not honour'd for these publick Shews, unless we consider him as a Person capable of giving the Pleasures of Admiration and Surprize to Multitudes. Honour then is the Opinion of others concerning our morally good Actions, or Abilitys presum'd to be apply'd that way; for Abilitys constantly apply'd to other Purposes, procure the greatest Infamy. Now, it is certain, that Ambition‖[43], or Love of Honour is really selfish‖; but then ‖[44] this‖ Determination to love Honour, presupposes a Sense of moral Virtue, both in the Persons who confer the Honour, and in him who pursues it. [224]

[45] And let it be observ'd, that if we knew an Agent had no other Motive of Action ‖[46] than‖ Ambition, we should apprehend no Virtue even in his most useful Actions, since they flow'd not from any Love to others, or Desire ‖[47] of‖ their Happiness. When Honour is thus constituted by Nature pleasant to us, it may be an additional Motive to Virtue, as we said above,‖[48]*‖ the Pleasure arising from Reflection on our Benevolence was: but the Person whom we imagine perfectly virtuous, acts immediately from the Love of others; however these refin'd Interests may be

* See Sect. iii. Art. 15. Par. 2.

joint Motives to him to set about such a Course of Actions, or to cultivate every kind Inclination, and to despise every contrary Interest, as giving a smaller Happiness than Reflection on his own Virtue, and Consciousness of the Esteem of others.

Shame is in the same manner constituted an immediate Evil, and influences us the same way to abstain from moral Evil; not that any Action or Omission would appear virtuous, where the sole Motive was Fear of Shame.

V. But to enquire further, how far the Opinions of our Company can raise a Sense of moral Good or Evil. If any Opinion [225] be universal in any Country, Men of little Reflection will probably embrace it. If an Action be believ'd to be advantageous to the Agent, we may be led to believe so too, and then Self-Love may make us undertake it; or may, the same way, make us shun an Action reputed pernicious to the Agent. If an Action pass for advantageous to the Publick, we may believe so too; and what next? If we have no disinterested Benevolence, what shall move us to undertake it? "Why, we love Honour; and to obtain this Pleasure, we will undertake the Action from Self-Interest." Now, is Honour only the Opinion of our Country that an Action is advantageous to the Publick? No: we see no Honour paid to the useful Treachery of an Enemy whom we have brib'd to our Side, to casual undesign'd Services, or to the most useful Effects of Compulsion on Cowards; and yet we see Honour paid to unsuccessful Attempts to serve the Publick from sincere Love to it. Honour then presupposes a Sense of something amiable besides Advantage, ||⁴⁹viz.|| a Sense of Excellence in a publick Spirit; and therefore the first Sense of moral Good must be antecedent to Honour, for Honour is founded upon it.⁵⁰ The Company we keep may lead us, without examining, to believe that certain Actions tend to the publick Good; but that our Company honours such Actions, and loves the Agent, must flow from a Sense of some [226] Excellence in this Love of the Publick, and serving its Interests.

Opinions flow from the Moral Sense.

"We therefore, say they again, pretend to love the Publick, altho we only desire the Pleasure of Honour; and we will applaud all who seem to act in that manner, either that we may reap Advantage from their

Actions, or that others may believe we really love the Publick." But shall any Man ever ||⁵¹ really love the Publick, or study the Good of others in his heart, if Self-love be|| the only spring of his Actions? No: that is impossible. Or, shall we ever really ||⁵² love|| Men who appear to love the Publick, without a moral Sense? ||⁵³ No: we could form no Idea of such a Temper; and as for these Pretenders to publick Love, we should hate|| them as Hypocrites, and our Rivals in Fame. Now this is all which could be effected by the Opinions of our Country, even supposing they had a moral Sense, provided we had none our selves: They never could make us admire Virtue, or virtuous Characters in others; but could only give us Opinions of Advantage, or Disadvantage in Actions, according as they tended ||⁵⁴ procure to|| us the Pleasures of Honour, or the Pain of Shame.

But if we suppose that Men have, by Nature, a moral Sense of Goodness in [227] Actions, and that they are capable of disinterested Love; all is easy. The Opinions of our Company may make us rashly conclude, that certain Actions tend to the universal Detriment, and are morally Evil, when perhaps they are not so; and then our Sense may determine us to have an Aversion to them, and their Authors; or we may, the same way, be led into implicit Prejudices in favour of Actions as good; and then our desire of Honour may co-operate with Benevolence, to move us to such Actions: but had we no Sense of moral Qualitys in Actions, ||⁵⁵ nor any|| Conceptions of them, ||⁵⁶ except|| as advantageous or hurtful, we never could have honour'd or lov'd Agents for publick Love, or had any regard to their Actions, further than they affected our selves in particular. We might have form'd the metaphysical Idea of publick Good, but we had never desir'd it,⁵⁷ further than it tended to our own private Interest, without a Principle of Benevolence; nor admir'd and lov'd those who ||⁵⁸ were|| studious of it, without a moral Sense. So far is Virtue from being (in the Language of a late*ⁱ Author) the Offspring of Flattery, begot upon Pride; that Pride, in the bad meaning of that Word, is the spurious Brood of Ignorance by our moral Sense, and Flattery only an

---

* Author of the *Fable of the Bees,* Pag. 37. 3d Ed.
i. Mandeville, *Fable of the Bees,* ed. Kaye, vol. 1, p. 51.

Engine, which the [228] Cunning may use to turn this moral Sense in others, to the Purposes of Self-love in the Flatterer.

VI. To explain what has been said of the Power of Honour. Suppose a State or Prince, observing the Money which is drawn out of England by Italian Musicians, ‖⁵⁹ should‖ decree Honours, Statues, Titles, for great Musicians: This would certainly excite all who had hopes of Success, to the Study of Musick; and ‖⁶⁰ Men of a good Ear would approve of‖ the good Performers as useful Subjects, as well as very entertaining. But would this give all Men a good Ear, or make them delight in Harmony? Or could it ever make us really love a Musician, who study'd nothing but his own Gain, in the same manner we do a Patriot, or a generous Friend? I doubt not. And yet Friendship, without the Assistance of Statues, or Honours, can make Persons appear exceedingly amiable.

Moral Sense, not from Love of Honour.

Let us take another Instance. Suppose Statues, and triumphal Arches were decreed, as well as a large Sum of Money, to the Discoverer of the Longitude, or any other useful Invention in Mathematicks: This would raise a universal Desire of such Knowledge from Self-Love; but would Men therefore love a Mathematician as they do a virtuous Man? Would a Mathema-[229]tician love every Person who had attain'd Perfection in that Knowledge, wherever he observ'd it, altho he knew that it was not accompany'd with any Love to Mankind, or Study of their Good, but with Ill-nature, Pride, Covetousness? In short, let us honour other Qualitys by external Shew as much as we please, if we do not discern a benevolent Intention in the Application, or presume upon it; we may look upon these Qualitys as useful, enriching, or otherwise advantageous to any one who is possess'd of them; but they shall never meet with those endearing Sentiments of Esteem and Love, which our nature determines us to appropriate to Benevolence, or Virtue.

Love of Honour, and Aversion to Shame, may often move us to do Actions for which others profess to honour us, even tho we see no Good in them our selves: And Compliance with the Inclinations of others, as it evidences Humanity, may procure some Love to the Agent, from Spectators who see no moral Good in the Action it self. But without some

Sense of Good in the Actions, Men shall never be fond of such Actions in Solitude, nor ever love any one for Perfection in them, or for practising them in Solitude; and much less shall they be dissatisfy'd with themselves when they act otherwise in Solitude. Now this is the case with us, as to Virtue; and therefore we must [230] have, by Nature, a moral Sense of it antecedent to Honour.

This will shew us with what Judgment a late*ⁱⁱ Author compares the Original of our Ideas of Virtue, and Approbation of it, to the manner of regulating the Behaviour of aukard Children by Commendation. It shall appear ||⁶¹ afterward||,† that our Approbation of some Gestures, and what we call Decency in Motion, depends upon some moral Ideas in People of advanc'd Years. But before Children come to observe this Relation, it is only good Nature, an Inclination to please, and Love of Praise, which makes them endeavour to behave as they are desir'd; and not any Perception of Excellence in this Behaviour. ||⁶² Hence|| they are not sollicitous about Gestures when alone, unless with a View to please when they return to Company; ||⁶³ nor do they ever|| love or approve others for ||⁶⁴ any|| Perfection of this kind, but rather envy or hate them; till they either discern the Connexion between Gestures, and moral Qualitys; or reflect on the good Nature, which is evidenc'd by such a Compliance with the desire of the Company. [231]

False Honour.   VII. The considering Honour in the manner above explain'd, may shew us the reason, why Men are often asham'd for things which are not vitious, and honour'd for what is not virtuous. For, if any Action only appears vitious to any Persons or Company, altho it be not so, they will have a bad Idea of the Agent; and then he may be asham'd, or suffer Uneasiness in being thought morally Evil. ||⁶⁵ The|| same way, those who look upon an Action as morally good, will honour the Agent, and he may be pleas'd with the Honour, altho he does not himself perceive any moral Good in what has procur'd it.

---

* See the *Fable of the Bees,* Page 38. 3d. Ed.
ii. Mandeville, *Fable of the Bees,* ed. Kaye, vol. 1, p. 52.
† See Sect. vi. Art. 4.

Again, we shall be asham'd of every Evidence of moral Incapacity, or Want of Ability; and with good ground, when this Want is occasion'd by our own Negligence. Nay further, if any Circumstance be look'd upon as indecent in any Country, offensive to others, ||⁶⁶ or|| deform'd; we shall, out of our ||⁶⁷ Love to|| the good Opinions of others, be asham'd to be found in such Circumstances, even when we are sensible that this Indecency or Offence is not founded on Nature, but is merely the Effect of Custom. Thus being observ'd in ||⁶⁸ those|| Functions of Nature which are counted indecent and offensive, will make us uneasy, altho we are sensible that they really do [232] not argue any Vice or Weakness. But on the contrary, since moral Abilitys of any kind, upon the general Presumption of a good Application, ⁶⁹ procure the Esteem of others, we shall value our selves upon them, or grow proud of them, and be asham'd of any Discovery of our want of such Abilitys. This is the reason that Wealth and Power, the great Engines of Virtue, when presum'd to be intended for benevolent Purposes, either toward our Friends or our Country, procure Honour from others, and are apt to beget Pride in the Possessor; which, as it is a general Passion which may be either good or evil, according as it is grounded, we may describe to be the Joy which arises from the real or imagin'd Possession of Honour, or Claim to it. ||⁷⁰ The|| same are the Effects of Knowledge, Sagacity, Strength; and hence it is that Men are apt to boast of them.

But whenever it appears that Men have only their private Advantage in view, in the application of these Abilitys, or natural Advantages, the Honour ceases, and we study to conceal them, or at least are not fond of displaying them; and much more when there is any Suspicion of an ill-natur'd Application. Thus some Misers are asham'd of their Wealth, and study to conceal it; as the malicious or selfish do their Power: Nay, this is very often done where there is [233] no positive evil Intention; because the diminishing their Abilitys, increases the moral Good of any little kind ||⁷¹ Action||, which they can find in their hearts to perform.

In short, we always see Actions which flow from publick Love, ac- company'd with generous Boldness and Openness; and not only malicious, but even selfish ones, the matter of Shame and Confusion; and that Men study to conceal them. The Love of private Pleasure is the ordinary occasion of Vice; and when Men have got any lively Notions of Virtue, they generally begin to be asham'd of every thing which betrays Selfishness, even in Instances where it is innocent. We are apt to imagine, that others observing us in such Pursuits, form mean Opinions of us, as too much set on private Pleasure; and hence we shall find such Enjoyments, in most polite Nations, conceal'd from those who do not partake with us. Such are venereal Pleasures between Persons marry'd, and even eating and drinking alone, any nicer sorts of Meats or Drinks; whereas a hospitable Table is rather matter of boasting; and so are all other kind, generous Offices between marry'd Persons, where there is no Suspicion of Self-love in the Agent; but he is imagin'd as acting from Love to his Associate. This, ||[72] I fancy, first introduc'd Ideas of Modesty in polite Nations, and Custom has strengthen'd [234] them wonderfully||; so that we are now asham'd of many things, upon some confus'd implicit Opinions of moral Evil, tho we know not upon what account.

Honour and Shame, often from some Associations of Ideas.

Here too we may see the reason, why we are not asham'd of any of the Methods of Grandeur, or high-Living. There is such a Mixture of moral Ideas, of Benevolence, of Abilitys kindly employ'd; so many Dependants supported, so many Friends entertain'd, assisted, protected; such a Capacity imagin'd for great and amiable Actions, that we are never asham'd, but rather boast of such things: We never affect Obscurity or Concealment, but rather desire that our State and Magnificence should be known. Were it not for this Conjunction of moral Ideas, no Mortal could bear the Drudgery of State, or abstain from laughing at those who did. Could any Man be pleas'd with a Company of Statues surrounding his Table, so artfully contriv'd as to consume his various Courses, and inspir'd by some Servant, like so many Puppets, to give the usual trifling Returns in praise of their Fare? Or with so many Machines to perform the Cringes and Whispers of a Levee?

The Shame we suffer from the Meanness of Dress, Table, Equipage, is entirely owing to the same reason. This Meanness is often imagin'd to argue Avarice, Meanness [235] of Spirit, want of Capacity, or Conduct in Life, of Industry, or moral Abilitys of one kind or other. To confirm this, let us observe that Men will glory in the Meanness of their Fare, when it was occasion'd by a good Action. How ||[73] many|| would be asham'd to be surpriz'd at a Dinner of cold Meat, who will boast of their having fed upon Dogs and Horses at the Siege of Derry?[iii] And they will all tell you that they were not, nor are asham'd of it.

This ordinary Connexion in our Imagination, between external Grandeur, Regularity in Dress, Equipage, Retinue, Badges of Honour, and some moral Abilitys greater than ordinary, is perhaps of more consequence in the World than some recluse Philosophers apprehend, who pique themselves upon despising these external Shews. This may possibly be a great, if not the only Cause of what some count miraculous, viz. That Civil Governors of no greater Capacity than their Neighbours, by some inexpressible Awe, and Authority, quell ||[74]the|| Spirits of the Vulgar, and keep them in subjection by such small Guards, as might easily be conquer'd by those Associations ||[75]which might be rais'd among|| the Disaffected, or Factious of any State; who are daring enough among their Equals, and shew a sufficient Contempt of Death for undertaking such an Enterprize. [236]

||[76]Hence also we may|| discover the reason, why the gratifying our superior Senses of Beauty and Harmony, or the Enjoyment of the ||[77]Pleasures|| of Knowledge, never occasions any Shame or Confusion, tho our Enjoyment were known to all the World. The Objects which furnish this Pleasure, are of such a nature, as to afford the same Delights to multitudes; nor is there any thing in the Enjoyment of them by one, which excludes any Mortal from a like Enjoyment. So that altho we pursue these Enjoyments from Self-love, yet||[78], since|| our Enjoyment cannot be prejudicial to ||[79]others, no|| Man is imagin'd any way inhumanly selfish, from the fullest Enjoyment of them which is possible. The same Regularity or Harmony which delights me, may at the same time delight multitudes; the same Theorem shall be equally fruitful of Pleasure, when it has entertain'd thousands. ||[80]Men therefore are not|| asham'd of such Pursuits, since they ||[81]never, of themselves,|| seduce us into any thing malicious, envious, or ill-natur'd; nor does any one ap-

---

iii. Overcrowded with some thirty thousand Protestant refugees, Londonderry (or Derry) withstood a siege by the dethroned King James II from April to July 1689.

prehend another too selfish, from ||[82]his|| pursuing Objects of unexhausted universal Pleasure.[83]

This View of Honour and Shame may also let us see the reason, why most Men are uneasy at being prais'd, when they themselves are present. Every one is delighted [237] with the Esteem of others, and must enjoy great Pleasure when he hears himself commended; but we are unwilling others should observe our Enjoyment of this Pleasure, which is really selfish; or that they should imagine us fond of it, or influenc'd by hopes of it in our good Actions: and therefore we chuse Secrecy for the Enjoyment of it, as we do with respect to other Pleasures, in which others do not share with us.

Compassion a motive to Virtue.

VIII. Let us next consider another Determination of our Mind, which strongly proves Benevolence to be natural to us, and that is Compassion; by which we are dispos'd to study the Interest of others, without any Views of private Advantage. This needs little Illustration. Every Mortal is made uneasy by any grievous Misery he sees another involv'd in, unless the Person be imagin'd ||[84]evil||, in a moral Sense: Nay, it is almost impossible for us to be unmov'd, even in that Case. Advantage may make us do a cruel Action, or may overcome Pity; but it scarce ever extinguishes it. A sudden Passion of Hatred or Anger may represent a Person as absolutely evil, and so extinguish Pity; but when the Passion is over, it often returns. Another disinterested View may even in cold blood overcome Pity; such as Love to our Country, or Zeal for Religion. Persecution is generally occasion'd by Love of Virtue, and [238] ||[85]a|| Desire of the eternal Happiness of Mankind, altho our Folly makes us chuse absurd Means ||[86]to promote it||; and is often accompany'd with Pity enough to make the Persecutor uneasy, in what, for prepollent Reasons, he chuses; unless his Opinion leads him to look upon the Heretick as absolutely and entirely evil.

We may here observe how wonderfully the Constitution of human Nature is adapted to move Compassion. Our ||[87]Misery or Distress immediately appears|| in our Countenance, if we do not study to prevent it, and propagates some Pain to all Spectators; who from Observation, universally understand the meaning of those dismal Airs. We mechanically send forth Shrieks and Groans upon any surprizing Apprehension of Evil; so that no regard to Decency can sometimes restrain them‖[88]. This is the Voice of Nature, understood by all Nations, by which‖ all who are present are rous'd to our Assistance, and sometimes our injurious Enemy is made to relent.

We observ'd above,* that we are not immediately excited by Compassion to desire the Removal of our own Pain: we think it just to be so affected upon the Occasion, and dislike those who are not so. But we [239] are excited directly to desire the Relief of the Miserable;‖[90] without any imagination that this Relief is a private Good to our selves: And‖ if we see this impossible, we may by Reflection discern it to be vain for us to indulge our Compassion any further; and then ‖[91] Self-love prompts us to‖ retire from the Object which occasions our Pain, and ‖[92] to endeavour‖ to divert our Thoughts. But where there is no such Reflection, People are hurry'd by a natural, kind Instinct, to see Objects of Compassion, and expose themselves to this Pain when they can give no reason for it; as in the Instance of publick Executions.

This same Principle leads men to Tragedys; only we are to observe, that another strong reason of this, is the moral Beauty of the Characters and Actions which we love to behold. For I doubt, whether any Audience would be ‖[93] pleas'd to‖ see fictitious Scenes of Misery, if they were kept strangers to the moral Qualitys of the Sufferers, or their Characters and Actions. As in such a case, there would be no Beauty to raise Desire of seeing such Representations, I fancy we would not expose our selves to Pain alone, from Misery which we knew to be fictitious.

It was the same Cause which crouded the Roman Theatres to see Gladiators. There [240] the People had frequent Instances of great Courage, and Contempt of Death, two great moral Abilitys, if not Virtues. Hence Cicero looks upon them as great Instructions in Fortitude. The Antagonist Gladiator bore all the blame of the Cruelty committed, among People of little Reflection; and the courageous and artful one, really obtain'd a Reputation of Virtue, and Favour among the Spectators, and was vindicated by the Necessity of Self-defence. In the mean

---

* See Sect. ii. Art. 8. ‖[89] Par. 2.‖

time they were inadvertent to this, that their crouding to such Sights, and favouring the Persons who presented them with such Spectacles of Courage, and with Opportunitys of following their natural Instinct to Compassion, was the true occasion of all the real Distress, or Assaults which they were sorry for.

What Sentiments can we imagine a Candidate would have rais'd of himself, had he presented his Countrymen only with Scenes of Misery; had he drain'd Hospitals and Infirmarys of all their pityable Inhabitants, or had he bound so many Slaves, and without[94] any Resistance, butcher'd them with his own Hands? I should very much question the Success of his Election, (however Compassion[95] might cause his Shews still to be frequented) if his Antagonist chose a Diversion apparently [241] more virtuous, or with a Mixture of Scenes of Virtue.

Compassion
natural.

How independent this Disposition to Compassion is ||[96]on|| Custom, Education, ||[97]or|| Instruction, will appear from the Prevalence of it in Women and Children, who are less influenc'd by these. That Children ||[98]delight in some Actions which|| are cruel and tormenting to Animals which they have in their Power, flows not from Malice, or want of Compassion, but from their Ignorance of those signs of Pain which many Creatures make; together with a Curiosity to see the various Contortions of their Bodys. For when they are more acquainted with these Creatures, or come by any means to know their Sufferings, their Compassion often becomes too strong for their Reason; as it generally does in beholding Executions, where as soon as they observe the evidences of Distress, or Pain in the Malefactor, they are apt to condemn this necessary Method of Self-defence in the ||[99]State.|| [242]

Concerning the Importance of this moral
Sense to the present Happiness of Mankind,
and its Influence on human Affairs.

I. It may now probably appear, that notwithstanding the Corruption of Manners so justly complain'd of every where, this moral Sense has a greater Influence on Mankind than is generally imagin'd, altho it is often directed by very partial imperfect Views of publick Good, and often overcome by Self-love. But we shall offer some further Considerations, to prove, "That it gives us more Pleasure and Pain than all our other Facultys." And to prevent Repetitions, let us observe, "That ||¹ where-ever|| any morally good Quality gives Pleasure from Reflection, or from Honour, the contrary evil one will give proportionable Pain, from Remorse and Shame." Now we shall consider the moral Pleasures, not only separately, but as they are the most delightful Ingredient in the ordinary Pleasures of Life. [243]

All ||²Men|| seem persuaded of some Excellency in the Possession of good moral Qualitys, which is superior to all other Enjoyments; and on the contrary, look upon a State of moral Evil, as worse and more wretched than any other whatsoever. We must not form our Judgment in this matter from the Actions of Men; for however they may be influenc'd by moral Sentiments, yet it is certain, that Self-interested Passions frequently overcome them, and partial Views of the Tendency of Actions, make us do what is really morally evil, apprehending it to be good. But let us examine the Sentiments which Men universally form of the State of others, when they are no way immediately concern'd; for in

Importance of the Moral Sense.

these Sentiments human Nature is calm and undisturb'd, and shews its true Face.

Now ||³should|| we imagine a rational Creature in a sufficiently happy State, ||⁴tho his|| Mind was, without Interruption, wholly occupy'd with pleasant Sensations of Smell, Taste, Touch, &c. if at the same time all other Ideas were excluded? ||⁵Should|| we not think the State low, mean and sordid, if there were no Society, no Love or Friendship, no good Offices? What then must that State be wherein there are no Pleasures but those of the external Senses, with such long Intervals as human Nature at present [244] must have? Do these short Fits of Pleasure make the Luxurious happy? How insipid and joyless are the Reflections on past Pleasure? And how poor a Recompence is the Return of the transient Sensation, for the nauseous Satietys, and Languors in the Intervals? This Frame of our Nature, so incapable of long Enjoyments of the external Senses, points out to us, "That there must be some other more durable Pleasure, without such tedious Interruptions, and nauseous Reflections."

Let us even join with the Pleasures of the external Senses, the Perceptions of Beauty, Order, Harmony. These are no doubt more noble Pleasures, and seem to inlarge the Mind; and yet how cold and joyless are they, if there be no moral Pleasures of Friendship, Love and Beneficence? Now if the bare Absence of moral Good, makes, in our Judgment, the State of a rational Agent contemptible; the Presence of contrary Dispositions is always imagin'd by us to sink him into a degree of Misery, from which no other Pleasures can relieve him. Would we ever wish to be in the same Condition with a wrathful, malicious, revengeful, or envious Being, tho we were at the same time to enjoy all ||⁶the Pleasures of the external and internal Senses? The internal Pleasures of Beauty and Harmony, contribute greatly indeed toward soothing|| the [245] Mind into a forgetfulness of Wrath, Malice or Revenge; and they must do so, before we can have any tolerable Delight or Enjoyment: for while these Affections possess the Mind, there is nothing but Torment and Misery.

Castle-builders prove it.   What Castle-builder, who forms to himself imaginary Scenes of Life, in which he thinks he ||⁷should|| be happy, ever made acknowledg'd

Treachery, Cruelty, or Ingratitude, the Steps by which he mounted to his wish'd for Elevation, or Parts of his Character, when he had attain'd it? We always conduct our selves in such Resveries, according to the Dictates of Honour, Faith, Generosity, Courage; and the lowest we can sink, is hoping we may be enrich'd by some innocent Accident.

> O si urnam Argenti Fors quà mihi monstret! ———*i

But Labour, Hunger, Thirst, Poverty, Pain, Danger, have nothing so detestable in them, that our Self-love cannot allow us to be often expos'd to them. ‖8On the contrary‖, the Virtues which these give us occasions of displaying, are so amiable and excellent, that scarce ever is any imaginary Hero in Romance, or Epic, brought to his high-[246]est Pitch of Happiness, without going thro them all. Where there is no Virtue, there is nothing worth Desire or Contemplation; the Romance, or Epos must end. Nay, the Difficulty,† or natural Evil, does so much increase the Virtue of the good Action which it accompanys, that we cannot easily sustain these Works after the Distress is over; and if we continue the Work, it must be by presenting a new Scene of Benevolence in a prosperous Fortune. A Scene of external Prosperity or natural Good, without any thing moral or virtuous, cannot entertain a Person of the dullest Imagination, had he ever so much interested himself in the Fortunes of his Hero; for where Virtue ceases, there remains nothing worth wishing to our Favourite, or which we can be delighted to view his Possession of, when we are most studious of his Happiness.

Let us take a particular Instance, to try how much we prefer the Possession of Virtue to all other Enjoyments, and how we look upon Vice as worse than any other Misery. Who could ever read the History of Regulus,ii 10 without concerning himself in the Fortunes of that gallant Man, sorrowing at his Sufferings, and wishing him a better Fate? But

Virtue own'd superior to all Pleasure.

---

* Hor. Lib. 2. Sat. 6. v. 10.

i. Translation: "O, that some lucky strike would disclose to me a pot of money. . . ." Horace, *Satires, Epistles, and Ars Poetica,* trans. H. Rushton Fairclough, Loeb Classical Library (Cambridge, Mass.: Harvard University Press, 1970), p. 210.

† Sect. iii. Art. xi. ‖9Axiom 6.‖

ii. See editor's note viii to Treatise II, Sect. I.

how ‖¹¹a better‖ Fate? Should [247] he have comply'd with the Terms
of the Carthaginians, and preserv'd himself from the intended Tortures,
tho to the detriment of his Country? Or should he have violated his
plighted Faith and Promise of returning? Will any Man say, that either
of these is the better Fate he wishes his Favourite? Had he acted thus,
that Virtue would have been gone, which interests every one in his Fortunes.—"Let him take his Fate like other common Mortals."—What
else do we wish then, but that the Carthaginians had relented of their
Cruelty, or that Providence, by some unexpected Event, had rescued him
out of their hands.

¹²Now may not this teach us, that we are indeed determin'd to judge
Virtue with Peace and Safety, preferable to Virtue with Distress; but that
at the same time we look upon the State of the Virtuous, the Publick-
spirited, even in the utmost natural Distress, as preferable to all affluence
of other Enjoyments? For this is what we chuse to have our Favourite
Hero in, notwithstanding all its Pains and natural Evils. We ‖¹³should‖
never have imagin'd him happier, had he acted otherwise; or thought
him in a more eligible State, with Liberty and Safety, at the expence of
his Virtue. We secretly judge the Purchase too dear; and therefore we
never imagine he acted foolishly in secu-[248]ring his Virtue, his Honour, at the expence of his Ease, his Pleasure, his Life. Nor can we think
these latter Enjoyments worth the keeping, when the former are entirely
lost.

Necessary
in other
Pleasures.

II. Let us in the same manner examine our Sentiments of the Happiness
of others in common Life. Wealth and External Pleasures bear no small
bulk in our Imaginations; but does there not always accompany this
Opinion of Happiness in Wealth, some suppos'd beneficent Intention
of doing good Offices to Persons dear to us, at least to our Familys, or
Kinsmen? And in our imagin'd Happiness ‖¹⁴from‖ external Pleasure,
‖¹⁵are not some Ideas‖ always included of some moral Enjoyments of
Society, some Communication of Pleasure, something of Love, of
Friendship, of Esteem, of Gratitude? Who ever pretended to a Taste
of ‖¹⁶these‖ Pleasures without Society? Or if any seem violent in pursuit
of ‖¹⁷them‖, how base and contemptible do they appear to all Persons,

even to those who could have no expectation of Advantage from their having a more generous Notion of Pleasure?

[18] Now were there no moral Sense, no Happiness in Benevolence, and did we act from no other Principle than Self-love; sure there is no Pleasure of the external Sen-[249]ses, which we could not ||[19] enjoy alone||, with less trouble and expence than in Society. But a Mixture of the moral Pleasures is what gives the alluring Relish; 'tis some Appearance of Friendship, of Love, of communicating Pleasure to others, which preserves the Pleasures of the Luxurious from being nauseous and insipid. And this partial Imagination of some good moral Qualitys, some Benevolence, in Actions which have many cruel, inhuman, and destructive Consequences toward others, is what has kept Vice more in countenance than any other Consideration.*

But to convince us further wherein the Happiness of Wealth, and external Pleasure lies; let us but suppose Malice, Wrath, Revenge; or only Solitude, Absence of Friendship, of Love, of Society, of Esteem, join'd with the Possession of them; and all the Happiness vanishes like a Dream. And yet Love, Friendship, Society, Humanity, tho accompany'd with Poverty and Toil, nay even with smaller degrees of Pain, such as do not wholly occupy the Mind, are not only the Object of Love from others, but even of a sort of Emulation: which plainly shews, "That Virtue is the chief Happiness in the ||[21] Judgment of all|| Mankind." [250]

III. There is a further Consideration which must not be pass'd over, concerning the External Beauty of Persons, which all allow to have ||[22] a|| great Power over human Minds. Now it is some apprehended Morality, some natural or imagin'd Indication of concomitant Virtue, which gives it this powerful Charm above all other kinds of Beauty. Let us consider the Characters of Beauty, which are commonly admir'd in Countenances, and we shall find them to be Sweetness, Mildness, Majesty, Dignity, Vivacity, Humility, Tenderness, Good-nature; that is, that certain Airs, Proportions, *je ne scai quoy's,* are natural Indications of such Vir-

The Charm in Beauty.

---

* See above, Sect. iv. Art. 4. Par. ||[20] 4, 5||.

tues, or of Abilitys or Dispositions toward them. As we observ'd above*
of Misery, or Distress appearing in Countenances; so it is certain, almost
all habitual Dispositions of Mind, form the countenance in such a manner, as to give some Indications of them to the Spectator. Our violent
Passions are obvious at first view in the Countenance; so that sometimes
no Art can conceal them: and smaller degrees of them give some less
obvious Turns to the Face, which an accurate Eye will observe. Now
when the natural Air of ||²⁴a|| Face approaches to that which any Passion
would form it unto, we make a [251] conjecture from this concerning
the leading Disposition of the Person's Mind.

As to those Fancys which prevail in certain Countrys toward large
Lips, little Noses, narrow Eyes; unless we knew from themselves under
what Idea ||²⁵ such Features|| are admir'd, whether as naturally beautiful
in Form, or Proportion to the rest of the Face; or as presum'd Indications
of some moral Qualitys; we may more probably conclude that it is the
latter; since this is so much the Ground of Approbation, or Aversion
||²⁶ towards|| Faces among our selves. And ||²⁷ as to those|| Features which
we count naturally disagreeable as to Form, we know the Aversion on
this account is so weak, that moral Qualitys shall procure a liking, even
to the Face, in Persons who are sensible of the Irregularity, or want of
that Regularity which is common in others. With us certain Features are
imagin'd to denote Dulness; as hollow Eyes, large Lips; a Colour of Hair,
Wantonness: and may we not conclude the like Association of Ideas,
||²⁸ perhaps in both Cases without Foundation in Nature,|| to be the
Ground of those Approbations which appear unaccountable to us?

In the same manner, when there is nothing grosly disproportion'd in
any Face, what is it we dispraise? ||²⁹ It is|| Pride, Haugh-[252]tiness, Sour-
ness, Ill-nature, Discontent, Folly, Levity, Wantonness; which some
Countenances discover in the manner above hinted at? And ||³⁰ these||
Airs, when brought by Custom upon the most regular Set of Features,
have often made them very disagreeable; as the contrary Airs have given
the strongest Charms to Countenances, which ||³¹ were|| far from Per-
fection in external Beauty.

* See Sect. ||²³V||. Art. 8. Par. 2.

‖ [32] One cannot but observe the Judgment of Homer, in his Character of Helen. Had he ever so much rais'd our Idea of her external Beauty, ‖ it would have been ridiculous to have engag'd his Countrymen in a War for such a Helen as Virgil has drawn her. He therefore still retains something ‖ [33] amiable in a moral Sense, ‖ amidst all her Weakness, and often suggests to his Reader,

——— Ἑλένης ὁρμήματά τε σοναχάς τε* iii

as the Spring of his Countrymens Indignation and Revenge.

This Consideration may shew us one Reason, among many others, for Mens different Fancys, or Relishes of Beauty. The Mind of Man, however generally dispos'd to esteem Benevolence and Virtue, yet by more particular Attention to some [253] kinds of it than others, may gain a stronger Admiration of some moral Dispositions than others. Military Men, may admire Courage more than other Virtues; Persons of smaller Courage, may admire Sweetness of Temper; Men of Thought and Reflection, who have more extensive Views, will admire the like Qualitys in others; Men of keen Passions, expect equal Returns of all the kind Affections, and are wonderfully charm'd by Compliance: the Proud, may like those of higher Spirit, as more suitable to their Dignity; tho Pride, join'd with Reflection and good Sense, will recommend to them Humility in the Person belov'd. Now as the various Tempers of Men make various Tempers of others agreeable to them, so they must differ in their Relishes of Beauty, according as it denotes the several Qualitys most agreeable to themselves.

> The Cause of different Fancys of Beauty.

This may also shew us, how in virtuous Love there may be the greatest Beauty, without the least Charm to engage a Rival. Love it self gives a Beauty to the Lover, in the Eyes of the Person belov'd, which no other Mortal is much affected with. And this perhaps is the strongest Charm possible, and that which will have the greatest Power, where there is not some very great Counter-ballance from worldly Interest, Vice, or gross Deformity. [254]

---

* See Homer, *Iliad* 2. v. 356, 590.
iii. Translation: "Helen's fear and lonesome sighs."

Air, Motion, Gestures.

IV. This same Consideration may be extended to the whole Air and Motion of any Person. Every thing we count agreeable, some way denotes Chearfulness, Ease, a Condescension, and Readiness to oblige, a Love of Company, with a Freedom and Boldness which always accompanys an honest, undesigning Heart. On the contrary, what is shocking in Air, or Motion, is Roughness, Ill-nature, a Disregard to others, or a foolish Shame-facedness, which evidences a Person to be unexperienc'd in Society, or Offices of Humanity.

With relation to these Airs, Motions, Gestures, we may observe, that considering the different Ceremonys, and Modes of shewing respect, which are practis'd in different Nations, we may indeed probably conclude that there is no natural Connexion between any of these Gestures, or Motions, and the Affections of Mind which they are by Custom made to express. But when Custom has made any of them pass for Expressions of such Affections, by a constant Association of Ideas, some shall become agreeable and lovely, and others extremely offensive, altho they were both, in their own Nature, perfectly indifferent. [255]

The Spring of Love between the Sexes.

V. Here we may remark the manner in which Nature leads Mankind to the Continuance of their Race, and by its strongest Power engages them to what occasions the greatest Toil and Anxiety of Life; and yet supports them under it with an inexpressible delight. We might have been excited to the Propagation of our Species, by such an uneasy Sensation as would have effectually determin'd us to it, without any great prospect of Happiness; as we see Hunger and Thirst determine us to preserve our Bodys, tho few look upon eating and drinking as any considerable Happiness. The Sexes might have been engag'd to Concurrence, ||[34] as|| we imagine the Brutes are, by Desire only, or by a Love of sensual Pleasure. But how dull and insipid had Life been, were there no more in Marriage? Who would have had Resolution enough to bear all the Cares of a Family, and Education of Children? Or who, from the general Motive of Benevolence ||[35] alone||, would have chosen to subject himself to natural Affection toward an Offspring, when he could ||[36] so easily foresee what|| Troubles it might occasion?

³⁷This Inclination therefore of the Sexes, is founded on something stronger, and more efficacious and joyful, than the Sollicitations of Uneasiness, or the bare desire of [256] sensible Pleasure. ³⁸Beauty gives a favourable Presumption of good moral Dispositions, and Acquaintance confirms this into a real Love of Esteem, or begets it, where there is little Beauty. This raises an expectation of the greatest moral Pleasures along with the sensible, and a thousand tender Sentiments of Humanity and Generosity; and makes us impatient for a Society which we imagine big with unspeakable moral Pleasures: where nothing is indifferent, and every trifling Service, being an Evidence of this strong Love ||³⁹of|| Esteem, is mutually receiv'd with the Rapture and Gratitude of the greatest Benefit, and of the most substantial Obligation. And where Prudence and Good-nature influence both sides, this Society may answer all their Expectations.

Nay, let us examine those of looser Conduct with relation to the fair Sex, and we shall find, ||⁴⁰that Love of sensible Pleasure is not|| the chief Motive of Debauchery, or false Gallantry. Were it so, the meanest Prostitutes would please as much as any. But we know sufficiently, that ||⁴¹Men|| are fond of Good-nature, Faith, Pleasantry of Temper, Wit, and many other moral Qualitys, even in a Mistress. And this may furnish us with a Reason for what appears pretty unaccountable, viz. "That Chastity it self has a powerful Charm in [257] the Eyes of the Dissolute, even when they are attempting to destroy it."

This powerful Determination even to a limited Benevolence, and other moral Sentiments, is observ'd to give a ||⁴²strong|| biass to our Minds ||⁴³toward|| a universal Goodness, Tenderness, Humanity, Generosity, and contempt of private Good in our whole Conduct; besides the obvious Improvement it occasions in our external Deportment, and in our relish of Beauty, Order, and Harmony. As soon as a Heart, before hard and obdurate, is soften'd in this Flame, we shall observe||⁴⁴, arising along with it,|| a Love of Poetry, Musick, the Beauty of Nature in rural Scenes, a Contempt of other selfish Pleasures of the external Senses, a neat Dress, a humane Deportment, a Delight in and Emulation of every thing which is gallant, generous and friendly.

Society,
Friendships,
from our
Moral Sense.

In the same manner we are determin'd to common Friendships and Acquaintances, not by the sullen Apprehensions of our Necessitys, or Prospects of Interest; but by an incredible variety of little agreeable, engaging Evidences of Love, Good-nature, and other morally amiable Qualitys in those we converse with. ‖⁴⁵And‖ among the rest, none of the least considerable is an Inclination to Chearfulness, a Delight to raise Mirth in others, which procures a secret [258] Approbation and Gratitude toward the Person who puts us in such an agreeable, innocent, good-natur'd, and easy state of Mind, as we are conscious of while we enjoy pleasant Conversation, enliven'd by moderate Laughter.

The Power
of Oratory
founded on it.

VI. Upon this moral Sense is founded all the Power of the Orator. The various Figures of Speech, are the several Manners which a lively Genius, warm'd with Passions suitable to the Occasion, naturally runs into, only a little diversify'd by Custom: and they only move the Hearers, by giving a lively Representation of the Passions of the Speaker; which are communicated to the Hearers, as we* observ'd above of one Passion, viz. Pity.

Now the Passions which the Orator attempts to raise, are all founded on moral Qualitys. All the bold Metaphors, or Descriptions, all the artificial Manners of Expostulation, Arguing, and addressing the Audience, all the Appeals to Mankind, are but more lively Methods of giving the Audience a stronger impression of the moral Qualitys of the Person accus'd, or defended; of the Action advis'd, or dissuaded: And all the Antitheses, or Witticisms; all the Cadences of sonorous Periods, whatever [259] inferior kind of Beauty they may have separately, are of no consequence to persuade, if we neglect moving the Passions by some Species of Morality. They may perhaps raise a little Admiration of the Speaker, among those who already favour his Party, but they oftner raise Contempt in his Adversarys. But when you display the Beneficence of any Action, the good Effect it shall have on the Publick in promoting the Welfare of the Innocent, and relieving the unjustly distressed; if you prove your Allegations, you make every Mortal approve the undertaking

* See Sect. v. Art. 8. Par. 2.

it. When any Person is to be recommended, display his Humanity, Generosity, Study of the publick Good, and Capacity to promote it, his Contempt of Dangers, and private Pleasures; and you are sure to procure
him Love and Esteem. If at the same time you shew his Distress, or the
Injurys he has suffer'd, you raise Pity, and every tender Affection.

On the contrary, represent the Barbarity, or Cruelty of any Action,
the Misery it shall procure to the Kind, the Faithful, the Generous, or
only to the Innocent; and you raise an Abhorrence of it in the Breasts
of the Audience, tho they were not the Persons who would have suffer'd
by it. The same way, would you make a Person infamous, and despis'd
and [260] hated, represent him as cruel, inhuman, or treacherous toward
the most distant rational Agents; or shew him only to be selfish, ||⁴⁶and||
given to solitary Luxury, without regard to any Friend, or the Interest
of others; and you have gain'd your Point as soon as you prove what you
alledge. Nay, ||⁴⁷how does it|| stop our Admiration of any celebrated Ac-
tion, to suggest, "That the Author of it was no Fool; he knew it would
turn to his own Advantage?"

Now, are the Learned and Polite the only Persons who are mov'd by
such Speeches? Must Men know the Schemes of the Moralists and Pol-
iticians, or the Art of Rhetorick, to be capable of being persuaded? Must
they be nicely conversant in all the Methods of promoting Self-Interest?
Nay, do we not see on the contrary, the rude undisciplin'd Multitude
most affected? Where had Oratory so much Power as in popular States,
and that too before the Perfection of the Sciences? Reflection, and Study,
may raise in Men a Suspicion of Design, and Caution of Assent, when
they have some knowledge of the various Topicks of Argument, and
find them employ'd upon themselves: but rude Nature is still open to
every moral Impression, and carry'd furiously along without Caution,
or Suspense. It was not the [261] Groves of the Academy, or the polish'd
Stones of the Portico, or the manag'd Horses of Greece, which listen'd
to the Harp of an Amphion, or an Orpheus; ⁱᵛ but the Trees, and Rocks,

---

iv. "The Groves of the Academy" refers to the Academy in Athens, the school of
philosophers founded by Plato; Zeno of Citium founded the school that derived its
name from the *stoa* ("portico" or colonnade), the Stoic school, also in Athens. Ac-

and Tygers of the Forest: which may shew us, "That there is some Sense of Morality antecedent to Instruction, or metaphysical Arguments proving the private Interest of the Person who is persuaded, to be connected with the publick Good."

Poetry pleases from this Moral Sense.

VII. We shall find ||⁴⁸this|| Sense to be the Foundation ||⁴⁹also|| of the chief Pleasures of Poetry. We hinted, in the former Treatise, at the Foundation of Delight in the Numbers, Measures, Metaphors, Similitudes.* But as the Contemplation of moral Objects, either of Vice or Virtue, affects us more strongly, and moves our Passions in a quite different and ||⁵⁰more|| powerful manner, than natural Beauty, or (what we commonly call) Deformity; so the most moving Beautys bear a Relation to our moral Sense, and affect us more vehemently, than the||⁵¹Representation|| of natural Objects in the liveliest Descriptions. Dramatic, and Epic Poetry, are entirely address'd to this Sense, and raise our Passions by the Fortunes of Characters, distinctly represented as morally good, or [262] evil; as might be seen more fully, were we to consider the Passions separately.

Where we are studying to raise any Desire, or Admiration of an Object really beautiful, we are not content with a bare Narration, but endeavour, if we can, to present the Object it self, or the most lively Image of it. And ||⁵²hence|| the Epic Poem, or Tragedy, ||⁵³gives|| a ||⁵⁴vastly|| greater Pleasure than the Writings of Philosophers, tho both aim at recommending Virtue. The representing the Actions themselves, if the Representation be judicious, natural, and lively, will make us admire the Good, and detest the Vitious, the Inhuman, the Treacherous and Cruel, by means of our moral Sense, without any Reflections of the Poet to guide our Sentiments. It is for this Reason that Horace has justly made Knowledge in Morals so necessary to a good Poet:

---

cording to legend, Amphion's lyre moved the stones into place for the city wall of Thebes; Orpheus could charm wild beasts, plants, and stones with his lyre-playing.

* See *Treatise* I. Sect. ii. Art. 13. Sect. iv. Art. 3.

Scribendi recte Sapere est & principium & fons.*ᵛ

And again:

Qui didicit Patriae quid debeat, & quid Amicis, [263]
Quo sit amore Parens, quo Frater amandus, & Hospes,
Quod sit Conscripti, quod Judicis officium, quae
Partes in bellum missi Ducis; ille profecto
Reddere Personae scit convenientia cuique.†ᵛⁱ

Upon this same Sense is founded the Power of that great Beauty in Poetry, the Prosopopoeia, by which every Affection is made a Person; every natural Event, Cause, Object, is animated by moral Epithets. For we join the Contemplation of moral Circumstances and Qualitys, along with natural Objects, to increase ‖⁵⁸ their‖ Beauty or Deformity; and ‖⁵⁹ we‖ affect the Hearer in a more lively manner with the Affections describ'd, by representing them as Persons. Thus a shady Wood must have its solemn venerable Genius, and proper rural Gods; every clear Fountain, its sacred chaste Nymph; and River, its bountiful God, with his Urn, and perhaps a Cornu-copia diffusing Plenty and Fruitfulness along ‖⁶⁰ its‖ Banks. The Day-light is holy, benign, and powerful to banish the pernicious Spirits of the Night. The Morning is a kind, officious Goddess, tripping over the dewy Mountains, and ushering [264] in Light to Gods and Men. War is an impetuous, cruel, undistinguishing Monster, whom no Virtue, no Circumstance of Compassion, can move from his bloody Purposes. The Steel is unrelenting; the Arrow and Spear are impatient to destroy, and carry Death on their Points. Our modern Engines of War are also frightful Personages, ‖⁶¹ counterfeiting with their rude Throats‖ the Thunder of Jove. The moral Imagery of Death is

Imagery in Poetry founded on the Moral Sense.

* Hor. *de Arte Poet.* ‖⁵⁵ v.‖ 309.
   v. Translation: "Of good writing the source and fount is wisdom." Horace, *Satires, Epistles, and Ars Poetica,* p. 476.
   † Hor. *de Arte Poet.* ‖⁵⁶ v.‖ 312 ‖⁵⁷ &c‖.
   vi. Translation: "He who has learned what he owes his country and his friends, what love is due a parent, a brother, and a guest, what is imposed on senator and judge, what is the function of a general sent to war, he surely knows to give each character his fitting part." Horace, ibid., p. 476.

every where known, viz. his Insensibility to Pity, his Inflexibility, and universal impartial Empire. Fortune is inimitably drawn by Horace,* with all her Retinue and Votaries, and with her rigid severe Minister, Necessity. The Qualitys of Mind too become Persons. Love becomes a Venus, or a Cupid; Courage, or Conduct, a Mars, or a Pallas protecting and assisting the Hero; before them march Terror and Dread, Flight and Pursuit, Shouts and Amazement. Nay, the most sacred Poets are often led into this Imagery, and represent Justice and Judgment as supporting the Almighty's Throne, and Mercy and Truth going before his Face: They shew us Peace as springing up from the Earth, and Mercy looking down from Heaven. [265]

Every one perceives a greater Beauty in this manner of Representation, this Imagery, this Conjunction of moral Ideas, than in the fullest Narration, or the most lively natural Description. When one reads the fourth Book of Homer, and is prepar'd, from the Council of the Gods, to imagine the bloody Sequel, and amidst the most beautiful Description which ever was imagin'd of shooting an Arrow, meets with its moral Epithet,

──────── μελαινάων ἔρμ᾽ ὀδυνάων,†
──────── The Source of blackest Woes; [vii]

he will find himself more mov'd by this Circumstance, than by all the Profusion of natural Description which Man could imagine.

History.   [63] VIII. History derives its chief Excellence from the representing the Manners and Characters; the Contemplation of which in Nature being very affecting, they must necessarily give Pleasure when well related.

Painting.   [64] IX. It is well known too, that a Collection of the best Pieces of Face-painting is but a poor Entertainment, when compar'd with those Pieces which represent moral Actions, Passions, and Characters. [65] [266]

* See Lib. 1. Od. 35.
† See Homer, *Iliad* 4. ‖[62]v.‖ 117.
vii. That is, Pandaros' arrow shot at Menelaos.

A Deduction of some Complex moral Ideas,
viz. of Obligation, and Right, Perfect, Imperfect,
and External, Alienable, and Unalienable, from
this moral Sense.

I. To conclude this Subject, we may, from what has been said, see the true Original of moral Ideas, viz. This moral Sense of Excellence in every Appearance, or Evidence of Benevolence‖¹. It remains to be explain'd, how we acquire more particular Ideas of Virtue and Vice, abstracting‖ from any Law, Human, or Divine.

If any one ask, Can we have any Sense of Obligation, ‖²abstracting‖ from the Laws of a Superior? We must answer according to the various Senses of the word Obligation. If by Obligation we understand a Determination, without regard to our own Interest, to approve Actions, and to perform them; which Determination shall also make us displeas'd with our selves, and uneasy upon having acted contrary to ‖³it‖; in this meaning of the word Obligation, [267] there is naturally an Obligation upon all Men to Benevolence; and they are still under its Influence, even when by false, or partial Opinions of the natural Tendency of ‖⁴their‖ Actions, this moral Sense leads them to Evil; unless by long inveterate Habits it be exceedingly weaken'd. For it scarce seems possible wholly to extinguish it. Or, which is to the same purpose, this internal Sense, and Instinct ‖⁵toward‖ Benevolence, will either influence our Actions, or ‖⁶else‖ make us very uneasy and dissatisfy'd; and we shall be conscious that we are in a base unhappy State, even without considering any Law whatsoever, or any external Advantages lost, or Disadvantages impend-

Obligation.

177

ing from its Sanctions. And further, there are still such Indications given us of what is in the whole ||⁷benevolent||, and what not; as may probably discover to us the true Tendency of every Action, and let us see, some time or other, the evil Tendency of what upon a partial View appear'd ||⁸benevolent||: ||⁹or if we have no Friends so faithful as to admonish us, the Persons injur'd will not fail to upbraid us.|| So that no Mortal can secure to himself a perpetual Serenity, Satisfaction, and Self-approbation, but by a serious Inquiry into the Tendency of his Actions, and a perpetual Study of universal Good||¹⁰, according to the justest Notions of it||. [268]

But if by Obligation, we understand a Motive from Self-interest, sufficient to determine all those who duly consider it, and pursue their own Advantage wisely, to a certain Course of Actions; we may have a Sense of such ||¹¹an|| Obligation, by reflecting on this Determination of our Nature to approve Virtue, to be pleas'd and happy when we reflect upon our having done virtuous Actions, and to be uneasy when we are conscious of having acted otherwise; and also by considering how much superior we esteem the Happiness of Virtue to any other Enjoyment.*
We may likewise have a Sense of this sort of Obligation, by considering those Reasons which prove a constant Course of benevolent and social Actions, to be the most probable means of promoting the natural Good of every Individual; as Cumberland and Puffendorf have prov'd: And all this without Relation to a Law.

But further, if our moral Sense be suppos'd exceedingly weaken'd, and the selfish Passions grown strong, either thro some general Corruption of Nature, or inveterate Habits; if our Understanding be weak, and we be often in danger of being hurry'd by our Passions into precipitate and rash [269] Judgments, that malicious Actions shall ||¹²promote our Advantage more|| than Beneficence; in such a Case, if it be inquir'd what is necessary to engage Men to beneficent Actions, or induce a steady Sense of an Obligation to act for the publick Good; then, no doubt, "A Law with Sanctions, given by a superior Being, of sufficient Power to make us happy or miserable, must be necessary to counter-ballance those

---

* See above, Sect. vi. Art. 1, 2.

apparent Motives of Interest, to calm our Passions, and give room for the recovery of our moral Sense, or at least for a just View of our Interest."

II. Now the principal Business of the moral Philosopher is to shew, from solid Reasons, "That universal Benevolence tends to the Happiness of the Benevolent, either from the Pleasures of Reflection, Honour, natural Tendency to engage the good Offices of Men, upon whose Aid we must depend for our Happiness in this World; or from the Sanctions of divine Laws discover'd to us by the Constitution of the Universe;" that so no apparent Views of Interest may counteract this natural Inclination: but not to attempt proving, "That Prospects of our own Advantage of any kind, can raise in us ‖ ¹³ real Love to‖ others." Let the Obstacles from Self-love be only remov'd, and Nature it self will incline us to Be-[270]nevolence. Let the Misery of excessive Selfishness, and all its Passions, be but once explain'd, that so Self-love may cease to counteract our natural Propensity to Benevolence, and when this noble Disposition gets loose from these Bonds of Ignorance, and false Views of Interest, it shall be assisted even by Self-love, and grow strong enough to make a noble virtuous Character. Then he is to enquire, by Reflection upon human Affairs, what Course of Action does most effectually promote the universal Good, what universal Rules or Maxims are to be observ'd, and in what Circumstances the Reason of them alters, so as to admit Exceptions; that so our good Inclinations may be directed by Reason, and a just Knowledge of the Interests of Mankind. But Virtue it self, or good Dispositions of Mind, are not directly taught, or produc'd by Instruction; ‖ ¹⁴ they must be originally implanted in our Nature, by its great Author; and afterwards strengthen'd and confirm'd by our own Cultivation. ‖

How far Virtue can be taught.

‖ ¹⁵ᵃ III. We are often told, "That there is no need of supposing such a Sense of Morality given to Men, since Reflection, and Instruction would recommend the same Actions from Arguments of Self-Interest, and engage us, from the acknowledg'd Principle of Self-love, [271] to the Practice of them, without this unintelligible Determination to Benevolence, or the occult Quality of a moral Sense."

Objection.

It is perhaps true, that Reflection and Reason might lead us to approve the same Actions as advantageous. But would not the same Reflection and Reason likewise, generally recommend the same Meats to us which our Taste represents as pleasant? And shall we thence conclude that we have no Sense of Tasting? Or that such a Sense is useless? No: The use is plain in both Cases. Notwithstanding the mighty Reason we boast of above other Animals, its Processes are too slow, too full of doubt and hesitation, to serve us in every Exigency, either for our own Preservation, without the external Senses, or to ||[16b]direct[b]|| our Actions for the Good of the Whole, without this moral Sense. Nor could we be so strongly determin'd at all times to what ||[17c]is[c]|| most conducive to either of these Ends, without these expeditious Monitors, and importunate Sollicitors; nor so nobly rewarded, when we act vigorously in pursuit of these Ends, by the calm dull Reflections of Self-Interest, as by those delightful Sensations.

This natural Determination to approve and admire, or hate and dislike Actions, is no doubt an occult Quality. But [272] is it any way more mysterious that the Idea of an Action should raise Esteem, or Contempt, than that the motion, or tearing of Flesh should give Pleasure, or Pain; or the Act of Volition should move Flesh and Bones? In the latter Case, we have got the Brain, and elastic Fibres, and animal Spirits, and elastic Fluids, like the Indian's Elephant, and Tortoise, to bear the Burden of the Difficulty: but go one step further, and you find the whole as difficult as at first, and equally a Mystery with this Determination to love and approve, or ||[18d]hate[d]|| and despise Actions and Agents, without any Views of Interest, as they appear benevolent, or the ||[19e]contrary.[e]||

When they offer it as a Presumption that there can be no such Sense, antecedent to all Prospect of Interest, "That these Actions for the most part are really advantageous, one way or other, to the Actor, the Approver, or Mankind in general, by whose Happiness our own State may be some way made better;" may we not ask, supposing the Deity intended to impress such a Sense of something amiable in Actions, (which is no impossible Supposition) what sort of Actions would a good God determine ||[20f]us[f]|| to approve? Must we deny the possibility of such a Determination, if it did not lead us to admire Actions of no Advantage to Man-[273]kind, or to love Agents for their being eminent Triflers? If then the Actions which a wise and good God must determine us to approve, if he give us any such Sense at all, must be Actions useful to the Publick, this Advantage can never be a Reason against the Sense it self. After the same manner, we should deny all Revelation which taught us good Sense, Humanity, Justice, and a rational Worship, because Reason and ‖[21g]Interest[g]‖ confirm and recommend such Principles, and Services; and should greedily embrace every Contradiction, Foppery, and Pageantry, as a truly divine Institution, without any thing humane, or useful to Mankind.

IV. The Writers upon opposite Schemes, who deduce all Ideas of Good and Evil from the private Advantage of the Actor, or from Relation to a Law and its Sanctions, either known from Reason, or Revelation, are perpetually recurring to this moral Sense which they deny; not only in calling the Laws of the Deity just and good, and alledging Justice and Right in the Deity to govern us; but by using a set of Words which import something different from what they will allow to be their only meaning. Obligation, with them, is ‖[22h]only[h]‖ such a Constitution, either of Nature, or some governing Power, as makes it advantageous for the Agent to [274] act in a certain manner. Let this Definition be substituted, wherever we meet with the words, *ought, should, must,* in a moral Sense, and many of their Sentences would seem very strange; as that the Deity *must* act rationally, *must* not, or *ought* not to punish the Innocent, *must* make the state of the Virtuous better than that of the Wicked, *must* observe Promises; substituting the Definition of the Words, *must, ought, should,* would make these Sentences either ridiculous, or very disputable.[a]‖

Moral Sense judges of Laws.

[23]V. But that our first Ideas of moral Good depend not on Laws, may plainly appear from our constant Inquirys into the Justice of Laws themselves; and that not only of human Laws, but of the divine. What else can be the meaning of that universal Opinion, "That the Laws of God are just, and holy, and good?" Human Laws may be call'd good, because of their Conformity to the Divine. But to call the Laws of the supreme

Deity good, or holy, or just, if all ||²⁴Goodness, Holiness||, and Justice be constituted by Laws, or the Will of a Superior any way reveal'd, must be an insignificant Tautology, amounting to no more than this, "That God wills what he wills."²⁵

²⁶It must then first be suppos'd, that there is something in Actions which is apprehend-[275]ed absolutely good; and this is Benevolence, or ||²⁷a Tendency to|| the publick natural happiness of rational Agents; and that our moral Sense perceives this Excellence. And then we call the Laws of the Deity good, when we imagine that they are contriv'd to promote the publick Good in the most effectual and impartial manner. And the Deity is call'd ||²⁸good||, in a moral Sense, when we apprehend that his whole Providence tends to the universal Happiness of his Creatures; whence we conclude his Benevolence, and ||²⁹Delight|| in their Happiness.

Some tell us, "That the Goodness of the divine Laws, consists in their Conformity to some essential Rectitude of his Nature."ⁱ But they must excuse us from assenting to this, till they make us understand the meaning of this Metaphor, essential Rectitude, and till we discern whether any thing more is meant by it than a perfectly wise, uniform, impartial Benevolence.

Difference between Constraint, and Obligation.
Hence we may see the Difference between Constraint, and Obligation. There is indeed no Difference between Constraint, and the second Sense of the word Obligation, viz. a Constitution which makes an Action eligible from Self-Interest, if we only mean external Interest, distinct from [276] the delightful Consciousness which arises from the moral Sense. The Reader need scarcely be told, that by Constraint, we do not understand ||³⁰an|| external Force moving our Limbs without our Consent, for in that Case we are not Agents at all; but that Constraint which arises from the threatening and presenting some Evil, in order to make us act in a certain manner. And yet there seems a universally acknowledg'd Difference between even this sort of Constraint, and Obligation.

i. See Samuel Clarke, *Discourse Concerning the Unchangeable Obligations of Natural Religion* (1706), chap. 1, sects. 3, 4, 6, in D. D. Raphael, *British Moralists 1650–1800* (Oxford: Clarendon Press, 1969), 199–214.

We never say we are oblig'd to do an Action which we count base, but we may be constrain'd to it; we never say that the divine Laws, by their Sanctions, constrain us, but oblige us; nor do we call Obedience to the Deity Constraint, unless by a Metaphor, ||³¹tho|| many own they are influenc'd by fear of Punishments. And yet supposing an almighty evil Being should require, under grievous Penaltys, Treachery, Cruelty, Ingratitude, we would call this Constraint. The difference is plainly this. When any ||³²Sanctions co-operate|| with our moral Sense, in exciting us to Actions which we count morally good, we say we are oblig'd; but when Sanctions of Rewards or ||³³Punishments|| oppose our moral Sense, then we say we are brib'd or constrain'd. In the former Case we call the Lawgiver good, as designing the publick Happiness; in the latter we call him evil, or unjust, for the suppos'd contrary [277] Intention. But were all our Ideas of moral Good or Evil, deriv'd solely from opinions of private Advantage or Loss in Actions, I see no possible difference which could be made in the meaning of these words.

³⁴VI. From this Sense too we derive our Ideas of Rights. Whenever it appears to us, that a Faculty of doing, demanding, or possessing any thing, universally allow'd in certain Circumstances, would in the whole tend to the general Good, we say that ||³⁵any Person|| in such Circumstances, has a Right to do, possess, or demand that Thing. And according as this Tendency to the publick Good is greater or less, the Right is greater or less.

    Rights.

The Rights call'd perfect, are of such necessity to the publick Good, that the universal Violation of them would make human Life intolerable; and it actually makes those miserable, whose Rights are thus ||³⁶violated. On|| the contrary, to fulfil these Rights in every Instance, tends to the publick Good, either directly, or by promoting the innocent Advantage of a Part. Hence it plainly follows, "That ||³⁷to allow|| a violent Defence, or Prosecution of such Rights, before Civil Government be constituted, cannot in any particular Case be more detrimental to the Publick, than the Violation of them with Impunity." [278] And as to the general Consequences, the universal use of Force in a ||³⁸State of Nature||, in pursuance of perfect Rights, seems exceedingly advanta-

    Perfect Rights.

geous to the Whole, by making every one dread any Attempts against the perfect Rights of others.

Right of
War, and
Punishment. [39] This is the moral Effect which attends proper Injury, or a Violation of the perfect Rights of others, viz. A Right to War, and all Violence which is necessary to oblige the Injurious to repair the Damage, and give Security against such Offences for the future. ||[40a] This is the sole Foundation of the Rights of punishing Criminals, and of violent Prosecutions of our Rights, in a ||[41b] State of Nature[b]||. And these Rights, ||[42c] belonging originally to the Persons injur'd, or their voluntary, or invited Assistants,[c]|| according to the Judgment of indifferent Arbitrators, ||[43d] in a State of Nature,[d]|| being by ||[44e] the[e]|| Consent of the ||[45f] Persons injur'd[f]||, transferr'd to the Magistrate in a Civil State, are the true Foundation of his Right of Punishment.[a]|| Instances of perfect Rights are those to our Lives; to the Fruits of our Labours; to demand Performance of Contracts upon valuable Considerations, from Men capable of performing them; to direct our own Actions either for publick, or innocent private Good, before we have submitted them to the Direction of others in any measure: and many others of like nature. [279]

Imperfect
Rights. Imperfect Rights are such as, when universally violated, would not necessarily make Men miserable. These Rights tend to the improvement and increase of positive Good in any Society, but are not absolutely necessary to prevent universal Misery. The Violation of them, only disappoints Men of the Happiness expected from the Humanity or Gratitude of others; but does not deprive Men of any Good which they had before. From this Description it appears, "That a violent Prosecution of such Rights, would generally occasion greater Evil than the Violation of them." Besides, the allowing of Force in such Cases, would deprive Men of the greatest Pleasure in Actions of Kindness, Humanity, Gratitude; which would cease to appear amiable, when Men could be constrain'd to perform them. Instances of imperfect Rights are those which the poor have to the Charity of the Wealthy; which all Men have to Offices of no trouble or expence to the Performer; which Benefactors have to returns of Gratitude, and such like.

[46] The Violation of imperfect Rights, only argues a Man to have such weak Benevolence, as not to study advancing the positive Good of oth-

ers, when in the least opposite to his own: but the Violation of per-
[280]fect Rights, argues the injurious Person to be positively evil or cruel;
or at least so immoderately selfish, as to be indifferent about the positive
Misery and Ruin of others, when he imagines he can find his Interest
in it. In violating the former, we shew a weak Desire of publick Happiness, which every small View of private Interest over-ballances; but in
violating the latter, we shew our selves so entirely negligent of the Misery
of others, that Views of increasing our own Good, overcome all our
Compassion toward their Sufferings. Now as the absence of Good, is
more easily born than the presence of Misery; ‖⁴⁷so‖ our good Wishes
toward the positive Good of others, ‖⁴⁸are‖ weaker than our Compassion toward their Misery. He then who violates imperfect Rights, shews
that his Self-love overcomes only the Desire of positive good to others;
but he who violates perfect Rights, betrays such a selfish Desire of advancing his own positive Good, as overcomes all ‖⁴⁹Compassion‖ toward
the Misery of others.

Beside these two sorts of Rights, there is a third call'd External; as
when the doing, possessing, or demanding of any thing is really detrimental to the Publick in any particular Instance, as being contrary to
the imperfect Right of another; but yet the ‖⁵⁰universally‖ denying Men
this Faculty [281] of doing, possessing, or demanding that Thing, or of
using Force in pursuance of it, would do more mischief than all the Evils
to be fear'd from the Use of this Faculty. And hence it appears, "That
there can be no Right to use Force in opposition even to external Rights,
since it tends to the universal Good to allow Force in pursuance of
them."

Civil Societys substitute Actions in Law, instead of the Force allow'd
in the State of Nature.

Instances of external Rights are these; that of a wealthy Miser to recal
his Loan from the most industrious poor Tradesman at any time; that
of demanding the Performance of a Covenant too burdensome on one
side; the Right of a wealthy Heir to refuse Payment of any Debts which
were contracted by him under Age, without Fraud in the Lender; the
Right of taking advantage of a positive Law, contrary to what was Equity
antecedent to that Law; as when a register'd Deed takes place of one not

External
Rights.

register'd, altho prior to it, and known to be so before the second
Contract.

What Rights,
can be
opposite.

Now whereas no action, Demand, or Possession, can at once be either
necessary to the publick Good, or conducive to it, and [282] at the same
time its contrary be either necessary or conducive to the same end; it
follows, "That there can be no Opposition of perfect Rights among
themselves, of imperfect among themselves, or between perfect and imperfect Rights." But it may often tend to the publick Good, to allow a
Right of doing, possessing, or demanding, and of using Force in pursuance of it, while perhaps it would have been more humane and kind
in any Person to have acted otherwise, and not have claim'd his Right.
But yet a violent Opposition to these Rights, would have been vastly
more pernicious than all the Inhumanity in the use of them. And there-
fore, ||⁵¹tho|| external Rights cannot be opposite among themselves; yet
they may be opposite to imperfect Rights, but imperfect Rights, tho vi-
olated, give no Right to ||⁵²Force. Hence|| it appears, "That there can
never be a Right to Force on both Sides, or a ||⁵³just War on both Sides||
at the same time."

Rights
alienable, and
unalienable.

⁵⁴VII. There is another important Difference of Rights, according as
they are Alienable, or Unalienable. To determine what Rights are alienable, and what not, we must take these two Marks:

1st. If the Alienation be within our natural Power, so that it be possible
for us in [283] Fact to transfer our Right; and if it be so, then,

2dly. It must appear, that ||⁵⁵to transfer|| such Rights may serve some
valuable Purpose.

By the first Mark it appears, "That the Right of private Judgment,
or of our inward Sentiments, is unalienable;" since we cannot command ourselves to think what either we our selves, or any other Person
||⁵⁶pleases. So|| are also our internal Affections, which necessarily arise
according to our Opinions of their Objects. By the second Mark it
appears, "That our Right of serving God, in the manner which we
think acceptable, is not alienable;" because it can never serve any valu-
able purpose, to make Men ||⁵⁷worship|| him in a way which seems to
them displeasing to him. The same way, a direct Right over our Lives

or Limbs, is not alienable to any Person; so that he might at Pleasure put us to death, or maim us. We have indeed a Right to hazard our Lives in any good Action which is of importance to the Publick; and it may often serve a most valuable end, to subject the direction of such perilous Actions to the Prudence of others in pursuing a publick Good; as Soldiers do to their General, or to a Council of War: and so far this Right is alienable. These may serve as [284] Instances to shew the use of the two Marks of alienable Rights, which must both concur to make them so, and will explain the manner of applying them in other Cases.

[58] VIII. That we may see the Foundation of some of the more important Rights of Mankind, let us observe, that probably nine Tenths, at least, of the things which are useful to Mankind, are owing to their Labour and Industry; and consequently, ||[59] when once Men become so numerous, that the natural Product of the Earth is not sufficient for their Support, or Ease, or innocent Pleasure; a necessity arises, for the support of the increasing System, that such a Tenour of Conduct be observ'd, as shall most effectually promote Industry; and that Men|| abstain from all Actions which would have the contrary effect. It is well known, that general Benevolence alone, is not a Motive strong enough to Industry, to bear Labour and Toil, and many other Difficultys which we are averse to from Self-love. For the strengthning therefore our Motives to Industry, we have the strongest Attractions of Blood, of Friendship, of Gratitude, and the additional Motives of Honour, and even of external Interest. Self-love is really as necessary to the Good of the Whole, as Benevolence; as that Attraction which causes the Cohesion of the Parts, is as necessary to the regular [285] State of the Whole, as Gravitation. Without these additional Motives, Self-love would generally oppose the Motions of Benevolence, and concur with Malice, or influence us to the same Actions which Malice would. "||[60] That|| Tenour of Action then, ||[61] which|| would take away the stronger Ties of Benevolence, or the additional Motives of Honour and Advantage, from our Minds, and so hinder us from pursuing industriously that Course which really increases the Good of the Whole, is evil; and we are oblig'd to shun it."

The Foundation of Property.

First then, the depriving any Person of the Fruits of his own innocent Labour, takes away all Motives ‖[62] to Industry from Self-love, or the nearer Ties; and leaves us no other Motive than general Benevolence:‖ nay, it exposes the Industrious as a constant Prey to the Slothful, and sets Self-love against Industry. This is the Ground of our Right of Dominion and Property in the Fruits of our Labours; without which Right, we could scarce hope for any Industry, or any thing beyond the Product of uncultivated Nature. Industry will be confin'd to our present Necessitys, and cease when they are provided for; at least it will only continue from the weak Motive of general Benevolence, if we are not allow'd to store up beyond present Necessity, and to dispose of what is above our Necessitys, [286] either in Barter for other kinds of Necessarys, or for the Service of our Friends or Familys. And hence appears the Right which Men have to lay up for the future, the Goods which will not be spoil'd by it; of alienating them in Trade; of Donation to Friends, Children, Relations: otherwise we deprive Industry of all the Motives of Self-love, Friendship, Gratitude, ‖[63] and‖ natural Affection. The same Foundation there is for the Right of Disposition by Testament. The Presumption of ‖[64] this‖ Disposition, is the Ground of the Right of Succession to the Intestate.

The external Right of the Miser to his useless Hoards, is founded also on this, that allowing Persons by Violence, or without Consent of the Acquirer, to take the Use of his Acquisitions, would discourage Industry, and take away all the Pleasures of Generosity, Honour, Charity, which cease when Men can be forc'd ‖[65] to‖ these Actions. Besides, there is no determining in many Cases, who is a Miser, and who is not.

Right of Marriage. Marriage must be so constituted as to ascertain the Offspring; otherwise we take away from the Males one of the strongest Motives to publick Good, viz. natural Affection; and discourage Industry, as has been shewn above. [287]

Commerce. The Labour of each Man cannot furnish him with all Necessarys, tho it may furnish him with a needless Plenty of one sort: Hence the Right of Commerce, and alienating our Goods; and also the Rights from Contracts and Promises, either to the Goods acquir'd by others, or to their Labours.

‖⁶⁶ᵃThe great Advantages which accrue to Mankind from unprej- **Right of Civil**
udic'd Arbitrators, impower'd to decide the Controversys which ordi- **Government.**
narily arise, thro the partiality of Self-love, among Neighbours; as also
from prudent Directors, who should not only instruct the Multitude in
the best Methods of promoting the publick Good, and of defending
themselves against mutual or foreign Injurys; but also be arm'd with
Force sufficient to make their Decrees or Orders effectual at home, and
the Society formidable abroad: these Advantages, I say, sufficiently shew
the Right Men have to constitute Civil Government, and to subject their
alienable Rights to the Disposal of their Governours, under such Lim-
itations as their Prudence suggests. And as far as the People have subjected their Rights, so far their Governours have an external Right at
least, to dispose of them, ‖⁶⁷ᵇas their Prudence shall directᵇ‖, for attain-
ing the Ends of their Institution; and no further.ᵃ‖ [288]

⁶⁸IX. These Instances may shew how our moral Sense, by a little Re- **Corollarys for**
flection upon the tendencys of actions, may adjust the Rights of Man- **comparing the**
kind. Let us now apply the general ‖⁶⁹Canon‖ laid down above,* for **degrees of**
Virtue and
comparing the Degrees of Virtue and Vice in Actions, in a few Corol- **Vice in**
larys besides that one already deduc'd.† **Actions.**

1. The Disappointment, in whole or in part, of any Attempt, Good **From Ability.**
or Evil, if it be occasion'd only by external Force, or any unforeseen
Accident, does not vary the moral Good, or Evil; for as in good Attempts,
the Moment of Good, ‖⁷²or [M]‖ is diminish'd, or vanishes in such a
case, so does the Ability, ‖⁷³or [A]‖ likewise: The Quotient then may still
be the same. ‖⁷⁴This holds equally‖ in evil Attempts. So that Actions are
not to be judg'd good or evil by the Events, any ‖⁷⁵further‖ than they
might have been foreseen by the Agent in evil Attempts; or were actually
intended, if they were good, in good Actions; for then only they argue
either Love or Hatred in the Agent.

2. Secular rewards annex'd to Virtue, and actually influencing the **Interest.**
Agent fur-[289]ther than his Benevolence would, diminish the moral

* See Sect. iii. Art. 11‖⁷⁰, 12‖.
† See Sect. iii. Art. 15. Par. ‖⁷¹3‖.

Good ||[76]as far|| as they were necessary to move the Agent to the action, or to make him do more Good than otherwise he would have done; for by increasing the Interest, ||[77]or [I] positive,|| to be subtracted, they diminish the Benevolence. But additional Interests which were not necessary to have mov'd the Agent, such as the Rewards of a good Being for Actions which he would have undertaken without a Reward, do not diminish the Virtue. In this however no Mortal is capable of judging another. Nor do the Prospects of grateful Returns for Benefits which we would have conferr'd gratuitously, diminish the Generosity. This Corollary may be apply'd to the Rewards of a future State, if any Person conceives them distinct from the Pleasures of virtue itself: If they be not conceiv'd as something distinct from those Pleasures, then the very Desire of them is a strong Evidence of a virtuous Disposition.

3. External Advantage exciting us to Actions of evil tendency to others, if without this Prospect of Advantage we would not have undertaken them, diminishes the Evil of the Action; such as the Prospects of great Rewards, of avoiding Tortures, or even the uneasy Sollicitations of violent selfish ||[78]Passions. This|| is com-[290]monly call'd the greatness of Temptation. The reason of this is the same with that in the former Case||[79], since $H = \frac{\mu - 1}{A}$||. We may here also remember again, that we are more uneasy upon the presence of Pain, than upon the absence of Good; and hence Torture is a more extenuating Circumstance than Bribes, engaging us to Evil, because ||[80][I] is greater.||

Detriment.

4. The surmounting the uneasy Sollicitations of the selfish Passions, increases the Virtue of a benevolent Action, and much more worldly Losses, Toil, &c. for now the Interest becomes negative; the Subtraction of which increases the Quantity.

5. A malicious Action is made the more odious by all its foreseen Disadvantages to the Agent, for the same reason: particularly,

Knowledge of Laws, how it affects Actions.

6. The Knowledge of a Law prohibiting an evil Action, increases the Evil by increasing the negative Interest to be subtracted; for then the ill-natur'd Inclination must be so strong as to surmount all the ||[81]Motives of Self-love, to avoid|| the Penaltys, and all the Motives of Gratitude toward the Law-giver. This is commonly call'd sinning against Conscience. [291]

7. Offices of no Toil or Expence, have little Virtue generally, because the ability is very great, and there is no contrary Interest surmounted.

8. But the refusing of them may be very vitious, as it argues an absence of good Affection, and ||⁸²often produces|| a great enough Moment of natural Evil. And,

9. In general, the fulfilling the perfect Rights of others has little Virtue in it; for thereby ||⁸³no|| Moment of Good is produc'd ||⁸⁴more than there was before||; and the Interest engaging to the Action is very great, even the avoiding all the Evils of War in a State of ||⁸⁵Nature.||

Degree of Right.

10. But the violating ||⁸⁶perfect, or even external Rights,|| is always exceedingly evil, either in the immediate, or more remote Consequences of the Action; and the selfish Motives surmounted by this vitious Inclination, are the same with those in the former Case.

11. The truest Matter of Praise are those Actions or Offices which others claim from us by an imperfect Right; and generally, the stronger their Right is, there is the less Virtue in fulfilling it, but the greater Vice in violating it. [292]

||⁸⁷Lemma. The stronger Ties of Benevolence, in equal Abilitys, must produce a greater Moment of Good, in equally good Characters, than the weaker Ties. Thus, natural Affection, Gratitude, Friendship, have greater Effects than general Benevolence. Hence,||

Strength of Ties.

12. In equal Moments of Good produc'd by two Agents, when one acts from general ||⁸⁸Benevolence||, and the other from a nearer Tie; there is greater Virtue in the Agent, who produces equal Good from the ||⁸⁹weaker|| Attachment, and less Virtue, where there is the ||⁹⁰stronger|| Attachment, which yet produces no ||⁹¹more||.

13. But the Omission of the good Offices of the stronger Ties, or Actions contrary to them, have greater Vice in them, than the like Omissions or Actions contrary to the weaker Ties; since our Selfishness or Malice must appear the greater, by the strength of the contrary Attachment which it surmounts. Thus, in co-operating with Gratitude, natural Affection, or Friendship, we evidence less Virtue in any given Moment of Good produc'd, than in equally important Actions of general Benevolence: But Ingratitude to a Benefactor, Negligence of the Interests of a Friend, or Relation; or Returns of evil Offices, are

vastly more [293] odious, than equal negligence, or evil Offices toward Strangers.

What Offices to be prefer'd, when there appears any Opposition.

14. When we cannot at once follow two different Inclinations of Benevolence, we are to prefer gratifying the stronger Inclination; according to the wise Order of Nature, ||⁹²who|| has constituted these Attachments. Thus, we are rather to be Grateful than Liberal, rather serve a Friend, or Kinsman, than a Stranger of only equal Virtue, when we cannot do both.

||⁹³ᵃ15. Or more generally, since there can be no Right, Claim, or Obligation to Impossibilitys; when two Actions to be done by any Agent, would both tend to the good of Mankind, but they cannot be perform'd both at once; that which occasions most Good is to be done, if the Omission of the other occasions no prepollent Evil. If the omission of either, will occasion some new natural Evil, that is to be omitted, whose Omission will occasion the least Evil. Thus, if two Persons of unequal Dignity be in Danger, we are to relieve the more valuable, when we cannot relieve both. Ingratitude, as it evidences a worse Temper than neglect of Beneficence; so it raises worse Sentiments in the Benefactor, and greater Diffidence, and Suspicion of his [294] Fellow-Creatures, than an Omission of an act of Beneficence: we ought therefore to be Grateful, rather than Beneficent, when we cannot (in any particular Case) evidence both Dispositions. If omitting of one Action will occasion new positive Evil, or continuance in a State of Pain, whereas the Omission of another would only prevent some new positive Good; since a State of Pain is a greater Evil, than the absence of Good, we ||⁹⁴ᵇareᵇ|| to follow Compassion, rather than Kindness; and relieve the Distressed, rather than increase the Pleasures of the Easy; when we cannot do both at once, and other Circumstances of the Objects are equal. In such Cases, we should not suppose contrary Obligations, or Dutys; the more important Office is our present Duty, and the Omission of the less important inconsistent Office at present, is no moral Evil.ᵃ||

The Original of Government.

||⁹⁵ᵃX. From Art. vii. ⁹⁶ᵇ it follows, "That all human Power, or Authority, must consist in a Right transferr'd to any Person or Council, to dispose of the alienable Rights of others; and that consequently, there can be no Government so absolute, as to have even an external Right to do or com-

mand every thing." For wherever any Invasion is made upon unalienable Rights, there must arise either a perfect, or external Right to Resistance. [295] The only Restraints of a moral Kind upon Subjects in such cases, are, when they foresee that, thro their want of Force, they shall probably by Resistance occasion greater Evils to the Publick, than those they attempt to remove; or when they find that Governours, in the main very useful to the Publick, have ||^{97c}by^c|| some unadvised Passion, done an Injury too small to overbalance the Advantages of their Administration, or the Evils which Resistance would in all likelihood occasion; especially when the Injury is of a private Nature, and not likely to be made a Precedent to the ruin of others. Unalienable Rights are essential Limitations in all Governments.

But by absolute Government, either in Prince, or Council, or in both jointly, we understand a Right to dispose of the natural Force, and Goods of a whole People, as far as they are naturally alienable, according to the Prudence of the Prince, Council, or of both jointly, for the publick Good of the State||^{98d}, or whole People^d||; without any Reservation as to the Quantity of ||^{99e}the^e|| Goods, manner of Levying, or the proportion of the Labours of the Subject, which they shall demand. But in all States this tacit Trust is presuppos'd, "that the Power ||^{100f}conferr'd^f|| shall be employ'd according to the best Judgment of the Rulers for the publick Good." So that [296] whenever the Governours openly profess a Design of ||^{101g}distroying^g|| the State, or act in such a manner as will necessarily do it; the essential Trust suppos'd in all ||^{102h}conveyance of Civil Power^h||, is violated, and the Grant thereby made void.

Absolute Government.

A Prince, or Council, or both jointly, may be variously Limited; either when the consent of the one may be necessary to the validity of the Acts of the other; or when, in the very Constitution of this supreme Power, certain Affairs are expresly exempted from the Jurisdiction of the Prince, or Council, ||^{103i}or both^i|| jointly: as when several independent States uniting, form a general Council, from whose Cognizance they expresly reserve certain Privileges, in the very Formation of this Council; or when in the very Constitution of any State, a certain Method of Election of the Person of the Prince, or of the Members of the supreme Council is determin'd, and the Intention of their Assembling declar'd. In all such

Limited Government.

cases, it is not in the Power of such Prince, Council, or both jointly, to alter the very Form of Government, or to take away that Right which the People have to be govern'd in such a manner, by a Prince, or Council thus elected, without the universal Consent of the very People who have subjected themselves to this Form of [297] Government. So that there may be a very regular State, where there is no universal absolute Power, lodg'd either in one Person, or Council, or in any other Assembly beside that of the whole People associated into that State. To say, that upon a Change attempted in the very Form of ‖ [104j] the[j] ‖ Government, by the supreme Power, the People have no Remedy according to the Constitution itself, will not prove that the supreme Power has such a Right; unless we confound all Ideas of Right with those of external Force. The only Remedy indeed in that Case, is an universal Insurrection against such perfidious Trustees.

The nature of despotick Power.

Despotick Power, is that which Persons injur'd may acquire over those Criminals, whose Lives, consistently with the publick Safety, they may prolong, that by their Labours they may repair the Damages they have done; or over those who stand oblig'd to a greater Value, than all their Goods and Labours can possibly amount to. This Power itself, is limited to the Goods and Labours only of the Criminals or Debtors; and includes no Right to Tortures, Prostitution, or any Rights of the Governed which are naturally Unalienable; or to any thing which is not of some Moment ‖ [105k] toward Repair[k] ‖ of Damage, Payment of Debt, or Security against future Offences. The Characteristick of de-[298]spotick Power, is this, "that it is solely intended for the good of the Governours, without any tacit Trust of consulting the good of the Governed." Despotick Government, in this Sense, is ‖ [106l] directly[l] ‖ inconsistent with the Notion of Civil Government.

From the Idea of Right, as above explain'd, we must necessarily conclude, "that there can be no Right, or Limitation of Right, inconsistent with, or opposite to the greatest publick Good." And therefore in Cases of extreme Necessity, when the State cannot otherwise be preserv'd from Ruin, it must certainly be Just and Good in limited Governours, or in any other Persons who can do it, to use the Force of the State for its own preservation, beyond the Limits fix'd by the Constitution, in some transitory acts, which are not to be made Precedents. And on the other hand, when an equal Necessity to avoid Ruin requires it, the Subjects may justly resume the Powers ordinarily lodg'd in their Governours, or may counteract them. This Privilege of flagrant Necessity, we all allow in defence of the most perfect private Rights: And if publick Rights are of more extensive Importance, so are also publick Necessitys. These Necessitys must be very grievous and flagrant, otherwise they can never over-ballance the Evils of vio-[299]lating a tolerable Constitution, by an arbitrary act of Power, on the one hand; or by an Insurrection, or Civil War, on the other. No Person, or State can be happy, where they do not think their important Rights are $\|$[107m]secur'd[m]$\|$ from the Cruelty, Avarice, Ambition, or Caprice of their Governours. Nor can any Magistracy be safe, or effectual for the ends of its Institution, where there are frequent Terrors of Insurrections. Whatever temporary acts therefore may be allow'd in extraordinary Cases; whatever may be lawful in the transitory act of a bold Legislator, who without previous Consent should rescue a slavish Nation, and place their Affairs so in the Hands of a Person, or Council, elected, or limited by themselves, that they should soon have confidence in their own Safety, and in the Wisdom of the Administration; yet, as to the fixed State which should ordinarily obtain in all Communitys, since no $\|$[108n]Assumer[n]$\|$ of Government, can so demonstrate his superior Wisdom or Goodness to the satisfaction and security of the Governed, as is necessary to their Happiness; this must follow,[a]$\|$ "That except when Men, for their own Interest, or out of $\|$[109]publick Love$\|$, have by Consent subjected their Actions, or their Goods within certain Limits to the $\|$[110]Disposal$\|$ of others; no Mortal can have a Right from his superior Wisdom, or [300] Goodness, or any other Quality, to give Laws to others without their Consent, express or tacit; or to dispose of the Fruits of their Labours, or of any other Right whatsoever." $\|$[111]And therefore superior Wisdom, or Goodness, gives no Right to Men to govern others.[b]$\|$

But then with relation to the Deity, suppos'd omniscient and benevolent, and secure from Indigence, the ordinary Cause of Injurys toward others; it must be amiable in such a Being, to assume the Government of weak, inconstant Creatures, often misled by Selfishness; and to give

Divine Government founded on Wisdom and Goodness.

them Laws. To these Laws every Mortal should submit from publick Love, as being contriv'd for the Good of the Whole, and for the greatest private Good consistent with it; and ‖ [112] every one may be sure, that he shall be better directed how to attain these Ends by the Divine Laws, than by his own greatest Prudence and‖ Circumspection. Hence we imagine, "That a good and wise God must have a perfect Right to govern the Universe; and that all Mortals are oblig'd to universal Obedience."

Divine Justice what.   The Justice of the Deity is only a Conception of his universal impartial Benevolence, as it shall influence him, if he gives any Laws, to attemper them to the universal Good, and inforce them with the [301] most effectual Sanctions of Rewards and Punishments.

Creation not the Ground of God's Dominion.   [113]XI. Some imagine that the Property the Creator has in all his Works, must be the true Foundation of his Right to govern. [ii] Among Men indeed, we find it necessary for the publick Good, that none should arbitrarily dispose of the Goods, acquir'd by the Labour of another, which we call his Property; and hence we imagine that Creation is the only Foundation of God's Dominion. But if the Reason‖ [114]*‖ of establishing the Rights of Property does not hold against a perfectly wise and benevolent Being, I see no Reason why Property should be necessary to his Dominion. ‖ [115]Now‖ the Reason does not hold: For an infinitely wise and good Being, could never ‖ [116]employ his assumed Authority to‖ counteract the universal Good. The tie of Gratitude is stronger indeed than bare Benevolence; and therefore supposing two equally wise and good Beings, the one our Creator, and the other not, we ‖ [117]should‖ think our selves more oblig'd to obey our Creator. But supposing our Creator malicious, [118] and a good Being condescending to rescue us, or govern us better, with sufficient Power to accomplish his kind Intentions; his Right to govern would be perfectly good. But [302] this is rather matter of curious Speculation than Use; since both Titles of Benevo-

---

ii. Compare John Locke's criticism of Robert Filmer in *Two Treatises of Government*, Treatise 1, vol. 5, chap. 3, pp. 222ff., from *The Works of John Locke*, 10 vols. (London, 1823).

* See Art. 10. Par. 6. of this Section.

lence and Property concur in the one only true Deity, as far as we can know, join'd with infinite Wisdom and Power.

[119]XII. If it be here enquir'd, "Could not the Deity have given us a different or contrary determination of Mind, viz. to approve Actions upon another Foundation than Benevolence?" ||[120]It is certain, there is|| nothing in this surpassing the natural Power of the Deity. But as in the first Treatise,* we resolv'd the Constitution of our present Sense of Beauty into the divine Goodness, so with much more obvious Reason may we ascribe the present Constitution of our moral Sense to his Goodness. For if the Deity be really benevolent, ||[122]or delights in|| the Happiness of others, he could not rationally act otherwise, or give us a moral Sense upon another Foundation, without counteracting his own benevolent Intentions. For, ||[123]even|| upon the Supposition of a contrary Sense, every rational Being must ||[124]still|| have been solicitous in some degree about his own external Happiness: Reflection on the Circumstances of Mankind in this World would have suggested, ||[125]that|| universal Benevolence and a social Temper, ||[126]or a certain Course of external|| Actions, [303] would most effectually promote the external Good of every one, according to the Reasonings of Cumberland and Puffendorf; while at the same time this perverted Sense of Morality would have made us uneasy in such a Course, and inclin'd us to the quite contrary, viz. Barbarity, Cruelty, and Fraud; and universal War, according to Mr. ||[127]Hobbs||,[iii] would really have been our natural State; so that in every Action we must have been distracted by two contrary Principles, and perpetually miserable, and dissatisfy'd when we follow'd the Directions of either.

Our Moral Sense the Effect of the Divine Goodness.

[128]XIII. It has ||[129]often been|| taken for granted in these Papers, "That the Deity is morally good;" tho the Reasoning is not at all built upon this Supposition. If we ||[130]enquire into|| the Reason of the great Agreement of Mankind in this Opinion, we shall perhaps find no demon-

Whence this universal Opinion of the Divine Goodness.

* Sect. viii. Art. 2. ||[121]Prop.|| 5.
    iii. Hobbes, *Leviathan*, pt. 1, chaps. 13, 14, 15; pt. 2, chap. 17; in *The English Works of Thomas Hobbes of Malmesbury; now first collected and edited by Sir William Molesworth*, vol. 3 (London, 1839; Scientia Verlag Aalen, 1966).

strative Arguments à priori, from the Idea of an Independent Being, to prove his Goodness. But there is abundant Probability, deduc'd from the whole Frame of Nature, which seems, as far as we know, plainly contriv'd for the Good of the Whole; and the casual Evils seem the necessary Concomitants of some Mechanism design'd for ||[131]vastly|| prepollent Good. ||[132]Nay||, this very moral Sense, implanted in rational Agents, to ||[133]delight in||, and admire whatever Actions flow from a [304] Study of the Good of others, is one of the strongest Evidences of Goodness in the Author of Nature.

[134]But these Reflections are ||[135]no way|| so universal as the Opinion, nor are they often inculcated ||[136]by any one||. What then more probably leads Mankind into that Opinion, is this. The obvious Frame of the World gives us Ideas of boundless Wisdom and Power in its Author. Such a Being we cannot conceive indigent, and must conclude happy, and in the best State possible, since he can still gratify himself. The best State of rational Agents, and their greatest and most worthy Happiness, we are necessarily led to imagine must consist in universal efficacious Benevolence: and hence we conclude the Deity benevolent in the most universal impartial manner. Nor can we well imagine what else deserves the Name of Perfection ||[137]but|| Benevolence, and those Capacitys or Abilitys which are necessary to make it effectual; such as Wisdom, and Power: at least we can have no ||[138]other valuable|| Conception of it.

FINIS.

TEXTUAL NOTES

Title Page

1. A1, A3: In which the principles of the late Earl of Shaftesbury are Explain'd and Defended, against the Author of the *Fable of the Bees:* and the Ideas of Moral Good and Evil are establish'd, according to the Sentiments of the Antient Moralists. With an Attempt to introduce a Mathematical Calculation in Subjects of Morality.

2. Not in A.

Dedication

3. Dedication not in A.

4. Omitted in D (p. vi).

Preface

5. A (p. iv): set

6. A (p. iv): about

7. In C and D always *farther* instead of *further.* Exception: *further* at the beginning of a paragraph (C and D, p. 20 and p. 57).

8. A (p. iv): latter to be more

9. A (p. iv): these

10. A (p. iv): about

11. A (p. iv): see Reason to imagine

12. D2, D3 [Corrigenda, p. 309]: are few Objects which are

13. A (p. v): shall find

14. C (p. xiii), D (p. xiii): commonly call

15. D2, D3 [Corrigenda, p. 309]: certain complex Forms

16. C (p. xiii), D (p. xiii): approve

17. C (p. xiv), D (p. xiv): Infirmities

18. A (p. vii): of Mankind could have

19. A (p. vii): may shew

20. D2, D3 [Corrigenda, p. 309]: some

21. C (p. xiv), D (p. xiv): He has given us strong Affections to be the Springs of each virtuous Action; and made Virtue a lovely Form, that we might easily distinguish it from its Contrary, and be made happy by the Pursuit of it.

22. A (p. vii): they are

23. D2, D3 (p. xv): private Interest

24. New paragraph in D2, D3 (p. xv).

25. D2, D3 (p. xv): It will perhaps be found, that the greater Part of the Ingenious Arts are calculated to please some Natural Powers, pretty different either from what we commonly call Reason, or the External Senses.

26. A (p. viii): is it

27. A (p. viii): perhaps will

28. A (p. viii): And we find to the full

29. D2, D3 (p. xvi): this

30. Not in A (p. viii).

31. A (p. ix): and thence

32. A (p. ix): do reflect

33. A (p. ix): And hence

34. A (p. ix): is full as

35. C (p. xvii), D (p. xvii): tho' these Objects present themselves to our Observation sooner than the other.

36. A (pp. ix–xi): Were not the Author diffident of his own Performance, as too inconsiderable to have any great Names mention'd in it, he would have publickly acknowledg'd his Obligations to a certain Lord (whose Name would have had no small Authority [x] with the learned World) for admitting him into his Acquaintance, and giving him some Remarks in Conversation, which have very much improv'd these Papers beyond what they were at first. The Author might have found good Materials for a modern Dedication from the active parts of his Life, as well as from his Learning and Reflection; but he knows him to be one of that sort,

Cui male si palpere, recalcitrat undique tutus.*

And therefore, when they come to his Hands again, he only repeats to him the old Dedication with which he first presented them ———

———— Si quid ego adjuvero, curamve levasso,
Si quae te coquat, aut verset in pectore fixa,
Jam pretium tulerim.†————

The same Consideration hinders the Author from Mentioning a Clergy-man, to whom he was much oblig'd for revising these Papers, and for some valuable Remarks. That Gentleman's Character is further known for every Quality becoming [xi] his Office, than the Author can well presume his Papers ever shall be; and therefore he thinks he can do him no honour by mentioning him.

*Hor. Lib. 2. Sat. I. v. 20. [Translation: "Who, being flattered clumsily, kicks back, protected from all sides."]

†Cicero de Senectute, in initio. [Editor's note: The exact quotation does not exist in any known Cicero text. The original lines read as follows: "si quid ego adiuero curamve levasso quae nunc te coquit et versat in pectore fixa, ecquid erit praemi." Translation: "should some aid of mine dispel / The cares that now within thy bosom dwell / And wring thy heart and torture thee with pain, / What then would be the measure of thy gain." (Cicero, De senectute, De amicitia, De divinatione, with an English translation by William Armistad Falconer, Cambridge, Mass.: Harvard University Press, 1971, p. 8.)]

37. A (p. xi): the Author's Performance, he

38. Not in A (p. xi). C (pp. xxi–xxii), D1 (p. xxi–xxii), D2, D3 (p. xxi): In [C (p. xxi): this third Edition] [D1 (p. xxi): this Edition] [D2, D3 (p. xxi): the later Editions], what Alterations are made, are partly owing to the Objections of some Gentlemen, who wrote very keenly against several Principles in this Book. The Author was convinc'd of some inaccurate Expressions, which are now alter'd; and some Arguments, he hopes, are now made clearer: but he has not yet seen Cause to renounce any of the Principles maintain'd in it. Nor is there any thing of Consequence added, except in Sect. II. of Treatise 2d; and the same Reasoning is found in Sect. I. of the Essay on the Passions.

D1 (p. xxi): In this [C (p. xxi): Third] [D2, D3 (p. xxi): 4th] Edition there are Additions interspersed, to prevent Objections which have been published against this Scheme by several Authors; and some Mathematical Expressions are left out, which upon second Thoughts, appear'd useless, and were disagreeable to some Readers.

Contents

39. C and D: relative or comparative

Treatise I, Section I

1. Divisional title page not in C and D.

2. D (p. 1): An Inquiry into the Original of our Ideas of Beauty and Virtue. Treatise I. Of Beauty, Order, Harmony, Design.

3. In A: Arabic numerals in Treatise I.

4. A (p. 1): that

5. In A: No marginal headings in Treatise I and Treatise II.

6. C (p. 2), D (p. 2): great

7. A (p. 2): that

8. Omitted in C (p. 2), D (p. 2).

9. D2, D3 [Corrigenda, p. 309]: Corporeal Substances

10. D2, D3 [Corrigenda, p. 309]: raise a clear enough Idea

11. A (p. 3): that

12. A (p. 3): he has not received any of these Ideas, or wants the Senses necessary for the Perception of them, no Definition can ever raise in him any Idea of that Sense in which he is deficient.

13. A (pp. 3–4): articles V and VI are interchanged. Instructions for alteration already in *Alterations and Additions* (p. 3).

14. Not in A (p. 4).

15. Not in A (p. 4).

16. Not in A (p. 4). Instructions for alteration already in *Alterations and Additions* (p. 3).

17. Not in A (p. 4).

18. Not in A (p. 5), C (p. 5).

19. A (p. 5): Aversion to

20. Omitted in C (p. 5), D (p. 5).

21. Not in A (p. 5).

22. A (p. 5): towards

23. Not in A (p. 5).

24. Addition already in *Alterations and Additions* (p. 3).

25. *Alterations and Additions* (p. 3): will

26. A (p. 5): in our Dress, and some other Affairs; and yet this may arise from a like accidental Conjunction of Ideas: as for instance,

27. D2, D3 [Corrigenda, p. 309]: including

28. Deleted in B [Errata, p. xxvi], C (p. 5), D (p. 6).

29. D2, D3 [Corrigenda, p. 310]: appears no

30. Not in A (p. 6).

31. Not in A (p. 6).

32. A (p. 6): that

33. C (p. 6), D (p. 6): many

34. C (p. 6), D (p. 6): far

35. A (p. 6): rising

36. Not in A (p. 7).

37. A (p. 8): relish

38. A (p. 8): wou'd

39. A (p. 8): Affairs

40. New paragraph added in D2, D3 (p. 9): We generally imagine the brute Animals endowed with the same sort of Powers of Perception as our External Senses, and having sometimes greater Acuteness in them: but we conceive few or none of them with any of these sublimer Powers of Perception here call'd Internal Senses; or at least if some of them have them, it is in a Degree much inferior to ours.

41. C (p. 9), D (p. 9): hereafter

42. D2, D3 (p. 10): Let one consider, first, That 'tis probable a Being may have the full Power of External Sensation, which we enjoy, so as to perceive each Colour, Line, Surface, as we do; yet, without the Power of comparing, or of discerning the Similitudes or Proportions: Again, It might discern these also, and yet have no Pleasure or Delight Accompanying these Perceptions. The bare Idea of the Form is something separable from Pleasure, as may appear from the different Tastes of men about the Beauty of Forms, where we don't imagine that they differ in any Ideas, either of the Primary or Secundary Qualities. Similitude, Proportion, Analogy, or Equality of Proportion, are Objects of the Understanding, and must be actually known before we know the natural Causes of our Pleasure. But Pleasure perhaps is not necessarily connected with the Perception of them: and may be felt where the Proportion is not known or attended to: and may not be felt where the Proportion is observed.

43. A (p. 9): imagine to be in

44. C (p. 10): much

45. A (p. 9): Sense

46. Not in A (p. 9).

47. A (p. 9): to receive

48. D2, D3 (p. 10): may often

49. Not in A (p. 10).

50. D2, D3 (p. 11): not numbered.

51. D2, D3 (p. 11): is different

52. D2, D3 (p. 11): we are struck at the first with the

53. Footnote in A (p. 10): *See above, Art. 5.

54. D2, D3 (p. 11): may bring along that peculiar kind of Pleasure, which attends

55. D2, D3 (p. 11): numbered XIII.

56. Not in A (p. 10).

57. D2, D3 (p. 12): numbered XIV.

58. Omitted in C (p. 12), D (p. 12).

59. A (p. 11): of even

60. Omitted in C (p. 13), D (p. 13).

61. Omitted in C (p. 13), D (p. 13).

62. D2, D3 (p. 13): but cannot

63. A (p. 12): Meats

64. A (p. 12): that were

65. C (p. 13), D (p. 13): The same holds true of

66. C (p. 13), D (p. 13): Interest

67. Omitted in C (p. 13), D (p. 13).

68. D2, D3 (p. 13): numbered XV.

69. Omitted in D2, D3 (p. 13).

70. A (p. 12): that

71. C (p. 13), D1 (p. 13): And Custom, Education, or Example, could never

D2, D3 (pp. 13–14): 'Tis true, what chiefly pleases in the Countenance, are the Indications of Moral Dispositions; and yet were we by the longest Acquaintance fully convinc'd of the best Moral Dispositions in any Person, with that Countenance we now think deform'd, this would never hinder our immediate Dislike of the Form, or our liking other Forms more: And Custom, Education, or Example, [p. 14] could never

72. A (p. 13): 6

73. XVI.

74. D2, D3 (p. 14): Beauty, in Corporeal Forms,

75. A (p. 13): noted

76. A (p. 13): that

77. A (p. 13): Heat

78. A (p. 13): that

79. C (p. 13), D (p. 14): otherwise

80. A (p. 14): that

81. A (p. 14): Pleasure as
82. Omitted in D2, D3 (p. 15).

Treatise I, Section II

1. A (p. 15): that
2. A (p. 15): that
3. Not in A (p. 15).
4. C (p. 16), D (p. 16): for there are many
5. C (p. 16), D (p. 16): and yet
6. Omitted in C (p. 16), D (p. 16).
7. A (p. 15): that
8. A (p. 16): that
9. A (p. 16): that shall be touched at* afterwards. [Same footnote.]
10. D2, D3 [Corrigenda, p. 310]: may seem probable, and hold pretty generally.
11. Not in A (p. 18). Instruction for addition already in *Alterations and Additions* (p. 4).
12. A (p. 17): which yet is
13. Not in C (p. 18), D (p. 18).
14. C (p. 19), D (p. 19): former
15. Omitted in C (p. 19), D (p. 19).
16. Omitted in C (p. 19), D (p. 19).
17. C (p. 19), D (p. 19): surprizing
18. Not in A (p. 18).
19. A (pp. 18–19): the [19] Structure, and Order
20. C (p. 20), D (p. 20): great
21. A (p. 19): and
22. No new paragraph in A (p. 19).
23. C (p. 21), D (p. 21): Thus
24. A (p. 20): various
25. C (p. 22), D (p. 22): great
26. C (p. 22), D (p. 22): how near the
27. C (p. 22), D (p. 22): in brackets.
28. D2, D3 [Corrigenda, p. 310]: minuter Parts, even of those,
29. Not in A (p. 21).
30. C (p. 22), D (p. 22): a very great
31. C (p. 22), D (p. 22): great

32. A (p. 21): or Leaf

33. Not in A (p. 21).

34. A (p. 21): shall spring

35. A (p. 21): shall sprout

36. C (p. 23), D (p. 23): each

37. Not in A (p. 22).

38. C (p. 23), D (p. 23): surprizing

39. A (p. 22): that

40. C (p. 24), D (p. 24): how universal is that Beauty which

41. Not in A (p. 23).

42. C (p. 25), D (p. 25): Mind. In Motion there is also a natural Beauty, when at fixed Periods like Gestures and Steps are regularly repeated, suiting the Time and Air of Music, which is observed in regular Dancing.

43. Not in A (p. 24).

44. C (p. 26), D (p. 26): great

45. C (p. 26), D (p. 26): considerable

46. D2, D3 [Corrigenda, p. 310]: and frequently

47. A (p. 25): Chords

48. A (p. 26): every second Vibration [Instruction for alteration already in *Alterations and Additions* (p. 4).]

49. A (p. 26): Chords. Now good Compositions, beside the Frequency of these Chords, must retain a general Unity of Key, an Uniformity among the Parts in Bars, Risings, Fallings, Closes. The Necessity of this will appear, by observing the Dissonance which would arise from tacking Parts of different Tunes together as one, altho both were separately agreeable. A greater

50. Instruction for addition already in *Alterations and Additions* (p. 4).

51. *Alterations and Additions* (p. 4): an artificial

52. Not in A (p. 26), and no new paragraph. Instruction for addition already in *Alterations and Additions* (pp. 4–5).

53. Not in *Alterations and Additions* (p. 4).

54. A (p. 26): afterwards

55. New footnote in D2, D3 (p. 29): *There is nothing singular in applying the Word Beauty to Sounds. The Antients observe the peculiar Dignity of the Senses of Seeing and Hearing, that in their Objects we discern the καλὸν [beauty], which we don't ascribe to the Objects of the other Senses.

56. D1 (p. 29): the
    D2, D3 (p. 29): these

Treatise I, Section III

1. A (p. 27): because

2. D2, D3 (p. 30): a Multitude

3. Omitted in D (p. 31).

4. A (p. 28, wrongly numbered p. 21): Thus also one Fluxional Calculation shall determine the Tangents of all Algebraick Curves; of these Curves there are infinite Orders and Species possible[,] of each Species infinite Sizes, or Magnitudes of Areas, of each Size infinite Individuals, of each Individual Curve an Infinity of Points, from which Tangents may be drawn. But all these Infinitys of Infinites are exactly comprehended in the general Theorem, which fixes the Lengths of the Subtangents, or their Proportion to the Abscissa. [Instruction for alteration already in *Alterations and Additions* (p. 5).]

5. D2, D3 (p. 31): find a like

6. D2, D3 (p. 31): many

7. D2, D3 (p. 31): innumerable

8. A (p. 28, wrongly numbered p. 21): which we are in [Omitted in D2, D3 (p. 31).]

9. D2, D3 (p. 31): are only

10. D1 (p. 32): make
    D2, D3 (p. 32): take

11. A (p. 29): Because however

12. A (p. 29): does contain

13. A (p. 29), C (p. 32), D (p. 32): of

14. D1 (p. 32): or
    D2, D3 (p. 32): and

15. Paragraph not in A (p. 29). Instruction for addition of this paragraph already in *Alterations and Additions* (pp. 5–6).

16. *Alterations and Additions* (p. 5): does also bisect

17. *Alterations and Additions* (p. 6): also

18. *Alterations and Additions* (p. 6): Joy

19. C (p. 33), D (p. 33): Truth. Another kind of Surprize in certain Theorems increases our Pleasure above that we have in Theorems of greater Extent; when we discover a general Truth, which upon some confused Notion we had reputed false: as that *Asymptotes always approaching should never meet the Curve.* This is like the Joy of unexpected Advantage where we dreaded Evil. But still the Unity of many Particulars in the general Theorem is necessary to give Pleasure in any Theorem.

20. A (p. 29): which cannot be omitted; which is this [Omitted in C (p. 34), D1 (p. 34), D2, D3 (p. 33).]

21. A (p. 29): shall contain

22. C (p. 34), D1 (p. 34), D2, D3 (p. 33): great

23. D2, D3 (p. 33): there are some leading, or fundamental Propertys, upon which a long Series of theorems can be naturally built

24. Not in D2, D3 (p. 34).

25. Not in A (p. 30).

26. D2, D3 (p. 34): others in higher Parts of Geometry

27. No new paragraph in A (p. 30), D2, D3 (p. 34).

28. D2, D3 (p. 34): What is the Aim of our ingenious Geometers? A continual Inlargement of theorems, or making them extensive, shewing how what was formerly known of one Figure extends to many others, to Figures very unlike the former in Appearance.

29. A (p. 31): Advantage in Life

30. A (p. 31): besides

31. A (p. 31): Whimsys

32. C (p. 35), D (p. 35): an Affectation

33. D2, D3 (p. 35): pleaded

34. D2, D3 (p. 35): boasts

35. Without footnote in A (p. 31). Omitted in D2, D3 (p. 35).

36. D2, D3 (p. 35): see

37. A (p. 32): Dr. Cumberland has taken a great deal of needless Pains to reduce the Laws of Nature to one general practical Proposition; and how

38. D2, D3 (p. 35): does Puffendorf

39. A (p. 32): As if they had not been better drawn, each respectively, from their immediate Sources, viz. Religion, Self-Love, and Sociableness.

40. Omitted in D2, D3 (p. 35).

41. C (p. 36), D1 (p. 36), D2, D3 (p. 35): perceive the Beauty of

42. A (p. 32): notwithstanding the Contortions of Common Sense they may be led into by pursuing it

D2, D3 (p. 36): since they are led into unnatural Deductions by pursuing it too far

43. D2, D3 (p. 36) add note: *Aristotle (*Ethic. Nicom.* I. ro. c. 3. [NE, X 2, 1174a 4–8]) justly observes, that we have certain natural Propensitys to certain Actions, or to the Exercise of certain natural Powers, without a View to, or Intention of, obtaining those Pleasures which naturally accompany them. Περὶ πολλὰ σπουδὴν ποιησαίμεθα ἄν, καὶ εἰ μηδεμίαν ἐπιφέροι ἡδονήν, οἷον

ὁρᾶν, μνημονεύειν, εἰδέναι, τὰς ἀρετὰς ἔχειν· εἰ δ' ἐξ ἀνάγκης ἕπονται του-
τοις ἡδοναί, οὐδὲν διαφέρει· ἑλοίμεθα γὰρ ἂν ταῦτα, καὶ εἰ μὴ γένοιτ' ἂν ἀπ'
αὐτῶν ἡδονή. [Translation: "Also there are many things which we should be
eager to possess even if they brought us no pleasure, for instance sight, memory, knowledge, virtue. It may be the case that these things are necessarily
attended by pleasure, but that makes no difference; for we should desire them
even if no pleasure resulted from them." Aristotle, *Nicomachean Ethics,* with
an English translation by H. Rackham (Cambridge, Mass.: Harvard University Press, 1975), p. 588.]

44. A (p. 33): that

45. Article not in A (p. 33), C (p. 37), D1 (p. 37), D2, D3 (pp. 36–37). Instruction for addition of the entire paragraph (without numeration and without footnote) already in *Alterations and Additions* (pp. 6–7).

46. A (p. 33): wrongly numbered VI. In C (p. 37), D (p. 37): numbered
VII.

47. Not in A (p. 33).

48. A (p. 33): to be constantly

49. C (p. 37), D (p. 37): great

50. Not in A (p. 34).

51. D2, D3 (p. 38): the

52. A (p. 34): numbered VII; C (p. 38), D (p. 38): numbered VIII.

53. A (p. 34): shall appear

Treatise I, Section IV

1. No new paragraph in A (p. 35).

2. C (p. 40), D (p. 40): represented. Nay, perhaps the Novelty may
make us prefer the Representation of Irregularity.

3. Omitted in D2, D3 [Corrigenda, p. 310].

4. A (p. 36): not out of choice

5. A (p. 36): the finest Characters possible for Virtue

6. B [Errata, p. xxvi]: whom

7. D1, D2, D3 (p. 41): Simile

8. D1, D2, D3 (p. 41): Similes

9. B [Errata, p. xxvi]: of those which seem very remote
C (p. 42), D (p. 42): of those which are very different from each other

10. Not in A (p. 38).

11. D (p. 43): of

12. B [Errata, p. xxvi], C (p. 43): Artificers

    D (p. 43): Artificer

13. B [Errata, p. xxvi]: them

    C (p. 43), D (p. 43): him

14. A (p. 39): Work

15. A (p. 41): We may only here observe the Pleasure which any one shall receive from

16. A (p. 41): as also that pleasant Sensation he shall have

17. New footnote in D2, D3 [Corrigenda, pp. 305–6]: *'Tis surprising to see the ingenious Author of *Alciphron*[i] alledging, that all Beauty observed is solely some Use perceived or imagined; for no other Reason than this, that the Apprehension of the Use intended, occurs continually, when we are judging of the Forms of Chairs, Doors, Tables, and some other Things of obvious Use; and that we like those Forms most, which are fittest for the Use. Whereas we see, that in these very Things Similitude of parts is regarded, where unlike Parts would be equally useful: thus the Feet of a Chair would be of the same Use, tho' unlike, were they equally long; tho' one were strait, and the other bended; or one bending outwards, and the other inwards: A Coffin-shape for a Door would bear a more manifest Aptitude to the human Shape, than that which Artists require. And then what is the Use of these Imitations of Nature, or of its Works, in Architecture? Why should a Pillar please which has some of the Human Proportions? Is the End or Use of a Pillar the same as of a Man? Why the Imitation of other natural or well-proportioned Things in the Entablature? Is there then a Sense of Imitation, relishing it where there is no other Use than this, that it naturally pleases? Again; Is no Man pleased with the Shapes of any Animals, but those which he expects Use from? The Shapes of the Horse or the Ox may promise [306] Use to the Owner; but is he the only Person who relishes the Beauty? And is there no Beauty discerned in Plants, in Flowers, in Animals, whose Use is to us unknown? But what is still more surprising, is his representing Aristotle as giving the ἐπαινετόν [laudable], for the Notion of the καλὸν [beauty]: when he has so often told us, "that the καλὸν is prior to it; that we love Praise from others, as it gives Testimony to, and confirms our Opinion of, our being possessed of Virtue, or the καλὸν; and that the superior Excellency of this, which we antecedently perceive, is the Reason why we love Praise." See *Ethic. Ad Nicom.* Lib. i. c. 5.[ii] and often elsewhere. 'Tis true that the καλὸν is laudable, and, as Plato asserts, all-wise, ἡδὺ, καὶ ὠφέλιμον [the pleasant and the profitable] at last; and so does every one maintain who asserts a Moral Sense, in that very As-

sertion. And yet the Doctor has found out the Art of making this an Objection to Moral Sense.

i. George Berkeley, *Alciphron, or The Minute Philosopher,* in *The Works of George Berkeley,* ed. A. A. Luce and T. E. Jessop, vol. 3 (London, 1950), Third Dialogue, sects. 4–12, pp. 118–32.

ii. Hutcheson paraphrases Aristotle and Plato using another paraphrase in Berkeley's *Alciphron,* p. 118. The passage indicated reads "men's motive in pursuing honour seems to be to assure themselves of their own merit." (Aristotle, *Nicomachean Ethics,* trans. and ed. H. Rackham [Cambridge, Mass.: Harvard University Press, 1937], p. 15; NE I 3, 1095b 22ff.); compare Plato, *Alcibiades,* II, 145c.

Treatise I, Section V

1. A (p. 42): antecedently
2. A (p. 42): may possibly
3. A (p. 42): do not seem
4. C (p. 46), D (p. 46): hereafter
5. A (p. 42): possible,
6. A (p. 43): This Expression is taken from the Cartesian Scheme, in which the Author of Nature is supposed to have designedly impress'd a general Force or *Conatus ad motum* upon the Mass of Matter, without any Direction whatsoever. This nonsensical Notion did so much prevail, and men have so many confused Conceptions of Nature and Chance, as real Beings operating without Wisdom or Design, that it may be useful to shew that their very absurd Postulatum is wholly insufficient, tho it were granted them, to answer the Appearances in the Regularity of the World. And this is what is attempted in the first fourteen Articles of this Section.
7. B [Errata, p. xxvi], C (p. 47), D (p. 47): The
8. D2, D3 [Corrigenda, p. 310]: below our Notice
9. Deleted in B [Errata, p. xxvi]. Printed again in C (p. 47), D (p. 47): possible
10. Not in A (p. 43).
11. A (p. 43): It is also certain that there is
12. A (p. 43): may
13. A (p. 44): shall be
14. A (p. 44): shall
15. No new paragraph in A (p. 44).
16. A (p. 44): Positions
17. A (p. 45): and hence

18. Not in A (p. 45).

19. A (p. 45): Whereas if different Senses of Beauty be in other Agents,

20. C (p. 50), D (p. 50): not immediately

21. Omitted in C (p. 50), D (p. 50).

22. A (p. 46): offered

23. A (p. 46): cubick Inches solid Content
    C (p. 51), D (p. 51): Parts whose solid Contents were each a cubick
Inch

24. A (p. 47): that

25. A (p. 47): meet

26. A (p. 47): Design as producing them,

27. A (p. 47): the

28. C (p. 51), D (p. 51): not

29. A (p. 47): are an infinity of other Forms possible, we could only expect from the casual Concourse of such a Mass as was suppos'd in the last
Case, one Prism of any Kind, since there are an Infinity of other Solids
possible

30. A (p. 47): Presumption for

31. A (p. 48): in this Affair but an undirected Force of Attraction
suppos'd

32. A (p. 48): given to

33. A (p. 48): shall

34. A (p. 49): even after

35. Not in A (p. 49).

36. A (p. 50): as is that of

37. A (p. 50): do determine

38. A (p. 51): might possibly

39. D (p. 55): does to

40. A (p. 52): are at least still an infinity

41. D2, D3 (p. 57): in

42. Not in A (p. 53).

43. D2, D3 (p. 57): infinites

44. D2, D3 (p. 57): arising daily in such Numbers in all Parts of the Earth
with such Similarity of Structure, should be the Effect of Chance, is beyond
all Conception or Expression.

45. Not in A (p. 54).

46. C (p. 58), D (p. 58): great

47. A (p. 54): like to

48. A (p. 54): as it

49. Omitted in D2, D3 (p. 58).

50. A (p. 55), C (p. 58), D (p. 58): should

51. A (p. 55): wrongly numbered 12. The following articles of this section wrongly numbered accordingly.

52. A (p. 55): only judge

53. Omitted in C (p. 59), D (p. 59).

54. C (p. 59), D (p. 59): might be retained

55. A (p. 56): numbered 13.

56. Not in A (p. 56).

57. A (p. 56): shall

58. A (p. 56): Minutes perhaps

59. A (p. 56): also are

60. A (p. 56): varying

61. A (p. 57): numbered 14.

62. C (p. 61), D (p. 61): sensibly different gross

63. Entire article not in A (p. 58). Instruction for addition of the entire paragraph (without numeration) already in *Alterations and Additions* (pp. 7–8).

64. *Alterations and Additions* (p. 7): further

65. *Alterations and Additions* (p. 7): an

66. *Alterations and Additions* (p. 7): man

67. *Alterations and Additions* (p. 8): 1000 to 1

68. C (p. 63), D (p. 63): may

69. *Alterations and Additions* (p. 8): all moral

70. *Alterations and Additions* (p. 8): Art, or Wisdom

71. A (p. 58): numbered 15.

72. A (p. 58): when he is not

73. A (p. 59): designed plainly

74. Not in A (p. 59).

75. A (p. 59): numbered 16.

76. C (p. 65), D (p. 65): Agents

77. C (p. 65), D (p. 65): them

78. No new paragraph in A (p. 60).

79. C (p. 65), D (p. 65): great

80. A (p. 61): numbered 17.

81. Omitted in C (p. 66), D (p. 66).

82. Omitted in C (p. 66), D (p. 66).

83. D (p. 67): an Uniformity,
84. A (p. 62): numbered 18.
85. A (p. 62): may perhaps* afterwards. [Footnote identical.]
86. A (p. 62): may possibly
87. A (p. 62): numbered 19.
88. A (p. 63): And yet
89. Not in A (p. 63).
90. A (p. 64): the
91. A (p. 64): numbered 20.

Treatise I, Section VI

1. A (p. 65): the
2. A (p. 65): which
3. A (p. 65): if
4. No new paragraph in A (p. 65).
5. A (p. 66): for
6. C (p. 71), D (p. 71): now call
7. D (p. 71): a positive
8. Omitted in C (p. 72), D (p. 72).
9. A (p. 67): what were
   C (p. 72), D (p. 72): if any thing were
10. Not in A (p. 67).
11. A (p. 67): towards
12. A (p. 67): these
13. A (p. 67): in ravenous
14. A (p. 68): afterwards
15. A (p. 68), C (p. 73), D (p. 73): Swine
16. A (p. 68): there is no
17. A (p. 69): do further extend their
18. Not in A (p. 69).
19. A (p. 69): not capable
20. Not in A (p. 69).
21. A (p. 69): Conveniency
22. A (p. 69): Time and Labour
23. C (p. 75), D (p. 75): might here
24. A (p. 70): or Eyes
25. A (p. 70): be however

26. A (p. 70): often may
27. No new paragraph in A (p. 71).
28. A (p. 71): some of the
29. A (p. 71): Regularity and Beauty
30. C (p. 76), D (p. 76): our Imaginations
31. Omitted in C (p. 77), D (p. 77).
32. A (p. 73): shall
33. C (p. 78), D (p. 78): rejected
34. A (p. 74): Advantage, or
35. Not in A (p. 75).
36. A (p. 77): Key,
37. No new paragraph in A (p. 78).
38. A (p. 78): conjoin'd

Treatise I, Section VII

1. C (p. 84), D (p. 84): Species
2. A (p. 80): no Custom could
3. A (p. 80): will
4. A (p. 80): the Taste
5. A (p. 80): different Sense from what
6. A (p. 80): like such as proved
7. A (p. 81): no Custom would
8. A (p. 81): were
9. A (p. 82): could
10. A (p. 82): necessarily the
11. Not in A (p. 82).
12. A (p. 82): when in reality the Object has
13. A (p. 83): Meats
14. A (p. 83): hear perhaps
15. A (p. 83): they
16. Not in A (p. 83).
17. A (p. 83): never could
18. Not in A (p. 84).
19. A (p. 84): repeat our Attention to
20. A (p. 84): shall
21. A (p. 85): seeing them
22. A (p. 86): hence are

23. A (p. 86): which we had an Aversion to

24. A (p. 86): Sense of Beauty or Harmony naturally

25. A (p. 87): without Examination conclude,

26. A (p. 87): And often

27. Not in A (p. 87).

28. Not in A (p. 87).

29. C (p. 92), D (p. 92): a livelier

30. A (p. 87): Ideas of Beauty

31. A (p. 87): when they do not perceive them
    C (p. 92), D (p. 92): than in reality they have

Treatise I, Section VIII

1. Entire paragraph not in A (p. 89). Instruction for addition of the entire paragraph already in *Alterations and Additions* (p. 9).

2. Omitted in C (p. 94), D (p. 94).

3. *Alterations and Additions* (p. 9): greatest

4. C (p. 94), D (p. 94): are

5. Not in C (p. 94), D (p. 94).

6. A (p. 89): Effect

7. C (p. 96), D (p. 96): is imagined

8. A (p. 90): Beside

9. Omitted in C (p. 96), D (p. 96).

10. A (p. 91): fitted

11. A (p. 91): Foundations

12. No new paragraph in A (p. 91).

13. A (p. 91): of

14. C (p. 97), D (p. 97): us

15. A (p. 92): to this Manner

16. A (p. 93): Circle pretty nearly

17. C (p. 99), D (p. 99): thus also other Figures, if they have any Regularity, are in every Point determined

18. A (p. 93): the last

19. A (p. 93): but equal in Use with

20. Not in A (p. 94).

21. A (p. 94): antecedently

22. A (p. 94): between the

23. C (p. 100), D (p. 100): no immediate

24. D (p. 100): Object

25. A (p. 94): one in its own Species

26. C (p. 100), D (p. 100): far

27. A (p. 94): their peculiar Beautys, than with the Beautys of a different Species

28. Omitted in C (p. 100), D (p. 100). In D2, D3 [Corrigenda, p. 310] this footnote follows: *See Cic. *de Nat. Deor.* Lib. I. c. 27.

29. A (p. 94): . This present Constitution is much more

30. A (p. 95): singular

31. A (p. 96): not numbered.

32. A (p. 96): Diversitys

33. C (p. 102), D (p. 102): have determined

34. C (p. 102), D (p. 102): stupendous

35. A (p. 96): that manner which should be

36. A (p. 97): this in

37. A (p. 97): a further Reason from a Sense still

38. A (p. 97): nor

39. Not in A (p. 97). Instruction for addition already in *Alterations and Additions* (pp. 9–10).

40. *Alterations and Additions* (p. 10): Effect

41. Not in *Alterations and Additions* (p. 10).

42. Not in A (p. 97), C (p. 103), D (p. 103). Instruction for addition in *Alterations and Additions* (p. 10): End of the first Treatise.

Treatise II, Introduction

1. Separate leaf in B with pagination 109. Entire page omitted in C and D. D (p. 105): The title "Treatise II." is displayed on the top of the first page of the text.

2. Not in A (p. 101).

3. C (p. 104), D (p. 105): attended with Desire of the Agent's Happiness.

4. C (p. 104), D (p. 105): Condemnation or Dislike. Approbation and Condemnation are probably simple Ideas, which cannot be farther explained.

5. A (p. 101): some general Foundation of

6. C (p. 105), D (p. 106): Approbation and Good-will

7. C (p. 105), D (p. 106): these

8. Omitted in C (p. 105), D (p. 106).

9. C (p. 105), D (p. 106): Approbation or Good-will

10. C (p. 105), D (p. 106): Dislike

11. Omitted in C (p. 105), D (p. 106).

12. Omitted in A (p. 102), C (p. 105), D (p. 106).

13. A (p. 103): them

14. A (p. 103): immediately; and such

15. Not in A (p. 103).

16. C (p. 108), D (p. 109): And

17. C (p. 108), D (p. 109): arising from reflection upon

18. C (p. 108), D (p. 109): arises from Reflection upon the Action, or some other future advantage.

19. C (p. 109), D (p. 110): approve the Actions of others, and perceive them to be their Perfection and Dignity, and are determin'd to love the Agent; a like Perception we have in reflecting on such Actions of our own

20. C (p. 109), D (p. 110): That the Affection Desire, or Intention, which gains Approbation to the Actions flowing from it, is not an Intention to obtain even this sensible Pleasure [D2, D3 (Corrigenda, p. 310) substitutes "pleasant Self-Approbation" for "sensible Pleasure" and wrongly attributes the alteration to p. 109].

21. C (p. 109), D (p. 110): from Self-Love, or Desire of private Good.

Treatise II, Section I

1. C (p. 110), D (p. 111): the Sensations and Affections

2. C (p. 111), D (p. 112): approve or love

3. C (p. 111), D (p. 112): us, or to any other Person

4. C (p. 111), D (p. 112): they study the Interest, and desire the Happiness of other Beings with whom they converse. [In A the text following this passage is not an independent paragraph.]

5. A (p. 108): Esteem
   C (p. 111), D (p. 112): Approbation

6. Not in A (p. 108).

7. C (p. 111), D (p. 112): Approbation

8. A (p. 109): which

9. C (p. 112), D (p. 113): from an ultimate Desire of our Happiness, or Good-will toward us;

10. A (p. 109): independently

11. Footnote not in A (p. 109).

12. A (p. 109): or

13. C (p. 112), D (p. 113): on both Occasions

14. C (p. 113), D (p. 114): Condemnation

15. A (p. 110): done toward

16. Not in A (p. 110).

17. A (p. 110): requires

18. Not in A (p. 110).

19. A (p. 110): which do not affect our selves, but other Persons,

20. A (p. 110): pleas'd with any

21. C (p. 113), D (p. 114): merely because

22. C (p. 114), D (p. 115): an ultimate Desire of

23. C (p. 114), D (p. 115): from Ill-will, Desire of the Misery of others without view to any prevalent Good to the Publick

24. A (p. 111): that of

25. A (p. 111): beneficent Actions toward them
      C (p. 114), D (p. 115): Actions which shew Good-will toward them

26. C (p. 114), D (p. 115): which makes benevolent Actions appear Beautiful

27. C (p. 115), D (p. 116): approve or condemn

28. Not in A (p. 112).

29. Inserted here in C (p. 115), D (p. 116): Would not the Parsimony of a Miser be as advantageous to his Heir, as the Generosity of a worthy Man is to his Friend? And cannot we as easily imagine ourselves Heirs to Misers, as the Favourites of Heroes? Why don't we then approve both alike?

30. Not in A (p. 112).

31. D2, D3 [Corrigenda, pp. 306–7] add: As Mr. Hobbes explains all the Sensations of Pity by our Fear of the like Evils [Editor's note: *Leviathan*, pt. 1, chap. 6], when by Imagination we place ourselves in the Case of the Sufferers; so others explain all Approbation and Condemnation of Actions in distant Ages or Nations, by a like Effort of Imagination: We place ourselves in the Case of others, and then discern an imaginary private Advantage or Disadvantage in these Actions. But as his Account of Pity will never explain how the Sensation increases, according to the apprehended Worth of the Sufferer, or according to the Affection we formerly had to him; since the Sufferings of any Stranger may suggest the same Possibility of our Suffering the like: So this Explication will ne[v]er account for our high Approbation of brave unsuccessful Attempts, which we see prove detr[i]mental both to the Agent, and to those for [307] whose Service they were intended; here there

is no private Advantage to be imagined. Nor will it account for our Abhorrence of such Injuries as we are incapable of suffering. Sure, when a Man abhors the Attempt of the young Tarquin, he does not imagine that he has chang'd his Sex like Caeneus. And then, when one corrects his Imagination, by remembring his own Situation, and Circumstances, we find the moral Approbation and Condemnation continues as lively as it was before, tho' the Imagination of Advantage is gone. [Editor's note: According to legend, Sextus, son of Tarquinius Superbus, raped Lucretia, sparking off the popular uprising that ended the Roman monarchy and ushered in the Roman republic. Caeneus, a mythical figure, was originally a woman and given a change of sex by Poseidon.]

32. C (p. 116), D (p. 117): Agents? Thus also an easy, indolent Simplicity, which exposes a Man of Wealth as a prey to others, may be as advantageous a Disposition as the most prudent Generosity, to those he converses with; and yet our Sentiments of this latter Temper are far nobler than of the former.

33. A (p. 113): and increase

34. No new paragraph in A (p. 114).

35. C (p. 118), D (p. 119): to judge certain Actions advantageous to us

36. No new paragraph in A (p. 115).

37. A (p. 115): did certainly perform

38. C (p. 118), D (p. 119): recommend Men to us only

39. Omitted in C (p. 119), D (p. 120).

40. No new paragraph in A (p. 116).

41. A (p. 117): more probably

42. C (p. 121), D (p. 122): hereafter

43. D2, D3 [Corrigenda, p. 310]: any Dispositions of Piety, or Thoughts of future Rewards

44. No new paragraph in A (p. 118).

45. Omitted in C (p. 122), D (p. 123).

46. C (p. 122), D (p. 123): recommend to me

47. C (p. 122), D (p. 123): make me like

48. Not in A (p. 119).

49. A (p. 119): is, "whether

50. A (p. 119): I may

51. Not in A (p. 119).

52. Not in A (p. 119).

53. A (p. 119): . The Sense of the moral Good, or Evil, cannot be over-ballanced by Interest.

54. C (p. 123), D (p. 124): Threatnings

55. A (p. 119): any Actions, such

56. D (p. 124): an

57. No new paragraph in A (p. 120).

58. A (p. 121): in the Contemplation or Reflection upon which they could be pleas'd.

59. C (p. 124), D (p. 125): Pleasure. Nay, what should excite a Cato or a Decius to desire Praise, if it is only the cold Opinion of others that they were useful to the State, without any Perception of Excellence in such Conduct?

60. A (p. 121): but in so

61. Not in A (p. 122).

62. C (p. 126), D (p. 127): sincerely approve and

63. C (p. 126), D (p. 127): Approbation of publick Spirit, nor Desire

64. C (p. 127), D (p. 128): private advantage

65. A (p. 123): abstractly from

66. A (p. 124): so

67. A (p. 124): Ideas, or

68. C (p. 128), D (p. 129): the simple Ideas of Approbation or Condemnation, from Actions observed

69. A (p. 124): they shall

70. A (p. 124): antecedently

71. C (pp. 128–30), D (pp. 129–31): Pleasure. That we may discern more distinctly the Difference between moral Perceptions and others, let us consider, when we taste a pleasant Fruit, we are conscious of Pleasure; when another tastes it, we only conclude or form an Opinion that he enjoys Pleasure; and, abstracting from some previous Good-Will or Anger, his enjoying this Pleasure is to us a matter wholly indifferent, raising no new Sentiment or Affection. But when we are under the Influence of a virtuous Temper, and thereby engaged in [C: p. 129, D: p. 130] virtuous Actions, we are not always conscious of any Pleasure, nor are we only pursuing private Pleasures, as will appear hereafter: 'tis only by reflex Acts upon our Temper and Conduct that we enjoy the Delights of Virtue [D2, D3 (Corrigenda, p. 310): "that Virtue never fails to give Pleasure" substitutes for "that we enjoy the Delights of Virtue"]. When also we judge the Temper of another to be virtuous, we do not necessarily imagine him then to enjoy Pleasure, tho' we know Reflection will give it to him: And farther, our Apprehension of his virtuous Temper raises Sentiments of Approbation, Esteem or Admiration, and the Affection of Good-will toward him. The Quality approved by our moral Sense is con-

ceived to reside in the Person approved, and to be a Perfection and Dignity in him: Approbation of another's Virtue is not conceived as making the Approver happy, or virtuous, or worthy, tho' 'tis attended with some small Pleasure. Virtue is then called Amiable or Lovely, from its raising Good-will or Love in Spectators toward the Agent; and not from the Agent's perceiving the virtuous Temper to be advantageous to him, or desiring to obtain it under that View. A virtuous Temper is called Good or Beatifick, not that it is always attended with Pleasure in the Agent; much less that some small Pleasure attends the Contemplation of it in the Approver: but from this, that every Spectator is persuaded that the reflex Acts of the virtuous Agent upon his own Temper will give him the highest Pleasures. The admired Qua-[C: p. 130, D: p. 131]lity is conceived as the Perfection of the Agent, and such a one as is distinct from the Pleasure either in the Agent or the Approver; tho' 'tis a sure source of Pleasure to the Agent. The Perception of the Approver, tho' attended with Pleasure, plainly represents something quite distinct from this Pleasure; even as the Perception of external Forms is attended with Pleasure, and yet represents something distinct from this Pleasure. This may prevent many Cavils upon this Subject.

Treatise II, Section II

1. C (p. 131), D (p. 132) introduce the marginal heading: Nature
2. C (p. 131), D (p. 132): sensitive Natures
3. A (p. 125): religious
4. No new paragraph in A (p. 126).
5. Not in A (p. 126).
6. Not in A (p. 126).
7. Not in A (p. 126).
8. A (p. 126): were
9. A (p. 126): have
10. A (p. 127): call virtuous, do spring from
    C (p. 133), D (p. 134): approve as virtuous, are either
11. C (p. 133), D (p. 134): That Virtue springs from some other Affection than Self-Love, or Desire of private Advantage. And where Self-Interest excites to the same Action, the Approbation is given only to the disinterested Principle.
12. C (p. 133), D (p. 134): are commonly included under the Names Love and Hatred

13. Omitted in C (p. 133), D (p. 134).

14. C (p. 134), D (p. 135): Malice. Complacence denotes Approbation of any Person by our Moral Sense; and is rather a Perception than an Affection; tho' the Affection of Good-will is ordinarily subsequent to it. Benevolence is the Desire of the Happiness of another. Their Opposites are called Dislike and Malice.

15. Omitted in C (p. 134), D (p. 135).

16. Omitted in C (p. 134), D (p. 135).

17. Omitted in C (p. 134), D (p. 135).

18. Omitted in C (p. 134), D (p. 135).

19. C (p. 134), D (p. 135): toward a

20. Omitted in C (p. 134), D (p. 135).

21. Omitted in C (p. 134), D (p. 135).

22. Omitted in C (p. 134), D (p. 135).

23. Omitted in C (p. 135), D (p. 136).

24. Deleted in B [Errata, p. xxvi].

25. C (p. 135), D (p. 136): disapprove

26. C (p. 135), D (p. 136): retain the same Opinion of his Temper and Intentions

27. C (p. 135), D (p. 136): false Opinion about his Temper

28. C (p. 135), D (p. 136): ultimate Desire of

29. D2, D3 [Corrigenda, p. 310]: real Good-will or Kindness

30. C (p. 136), D (p. 137): others. To raise Benevolence, no more is required than calmly to consider any sensitive Nature not pernicious to others. Gratitude arises from Benefits conferred from Good-will on ourselves, or those we love; Complacence is a Perception of the moral Sense. Gratitude includes some Complacence, and Complacence still raises a stronger Good-will than that we have toward indifferent Characters, where there is no opposition of Interests.

31. A (p. 130): and

32. Not in A (p. 130), C (p. 137), D (p. 138). Instruction for addition already in *Alterations and Additions* (p. 10).

33. The following two paragraphs are not in C (p. 137) and D (p. 138); instead, fourteen new pages are added: [Margin heading: Benevolence is disinterested.] IV. There are two ways in which some may deduce Benevolence from Self-Love, the one supposing that "we voluntarily bring this Affection upon ourselves, whenever we have an Opinion that it will be for our Interest to have this Affection, either as it may be immediately pleasant, or

may afford pleasant Reflection afterwards by our Moral Sense, or as it may tend to procure some external Reward from God or Man." The other Scheme alledges no such Power in us of raising Desire or Affection of any kind by our Choice or Volition; but "supposes our Minds determined by the Frame of their Nature to desire whatever is apprehended [C: p. 138, D: p. 139] as the Means of any private Happiness; and that the Observation of the Happiness of other Persons, in many Cases is made the necessary Occasion of Pleasure to the Observer, as their Misery is the Occasion of his Uneasiness: and in Consequence of this Connexion, as soon as we have observed it, we begin to desire the Happiness of others as the Means of obtaining this Happiness to ourselves, which we expect from the Contemplation of others in a happy State. They alledge it to be impossible to desire either the Happiness of another, or any Event whatsoever, without conceiving it as the Means of some Happiness or Pleasure to ourselves; but own at the same time, that Desire is not raised in us directly by any Volition, but arises necessarily upon our apprehending any Object or Event to be conducive to our Happiness.

[Margin heading: The first contrary Opinion confuted.] That the former Scheme is not just, may appear from this general Consideration, that "neither Benevolence nor any other Affection or Desire can be directly raised by Volition." If they could, then we could be bribed into any Affection whatsoever toward any Object, even the most improper: we might raise Jealousy, Fear, Anger, Love, toward any sort of Persons indifferently by an Hire, even as we engage Men to external Actions, or to the [C: p. 139, D: p. 140] Dissimulation of Passions; but this every Person will by his own Reflection find to be impossible. The Prospect of any Advantage to arise to us from having any Affection, may indeed turn our Attention to those Qualitys in the Object, which are naturally constituted the necessary Causes or Occasions of the advantageous Affection; and if we find such Qualitys in the Object, the Affection will certainly arise. Thus indirectly the Prospect of Advantage may tend to raise any Affection; but if these Qualitys be not found or apprehended in the Object, no Volition of ours, nor Desire, will ever raise any Affection in us.

But more particularly, that Desire of the Good of others, which we approve as virtuous, cannot be alledged to be voluntarily raised from Prospect of any Pleasure accompanying the Affection itself: for 'tis plain that our Benevolence is not always accompanied with Pleasure; nay, 'tis often attended with Pain, when the Object is in Distress. Desire in general is rather uneasy than pleasant. 'Tis true, indeed, all the Passions and Affections justify themselves; while they continue, (as Malebranch expresses it) we generally approve our being thus affected on this Occasion, as an innocent Disposition, or a just one, and condemn a Person who would be otherwise affected on the like Occasion. So the Sorrowful, the Angry, the [C: p. 140, D: p. 141] Jealous, the Compassionate, approve their several Passions on the apprehended Occasion; but we should not therefore conclude, that Sorrow, Anger, Jealousy or Pity are pleasant, or chosen for their concomitant Pleasure. The Case is plainly thus: The Frame of our Nature on the Occasions which move these Passions, determines us to be thus affected, and to approve our Affection at least as innocent. Uneasiness generally attends our Desires of any kind; and this Sensation tends to fix our Attention, and to continue the Desire. But the Desire does not terminate upon the Removal of the Pain accompanying the Desire, but upon some other Event: the concomitant Pain is what we seldom reflect upon, unless when it is very violent. Nor does any Desire or Affection terminate upon the Pleasure which may accompany the Affection; much less is it raised by an Act of our Will, with a View to obtain this Pleasure.

The same Reflection will shew, that we do not by an Act of our Will raise in ourselves that Benevolence which we approve as virtuous, with a View to obtain future Pleasures of Self-Approbation by our Moral Sense. Could we raise Affections in this manner, we should be engaged to any Affection by the Prospect of an Interest [C: p. 141, D: p. 142] equivalent to this of Self-Approbation, such as Wealth or sensual Pleasure, which with many Tempers are more powerful; and yet we universally own, that that Disposition to do good Offices to others, which is raised by these Motives, is not virtuous: how can we then imagine, that the virtuous Benevolence is brought upon us by a Motive equally selfish?

But what will most effectually convince us of the Truth on this Point, is Reflection upon our own Hearts, whether we have not a Desire of the Good of others, generally without any Consideration or Intention of obtaining these pleasant Reflections on our own Virtue: nay, often this Desire is strongest where we least imagine Virtue, in natural Affection toward Offspring, and in Gratitude to a great Benefactor; the Absence of which is indeed the greatest Vice, but the Affections themselves are not esteemed in any considerable degree virtuous. The same Reflection will also convince us, that these Desires or Affections are not produced by Choice, with a View to obtain this private Good.

In like manner, if no Volition of ours can directly raise Affections from the former Prospects of Interest, no more can any Volition raise them from

Prospects of eternal Rewards, or to avoid eternal Punishments. The former Motives differ from these only [C: p. 142, D: p. 143] as smaller from greater, shorter from more durable. If Affections could be directly raised by Volition, the same Consideration would make us angry at the most innocent or virtuous Character, and jealous of the most faithful and affectionate, or sorrowful for the Prosperity of a Friend; which we all find to be impossible. The Prospect of a future State, may, no doubt, have a greater indirect Influence, by turning our Attention to the Qualitys in the Objects naturally apt to raise the required Affection, than any other Consideration.* [C: p. 143, D: p. 144]

'Tis indeed probably true in Fact, that those who are engaged by Prospect of future Rewards to do good Offices to Mankind, have generally the virtuous Benevolence jointly exciting them to Action; because, as it may appear hereafter, Benevolence is natural to Mankind, and still operates where there is no Opposition of apparent Interest, or where any contrary apparent Interest is overbalanced by a greater Interest. Men, conscious of this, do generally approve good Offices, to which Motives of a future State partly excited the Agent. But that the Approbation is founded upon the Apprehension of a disinterested Desire partly exciting the Agent, is plain from this, that not only Obedience to an evil Deity in doing Mischief, or even in performing trifling Ceremonies, only from Hope of Reward, or Prospect of avoiding Punishment, but even Obedience to a good Deity only from the same Motives, without any Love or Gratitude towards him, and with a perfect Indifference about the Happiness or Misery of Mankind, abstracting from this private Interest, would meet with no Approbation. We plainly see that [C: p. 144, D: p. 145] a Change of external Circumstances of Interest under an evil Deity, without any Change in the Disposition of the Agent, would lead him into every Cruelty and Inhumanity.

Gratitude toward the Deity is indeed disinterested, as it will appear hereafter. This Affection therefore may obtain our Approbation, where it excites to Action, tho' there were no other Benevolence exciting the Agent. But this Case scarce occurs among Men. But where the Sanction of the Law is the only Motive of Action, we could expect no more Benevolence, nor no other Affection, than those in one forced by the Law to be Curator to a Person for whom he has not the least Regard. The Agent would so manage as to save himself harmless if he could, but would be under no Concern about the Success of his Attempts, or the Happiness of the Person whom he served, provided he performed the Task required by Law; nor would any Spectator approve this Conduct.

[Margin heading: The second Opinion confuted.] V. The other Scheme is more plausible: That Benevolence is not raised by any Volition upon Prospect of Advantage; but that we desire the Happiness of others, as conceiving it necessary to procure some pleasant Sensations which we expect to feel [C: p. 145, D: p. 146] upon seeing others happy; and that for like Reason we have Aversion to their Misery. This Connection between the Happiness of others and our Pleasure, say they, is chiefly felt among Friends, Parents and Children, and eminently virtuous Characters. But this Benevolence flows as directly from Self-Love as any other Desire.

To shew that this Scheme is not true in Fact, let us consider, that if in our Benevolence we only desired the Happiness of others as the Means of this Pleasure to ourselves, whence is it that no Man approves the Desire of the Happiness of others as a means of procuring Wealth or sensual Pleasure to ourselves? If a Person had wagered concerning the future Happiness of a Man of such Veracity, that he would sincerely confess whether he were happy or not; would this Wagerer's Desire of the Happiness of another, in order to win the Wager, be approved as virtuous? If not, wherein does this Desire differ from the former? except that in one case there is one pleasant Sensation expected, and in the other case other sensations: For by increasing or diminishing the Sum wagered, the Interest in this case may be made either greater or less than that in the other.

Reflecting on our own Minds again will best discover the Truth. Many have never thought upon this Connection: nor do [C: p. 146, D: p. 147] we ordinarily intend the obtaining of any such Pleasure. When we do generous Offices, we all often feel Delight upon seeing others happy, but during our Pursuit of their Happiness we have no Intention of obtaining this delight. We often feel the Pain of Compassion; but were our sole ultimate Intention or Desire the freeing ourselves from this Pain, would the Deity offer to us either wholly to blot out all Memory of the Person in Distress, (C, p. 146: "or"; omitted in D, p. 147) to take away this Connection, so that we should be easy during the Misery of our Friend on the one hand, or on the other would relieve him from his Misery, we should be as ready to choose the former way as the latter; since either of them would free us from our Pain, which upon this Scheme is the sole End proposed by the compassionate Person.— Don't we find in ourselves that our Desire does not terminate upon the Removal of our own Pain? Were this our sole Intention, we would run away, shut our Eyes, or divert our Thoughts from the miserable Object, as the readiest way of removing our Pain: This we seldom do, nay, we croud about such

Objects, and voluntarily expose ourselves to this Pain, unless calm Reflection upon our Inability to relieve the Miserable, countermand our Inclination, or some selfish Affection, as Fear of Danger, over-power it. [C: p. 147, D: p. 148]

To make this yet clearer, suppose that the Deity should declare to a good Man that he should be suddenly annihilated, but at the Instant of his Exit it should be left to his Choice whether his Friend, his Children, or his Country should be made happy or miserable for the Future, when he himself could have no Sense of either Pleasure or Pain from their State. Pray would he be any more indifferent about their State now, that he neither hoped or feared any thing to himself from it, than he was in any prior Period of his Life?** Nay, is it not a pretty common Opinion among us, that after our Decease we know nothing of what befalls those who survive us? How comes it then that we do not lose, at the Approach of Death, all Concern for our Families, Friends, or Country? Can there be any Instance given of our desiring any Thing only as the Means of private Good, as violently when we know that we shall not enjoy this Good many Minutes, as if we expected the Possession of this good for many Years? Is this the way we compute the Value of Annuities?

How the disinterested Desire of the Good of others should seem inconceivable, 'tis hard to account: perhaps 'tis owing to the Attempts of some great Men to give Definitions of simple Ideas.—Desire, say they, is Uneasiness, or uneasy Sensation upon the Absence [C: p. 148, D: p. 149] of any Good.—Whereas Desire is as distinct from Uneasiness, as Volition is from Sensation. Don't they themselves often speak of our desiring to remove Uneasiness? Desire then is different from Uneasiness, however a Sense of Uneasiness accompanies it, as Extension does the Idea of Colour, which yet is a very distinct Idea. Now wherein lies the Impossibility of desiring the Happiness of another without conceiving it as the Means of obtaining any thing farther, even as we desire our own Happiness without farther View? If any alledge, that we desire our own Happiness as the Means of removing the Uneasiness we feel in the Absence of Happiness, then at least the Desire of removing our own Uneasiness is an ultimate Desire: and why may we not have other ultimate Desires?

"But can any Being be concerned about the Absence of an Event which gives it no Uneasiness?" Perhaps superior Natures desire without uneasy Sensation. But what if we cannot? We may be uneasy while a desired Event is in Suspence, and yet not desire this Event only as the Means of removing this Uneasiness: Nay, if we did not desire the Event without View to this Uneasiness, we should never have brought the Uneasiness upon ourselves by desiring it. So likewise we may feel Delight upon the Existence of a desired Event, when yet we did not desire the Event only as the Means of obtaining this [C: p. 149, D: p. 150] Delight; even as we often receive Delight from Events which we had an Aversion to.

VI. If any one should ask, since none of these Motives of Self-Interest excite our Benevolence, but we are in virtuous Actions intending solely the Good of others, to what Purpose serves our moral Sense, our Sense of Pleasure from the Happiness of others? To what Purpose serves the wise Order of Nature, by which Virtue is even made generally advantageous in this Life? To what End are eternal Rewards appointed and revealed? The Answer to these Questions was given partly already: all these Motives may make us desire to have benevolent Affections, and consequently turn our Attention to those Qualities in Objects which excite them; they may overbalance all apparent contrary Motives, and all Temptations to Vice. But farther, I hope it will be still thought an End worthy of the Deity, to make the Virtuous happy, by a wise Constitution of Nature, whether the Virtues [D2, D3 (Corrigenda, p. 310) substitute "Virtuous" for "Virtues"] were in every Action intending to obtain this Happiness or not. Beneficent Actions tend to the publick Good; it is therefore good and kind to give all possible additional Motives to them; and to excite Men, who have some weak Degrees of good Affection, to promote the publick Good more vigorously by Motives of Self-Interest; or even to excite those who have no Virtue at all to external Acts [C: p. 150, D: p. 151] of Beneficence, and to restrain them from Vice.*** [C: p. 151, D: p. 152]

From the Whole it may appear, that there is in human Nature a disinterested ultimate Desire of the Happiness of others; and that our moral Sense determines us [C, p. 151, D1, p. 152, D3, p. 152: only] [D2, p. 152: instead of "only" a lacuna of approximately four letters] to approve [D2, D3 (Corrigenda, p. 310): only such] Actions as virtuous, which are apprehended to proceed partly at least from such Desire.

*These several Motives of Interest, which, some alledge, do excite us to Benevolence, operate upon us in a very different Manner. Prospect of external Advantage of any kind in this Life from our Fellows, is only a Motive to the Volition of external Actions immediately, and not to raise Desire of the Happiness of others. Now being willing to do external Actions which we know do in Fact promote the Happiness of others, without any Desire of their Happiness, is not approved as virtuous: Otherwise it were Virtue to do a beneficent Action for a Bribe of Money.

The Prospect of Rewards from the Deity, of future Pleasures from the Self-

Approbation of our Moral Sense, or of any Pleasure attending an Affection itself, are only Motives to us to desire or wish to have the Affection of Benevolence in our Hearts; and consequently, if our Volition could raise Affections in us, these Motives would make us will or choose to raise benevolent Affections: But these Prospects cannot be Motives to us from Self-Love, to desire the Happiness of others; for, from Self-Love we only desire what we apprehend to be the Means of private Good. Now the having those Affections is the Means of obtaining these private Goods, and not the actual Happiness of others; for the Pleasure of Self-Approbation, and Divine Re-[C: p. 143, D: p. 144]wards, are not obtained or lost according as others are happy or miserable, but according to the Goodness of our Affections. If therefore Affections are not directly raised by Volition or Choice, Prospects of future Rewards, or of Self-Approbation, cannot directly raise them.

**[Note added in D2, D3 (Corrigenda, p. 307)]: Cic. *de Finib.* lib. ii. c. 31. [today: II, 99] Ista commendatio puerorum, memoria et caritas amicitiae, summorum officiorum in extremo spiritu conservatio, indicat innatam esse homini probitatem gratuitam, non invitatam voluptatibus, nec praemiorum mercedibus evocatam, &c. [Translation: "That provision for the care of children, that loyalty to friendship and affection, that observance of these solemn duties with his latest breath, prove that there was innate in the man a disinterested uprightness, not evoked by pleasure nor elicited by prizes and rewards." Cicero, *De finibus bonorum et malorum,* with an English translation by H. Rackham (Cambridge, Mass.: Harvard University Press, 1967), p. 190.]

***Let it be also remembered, that every Consideration suggested in the Gospel, as an additional Motive to beneficent Actions, is not immediately to be looked upon as the proper Motive to Virtue, or what would engage our Approbation of Actions flowing from it alone. We have the Promises of this Life as well as of the next, and yet the former alone was never thought a virtuous Principle. Some Texts are also brought to confute this Scheme of disinterested Affections as the only truly virtuous Principle, such as i Corinth. Ch. XV. ver. 32. which imports no more than this, "That if there were no resurrection, and consequently Christ had not risen, and therefore his Religion only an Imposture, it had been the greatest Folly in the Apostle to have exposed himself to Persecution:" Not that the Prospect of a future Reward was the only Motive to Virtue, or that the only Affection of Mind which made the Apostle bear Persecution was, Hope of Reward.

Another Text insisted on is, Heb. XI. ver. 6. But this only means, either "that no Man can perform religious Acts acceptably to God, who does not believe his Existence and Goodness," which is self-evident: Or it is to be understood of "embracing the true Religion, and adhering to it under the most severe Persecutions, which we may allow no Man could do without Hopes of future Reward." Now this does not prove either that our sole, or our strongest Incitement to virtuous Actions is a Prospect of Interest, nor even that any Action is approved, because it springs from Hope of Reward.

Heb. XII. ver. 2. is chiefly urged, but with least Ground: if we have it well translated, it only asserts, "That the Hope of future Joy was one Incitement to our Saviour in enduring Sufferings," not that this was the principal Spring of his beneficent Actions, or that they were made amiable by arising from it. Nay, this Joy may be understood metonymically, for its Object, viz. the Salvation of Mankind. Not to mention another Translation long ago known to Criticks; some of whom insist that ἀντί is seldom used for the final Cause; but means instead of, in this Place, as well as in Texts debated with the Socinians: And then this Verse may be thus translated; [C: p. 151, D: p. 152] "Who instead of that Joy which was ready at hand, or in his Power to have enjoyed, as he had from the Beginning, he submitted to the Cross." Nor is there any thing to confute this Translation; save that some Antithesis between our suffering from Faith in a Reward, and his suffering in like manner, is not kept up so well; as if it were a necessary Perfection in the Scriptures to abound in such Antitheses. For in this Translation there is good Reasoning, in shewing how our Saviour's sufferings are enhanced by his exchanging a State of Joy for them, parallel to Philip. II. ver. 6, 7.

Whoever would appeal to the general Strain of the Christian Exhortations, will find disinterested Love more inculcated, and Motives of Gratitude more frequently suggested, than any others.

34. Not in A (p. 132), no new paragraph. In C (p. 151), D (p. 152): numbered VII.

35. C (p. 151), D (p. 152): ultimate Desire of

36. A (p. 132): Interests

37. Not in A (p. 133).

38. A (p. 133): would rather

39. Not in A (p. 133).

40. C (p. 153), D (p. 154): ultimate Desire of

41. C (p. 153), D (p. 154): calm Ill-will

42. C (p. 153), D (p. 154): yet

43. A (p. 134): Now having
C (p. 153), D (p. 154): numbered VIII.

44. C (p. 153), D (p. 154): neither our Esteem nor Benevolence, is founded on Self-Love

45. Omitted in C (p. 154), D (p. 155).

46. A (p. 134): were

47. C (p. 154), D (p. 155): been reputed virtuous

48. C (p. 154), D (p. 155): numbered IX.

49. C (p. 154), D (p. 155): Good-Will

50. A (p. 135): procures

51. Not in A (135). In C (p. 154), D (p. 155): , and especially toward ourselves

52. C (p. 154), D (p. 155): wish well to

53. C (p. 154), D (p. 155): do so

54. A (p. 135): And further
C (p. 155), D (p. 156): Nay, farther

No new paragraph in A (p. 135), C (p. 155), D (p. 156).

55. C (p. 155), D (p. 156): Good-will

56. C (p. 155), D (p. 156): will

57. New paragraph in C (p. 155), D (p. 156).

58. C (p. 155), D (p. 156): Beneficence then must increase our Good-will, as it raises Complacence, which is still attended with stronger degrees of Benevolence

59. A (p. 136): hence it is that we

60. Omitted in C (pp. 155–56), D (pp. 156–57).

61. A (p. 136): much more powerful to excite

62. A (p. 136): by

63. Not in A (p. 137).

64. Not in A (p. 137).

65. C (p. 156), D (p. 157): Good-will

66. C (p. 156), D (p. 157): Good-will
    D2, D3 [Corrigenda, p. 310]: ultimate Good-will

67. C (p. 156), D (p. 157): arises from

68. C (p. 156), D (p. 157): Good-will
    D2, D3 [Corrigenda, p. 310]: such Good-will

69. Omitted in C (p. 156), D (p. 157).

70. C (p. 156), D (p. 157): Affection

71. Paragraph omitted in C (p. 156), D (p. 157).

72. A (p. 137): taken

73. B [Errata, p. xxvi]: 5

74. Not in A (p. 138).

75. A (p. 138): does scarce deserve

76. A (p. 138): any farther

77. No new paragraph in A (p. 138). In C (p. 156), D (p. 157): Had we no other ultimate Desire but that of private Advantage

78. A (p. 138): but

79. A (p. 138): must only act

80. A (p. 138): we can have no reason to imagine that

81. C (p. 157), D (p. 158): by many who yet expect Mercy and Beneficence in the Deity

82. A (p. 139): this

83. Not in A (p. 139).

84. No new paragraph in A (p. 139).

85. C (p. 158), D (p. 159): infinite Power and Art

86. Not in A (p. 139).

87. A (p. 140): be as capable of giving him

88. Entire article VIII omitted in C (p. 158), D (p. 159).

89. A (p. 140): perhaps Virtue

90. No new paragraph in A (p. 140).

91. A (p. 140): such a

92. A (p. 140): such an Occasion

93. A (p. 141): And then this

94. A (p. 141): Passions are not from Self-Love [Instruction for alteration already in *Alterations and Additions* (p. 11).]

95. *Alterations and Additions* (p. 10): on

96. A (p. 141): do tend generally in fact

97. A (p. 141): removal of our Pain is not directly intended; for then [Instruction for alteration already in *Alterations and Additions* (p. 11).]

98. *Alterations and Additions* (p. 11): were

99. A (p. 141): run into

100. C (p. 158), D (p. 159): numbered X.

101. A (p. 143): falsely suppos'd

102. A (p. 143): those Actions which are counted Virtuous

103. A (p. 143): suppos'd

104. C (p. 159), D (p. 160): Spring

105. Not in A (p. 144).

106. A (p. 144): bustles

107. D (p. 160): for

108. C (p. 160), D (p. 161): his Children are

109. C (p. 160), D (p. 161): No; but his naturally implanted Desire of their Good, and Aversion to their misery, makes him affected with Joy or Sorrow from their Pleasures or Pains. This Desire

110. C (p. 160), D (p. 161): it

111. D2, D3 [Corrigenda, p. 310]: say others

112. D2, D3 [Corrigenda, pp. 307–8]: it. Another Author thinks all this easily deducible from Self-Love. "Children are not only made of our Bodies, but resemble us in Body and Mind; they are rational agents as we are, and we only love our own Likeness in them." Very good all this. What is Likeness? 'Tis not individual Sameness; 'tis only being included under one general or specifical Idea. Thus there is Likeness between us and other Mens Children, thus any Man is like any other, in some Respects; a Man is also like an Angel, and in some Respects like a Brute. Is there then a natural Disposition in every

Man to love his Like, to wish well not only to his individual Self, but to any other like rational or sensitive Being? and this Disposition strongest, where there is the greatest Likeness in the more noble Qualities? If all this is called by the Name Self-Love; be it so: The highest Mystick needs no more-disinterested Principle; 'tis not confined [308] to the Individual, but termi-nates ultimately on the Good of others, and may extend to all; since each one some way resembles each other. Nothing can be better than this Self-Love, nothing more generous.

If any allege, That "Parents always derive Pleasure, often Honour, and sometimes Wealth, from the Wisdom and Prosperity of their Children, and hence all Parental Solicitude arises;" let us recollect what was said above; all these Motives cease upon Approach of Death, and yet the Affection is as strong then as ever. Let Parents examine their own Hearts, and see if these views are the only Springs of their Affection, and that toward the most infirm, from whom there is least Hope.

113. No new paragraph in A (p. 145).

114. A (p. 145): were

115. Not in A (p. 145).

116. A (p. 145): appear to be moral

117. C (p. 161), D (p. 162): numbered XI.

118. C (p. 162), D (p. 163): more desire

119. C (p. 162), D (p. 163): would he not rather desire the Prosperity of his Country

120. C (p. 162), D (p. 163): readily wish

121. Not in A (p. 147).

122. A (p. 147): and Design, and Study

123. A (p. 147): argues a Benevolence in

124. C (p. 163), D (p. 164): desire

125. C (p. 163), D (p. 164): Happiness. And that all these Affections, whether more or less extensive, are properly disinterested, not even founded on any Desire of that Happiness we may expect in seeing their prosperous Condition; may appear from this, that they would continue even at the In-stant of our Death, or intire Destruction, as was already observed, Art. IV. of this Section.

126. C (p. 163), D (p. 164): numbered XII.

127. C (p. 164), D (p. 165): those

128. A (p. 148): and Faction

129. B [Errata, p. xxvi]: or

130. A (p. 149): but
131. A (p. 149): may be

Treatise II, Section III

1. D2, D3 [Corrigenda, p. 310]: generally
2. A (p. 150): the Love of others
   C (p. 165), D (p. 166): Good-will to others
3. Not in A (p. 150).
4. B [Errata, p. xxvi]: 6. Par. 3
   C (p. 166), D (p. 167): 9. Par. 2
5. A (p. 151): know that
6. D (p. 167): towards
7. A (p. 151): Hence it is, that those
8. No marginal heading in D (p. 167).
9. A (pp. 152–53): Beneficiary
10. D (p. 168): belov'd
11. A (p. 152): Beneficiary
12. D (p. 168): but
13. Omitted in D2, D3 [Corrigenda, p. 310].
14. Omitted in C (p. 168), D (p. 169).
15. Not in A (p. 153).
16. A (p. 155): tended
17. A (p. 155): was
18. C (p. 171), D (p. 172): the one
19. D2, D3 [Corrigenda, p. 310]: manifest
20. A (p. 156): be acted
21. A (p. 156): by
22. C (p. 171), D (p. 172): ultimate Desire of
23. C (p. 172), D (p. 173): desire
24. A (p. 157): conceiv'd to be no
25. D3 (pp. 173–74): The frequent, and seemingly unprovoked Cruelties of the Nero's and Domitian's, are often alleged in Opposition to all this; but perhaps unjustly. Such Tyrants are conscious that they are hated by all those whom the World repute virtuous, and they apprehend Danger from them: A Tyrant looks upon such Men as designing, artful, or ambitious, under a false Shew of Virtue. He imagines the surest Means of his own Safety is to appear terrible, and to deprive his Enemys of all Hopes of escaping by his

Compassion. The Fame of Virtue in eminent Subjects is matter of Envy, and is a Reproach upon the Tyrant: it weakens his Power, and makes them dangerous to him. Power becomes the Object of Delight to the Tyrant; and in Ostentation of it, he may break through all regards to Justice and Humanity. Habits of Cruelty can be acquired in such a Course. Any of these apparent interests seem better to account for the Crueltys of Tyrants, than [174] the supposing in them

26. A (p. 157): conscious that he

27. Omitted in D3 (p. 174).

28. Omitted in D3 (p. 174).

29. A (p. 158), C (p. 173), D (p. 174): were

30. A (p. 158): that it is

31. A (p. 158): only Self-Love, and not Malice, which was his Motive; or
C (p. 173), D (p. 174): he acted from Self-Love, and not Malice, or,

32. A (p. 158): Mankind

33. D3 (p. 174): they are

34. C (p. 174), D (p. 175): Spring

35. Not in A (p. 159).

36. A (p. 159): must then be supposed to be

37. A (p. 159): too

38. A (p. 159): so as

39. D3 (p. 175) adds: or such strong Appetites, or Passions either selfish, or toward some narrow Systems, as overcome our Regard to Publick Good;

40. A (p. 159): had mutually

41. Not in A (p. 159).

42. Omitted in D3 (p. 175).

43. D3 (pp. 175–76): seem of a middle Nature, neither virtuous nor vitious.

44. A (p. 160): discover indeed

45. A (p. 160): And hence

46. Omitted in C (p. 175), D (p. 176).

47. A (p. 161): is

48. A (p. 161): run into any

49. A (p. 161): Mankind

50. D3 (pp. 177–78) inserts a new article with the margin heading "Benevolence of different Kinds" and numbered VI. The remaining articles of section III are renumbered accordingly. VI. Benevolence is a Word fit enough in general, to denote the internal Spring of Virtue, as Bishop Cumberland

always uses it. But to understand this more distinctly, 'tis highly necessary to observe, that under this Name are included very different Dispositions of the Soul. Sometimes it denotes a calm, extensive Affection, or Good-will toward all Beings capable of Happiness or Misery: Sometimes, 2. A calm deliberate Affection of the Soul toward the Happiness of certain smaller Systems or Individuals; such as Patriotism, or Love of a Country, Friendship, Parental Affection, as it is in Persons of Wisdom and Self-Government: Or, 3. The several kind particular Passions of Love, Pity, Sympathy, Congratulation. This Distinction between the calm Motions of the Will, Affections, Dispositions, or Instincts of the Soul, and the several turbulent Passions, is elsewhere more fully considered.* [p. 178]

Now tho' all these different Dispositions come under the general Character of benevolent, yet as they are in Nature different, so they have very different Degrees of Moral Beauty. The first Sort is above all amiable and excellent: 'Tis perhaps the sole Moral Perfection of some superior Natures; and the more this prevails and rules in any human Mind, the more amiable the Person appears, even when it not only checks and limits our lower Appetites, but when it controuls our kind particular Passions, or counteracts them. The second Sort of Benevolence is more amiable than the third, when it is sufficiently strong to influence our Conduct: And the third Sort, tho' of a lesser Moral Dignity, is also beautiful, when it is no way opposite to these more noble Principles. And when it is opposite, tho' it does not justify such Actions as are really detrimental to greater Systems, yet it is strong extenuating Circumstance, and much alleviates the Moral Deformity. We are all sensible of this, when any Person, from Friendship, Parental-Affection, or Pity, has done something hurtful to larger Societys.

*See *Treatise* III. Sect. ii. Art. 3 and *Treatise* IV. Sect. vi. Art. 4. [Editor's note: Hutcheson thought of the *Inquiry* and the *Essay* as a coherent whole. Consequently he is here referring to the two Treatises making up the *Essay*, namely, *An Essay on the Nature and Conduct of the Passions* and *Illustrations upon the Moral Sense,* London, 1728.]

51. A (p. 161): requires that every one should be

52. D3 (p. 179a): the Strength of some particular kind Attachment, or of [In D3 the page numbers are used twice subsequently. The first page 179 begins with "in part"; the first page 180 begins with "in such." The second page 179 begins with "Happiness"; the second page 180 begins with "nevolence".]

53. A (p. 161): shews it to be founded upon a mistaken Opinion of the Tendency of an Action to the publick Good, which does not in Reality tend to it: so that a wise

54. D3 (p. 179a): by the calm extensive Benevolence, how strong soever it were

55. D3 (p. 179a): strong virtuous Disposition

56. A (p. 162): further were there any Good

57. Not in A (p. 162). Instruction for addition of the following two paragraphs already in *Alterations and Additions* (pp. 11–13).

58. C (p. 177), D1, D2 (p. 178), D3 (p. 180a): what

59. D3 (p. 180a): Proportion

60. D3 (p. 180a): Yet Gifts

61. Omitted in D3 (p. 180a).

62. Not in *Alterations and Additions* (p. 13).

63. Wrongly corrected in D2 [Corrigenda, p. 310]: VIII. In D3 this correction is correct [Corrigenda, p. 310, referring to p. 179b].

64. A (p. 162): than as

65. A (p. 163): injurious

66. Omitted in C (p. 179), D1, D2 (p. 180), D3 (p. 180b).

67. D2, D3 [Corrigenda, p. 310] instruct to delete the number.

68. A (p. 163): thus to judge

69. A (p. 164): And in

70. A (p. 164): accomplishes

71. C (p. 180), D (p. 181): not numbered.

72. Not in A (p. 164).

73. A (pp. 164–65): But by the Consequences of Actions, we are not only to understand the immediate Effects directly produc'd by them, but also all those Events which otherwise would not have happen'd. Thus many Actions which have no immediate evil Effects; nay, which actually produce good Effects, may be evil, if their universal Al-[165]lowance would be more detrimental to Mankind than their universal Prohibition; or if there be no fixed Standard, that Men may easily know when such Actions are allow'd, and when prohibited; or when such Actions, however useful in particular Instances, might be Precedents to the greatest Mischief. As for Example, the Execution of Justice by private Persons on Offenders, in any State not entirely perverted from the Ends of Government; the violating the Rights of worthless Persons, in favor of those of great moral Capacitys, and of great Benevolence; the protecting the Innocent by false Testimony in a Court of Justice, and such like, may be very useful in singular Instances: but then the Allowance of such Actions would lead into the greatest Mischief, since every one would judge for himself what Cases were proper, and what not, and then

there could be no Certainty of Life, Possessions, and Evidences: and hence such Practices are universally counted evil. [Instruction for alteration of the following two paragraphs already in *Alterations and Additions* (pp. 13–14).]

74. *Alterations and Additions* (p. 13): Thus

75. *Alterations and Additions* (p. 13): the accidental evil

76. *Alterations and Additions* (p. 13): good effects he proposes to attain by the Action

77. *Alterations and Additions* (p. 13): it

78. C (p. 181), D (p. 182): Mistake

79. *Alterations and Additions* (p. 14): to

80. *Alterations and Additions* (p. 14): are probably greater

81. *Alterations and Additions* (p. 14): these

82. C (pp. 182–83), D (pp. 183–84): it. [new article] (D2, D3 [Corrigenda, p. 310] instruct to delete the number.) IX. 'Tis here to be observed, that tho' every kind Affection abstractly considered, is approved by our moral Sense, yet all sorts of Affections or Passions which pursue the Good of others are not equally approved, or do not seem in the same degree virtuous. Our calm Affections, either private or publick, are plainly distinct from our particular Passions; calm Self-Love quite distinct from Hunger, Thirst, Ambition, Lust, or Anger; so calm Good-will toward others is different from Pity, passionate Love, the parental Affection, or the Passion of particular Friends. Now every kind Passion which is not pernicious to others, is indeed approved as virtuous and lovely: And yet a calm Good-will toward the same Persons appears more lovely. So calm Good-will toward a small System is lovely and preferable to more passionate Attachments; and yet a more extensive calm Benevolence is still more beautiful and virtuous; and the highest Perfection of Virtue is an universal calm Good-will toward all sensitive Natures. Hence it is, that we condemn particular Attachments, when inconsistent [C: p. 183, D: p. 184] with the Interest of great Societies, because they argue some defect in that more noble Principle, which is the Perfection of Virtue.*

*See *Essay on Passions,* Sect. 2. Art. 3. And *Illustrations,* Sect. 6. Art. 4.

83. D2, D3 [Corrigenda, p. 310] instruct to read IX.

84. C (p. 183), D (p. 184): these

85. A (p. 165): extend

86. C (p. 183), D (p. 184): Beneficence

87. A (p. 166): if

88. C (p. 183), D (p. 184): even

89. C (p. 183), D (p. 184): except

90. C (p. 183), D (p. 184): does

91. A (p. 166): is

92. D2, D3 (p. 185): he would condemn a great

93. C (pp. 184–85), D (pp. 185–86): This Constitution of our Sense, whereby the moral Beauty of Actions, or Dispositions, increases according to the Number of Persons to whom the good Effects of them extend; whence also Actions which flow from the nearer Attachments of Nature, such as that between the Sexes, and the Love of our Offspring, do not appear so virtuous as Actions of equal Moment of Good towards Persons less attach'd to us; has been chosen by the Author of Nature for this good Reason, "That the more limited Instincts tend to produce a smaller Moment of Good, be-[C: p. 185, D: p. 186]cause confined to small numbers. Whereas the more extensive calm Instinct of Good-will, attended with Power, would have no Bounds in its good Effects, and would never lead into any Evil, as the particular Passions may: and hence it is made more lovely to our Sense, that we might be induced to cultivate and strengthen it; and make it check even kind Passions, when they are opposite to a greater Good."

94. A (p. 167): were it

95. D2, D3 (p. 186): numbered X.

96. D2, D3 (p. 186): may arise a Notion of moral

97. D2, D3 (p. 186): or are natural Indications of a good Temper, and usually accompany it

98. C (p. 185), D (p. 186): Approbation of

99. A (p. 168): Qualitys Good or Evil. Now, a Veneration for these Qualitys, any further than as they are employ'd for the publick Good, is foolish, and flows from our moral Sense, grounded upon a false Opinion; for if

D2, D3 (p. 186): Qualitys: And we seem to have a natural Relish for them distinct from moral Approbation. But if

100. D2, D3 (p. 187): Rule

101. In D2, D3 (pp. 187–88) all formulae are omitted, and the axioms read as follows:

1. The moral Importance of any Agent, or the Quantity of publick Good he produces, is in a compound Proportion of his Benevolence and Abilitys. For 'tis plain that his good Offices depend upon these two jointly. In like manner, the Quantity of private Good which any Agent obtains for himself, is in a like compound Proportion of his selfish Principles, and

his Abilitys. We speak here only of the external Goods of this World, which one pursues from some selfish Principles. For as to internal Goods of the Mind, these are most effectually obtain'd by the Exercise of other Affections than those called Selfish, even those which carry the Agent beyond himself toward the Good of others.

2. In comparing the Virtues of different Agents, when the Abilitys are equal, the Moments of publick Good are proportioned to the Goodness of the Temper, or the Benevolence; and when the Tempers are equal, the Quantitys of Good are as the Abilitys.

3. The Virtue then or Goodness of Temper is directly as the Moment of Good, [188] when other Circumstances are equal, and inversly as the Abilitys. That is to say, where the Abilitys are greatest, there is less Virtue evidenced in any given Moment of Good produced.

4. But as the natural Consequences of our Actions are various, some good to ourselves, and evil to the Publick; and others evil to ourselves, and good to the Publick; or either useful both to ourselves and others, or pernicious to both; the intire Spring of good Actions is not always Benevolence alone; or of Evil, Malice alone (nay, sedate Malice is rarely found); but in most Actions we must look upon Self-Love as another Force, sometimes conspiring with Benevolence, and assisting it, when we are excited by Views of private Interest, as well as publick Good; and sometimes opposing Benevolence, when the good Action is any way difficult or painful in the Performance, or detrimental in its Consequences to the Agent.

102. A (p. 168): Character

103. Not in A (p. 168). The following axioms are numbered accordingly, 2, 3, 4, 5. Instruction for addition of this paragraph (without numeration) already in *Alterations and Additions* (p. 14).

104. Not in *Alterations and Additions* (p. 14).

105. C (p. 186), D1 (p. 187): Agents, the Abilitys are

106. A (p. 169): Benevolence is as the Moment of publick Good, produced by them in like Circumstances: or B = M × 1.

107. D1 (p. 187): B

108. C (p. 187), D1 (p. 188): Spring of

109. C (p. 187), D1 (p. 188): or of Evil

110. C (p. 187), D1 (p. 188): sedate Malice is rarely found

111. Not in A (p. 169). Instruction for addition already in *Alterations and Additions* (p. 15).

112. A (p. 170): afterwards

113. Not in A (p. 170).

114. A (p. 170): in one

115. Not in A (p. 170).

116. A (p. 170): And in

117. Omitted in D2, D3 (p. 189).

118. A (p. 171): tend to

119. A (p. 171): only then

120. Not in A (p. 171).

121. C (p. 189), D (p. 190): done by

122. A (p. 171): nor

123. A (p. 171): fifth

124. A (p. 171): have surmounted

125. D2, D3 (p. 190): in judging of the Goodness of Temper in any Agent, the Abilitys must come into Computation, as is above-mentioned, and none can act beyond their natural Abilitys

126. D2, D3 (p. 190): the Moment of Good produced equals the Ability

127. A (p. 172): its

128. Omitted in D2, D3 (p. 190).

129. A (p. 172): its

130. Omitted in D2, D3 (p. 190).

131. Omitted in D2, D3 (p. 191).

132. D2, D3 (p. 191): XII. In the same Manner we may compute the Degree of Depravity of any Temper, directly as the Moment of Evil effected, and inversly as the Abilitys. The Springs of vicious Actions however are seldom any real ultimate Intention of Mischief, and never ultimate deliberate Malice; but only sudden Anger, Self-Love, some selfish Passion or Appetite, some kind Attachments to Parties, or particular kind Passions.

The Motives of Interest may sometimes strongly cooperate with a depraved Temper, or may oppose it, in the same Manner that they cooperate with or oppose a good Temper. When they cooperate, they diminish the Moral Evil; when they oppose, they may argue the Depravity of Temper to be greater, which is able to surmount such Motives of Interest.

133. B [Errata, p. xxvi]: $\mu = H \times 1$

134. A (p. 173): or the Degree of Vice

135. A (p. 173): be co-operating with Hatred or opposing

136. Footnote in D2, D3 (p. 191): *See Treatise IV. § 6.

137. The following three paragraphs not in A (p. 174). Instruction for addition of the following three paragraphs already in *Alterations and Additions* (pp. 15–16).

138. *Alterations and Additions* (p. 16): or the secret

139. *Alterations and Additions* (p. 16): Laws, and Governours

140. *Alterations and Additions* (p. 16): which in fact tend

141. *Alterations and Additions* (p. 16): the

142. A (p. 174): From Axiom the 4th

     D2, D3 (p. 193): From the former Reasonings

143. A (p. 174): would

144. A (p. 175): these do

145. A (p. 175): Affections may

146. D2, D3 (p. 194): Beneficence; and makes us

147. D2, D3 (p. 194): their Interests

148. D2, D3 (pp. 195–96): Some will not allow that Virtue can spring from Passions, Instincts, or Affections of any Kind. 'Tis true, kind particular Passions are but a lower Kind of Goodness, even when they are not opposite to the general Good. Those calmer Determinations of the Will, whether of greater or less Extent, or sedate strong Affections, or Desires of the Good of others, are more amiable. These may be as much rooted in the Frame of the Soul, or there may be as natural a Disposition to them as to particular Passions. They tell us, That "Virtue should wholly spring from Reason;" as if Reason or Knowledge of any true Proposition could ever move to Action where there is no End proposed, and no Affection or Desire toward that End.* For this see *Treatise* IV. Sect. i and ii.

The ultimate End, according to many of our Moralists, is to each one his own Hap-[196]piness; and yet this he seeks by Instinct.

*These Gentlemen should either remember the common Doctrine of the Schools, or else confute it better; that the προαίρεσις [choice] which is necessary in virtuous Actions is ὄρεξις βουλευτικὴ [intention of will]: And that Virtue needs not only the λογὸν ἀληθῆ [logical truth], but the ὄρεξις ὀρθήν [right intention]. These very Authors who deny any Affections or Motions of the Will to be the proper Springs of sublime Virtue, yet, inconsistently with themselves, must allow in Men of sublime Virtue, and even in the Deity too, a settled Disposition of Will, or a constant Determination, or Desire to act in Conformity to Reason, or a fixed Affection toward a certain Manner of Conduct. Now an ill-natur'd Adversary would call this an Instinct, an Essential or Natural Disposition of Will, an Affectionate Determination toward a very sublime Object presented by the Understanding. See Aristotle's *Magn. Moral.* Lib. i. c. 18, 35. and Lib. ii. c. 7 & 8. [MM I 18, 1189b 32ff.; I 35, 1196b 4ff.; and II 7–8, 1204a 19ff.] and in many other Places.

149. Omitted in D2, D3 (p. 196).

150. A (p. 176): towards

151. D2, D3 (p. 196): End consistently with the general Good.

152. Omitted in D2, D3 (p. 196).

153. A (p. 176): generally

154. No new paragraph in A (p. 176), D2, D3 (p. 196). Not in Errata.

155. A (p. 176): not so much the

156. Not in A (p. 176).

157. A (p. 176): Self-Love: And I see

158. A (p. 176): to be engag'd into Actions only as they shall appear to tend to their own private Good.

      C (p. 196), D1 (p. 197), D2, D3 (p. 196): until some prospect of Interest allures them to it.

159. A (p. 177): it may appear afterwards

160. A (p. 177): resolve, as much as possible, to cultivate

161. C (p. 196), D (p. 197): arises from

162. C (p. 197), D1 (p. 198), D2, D3 (p. 197): in studying to raise these kind Affections, and to

163. New footnote in D2, D3 (pp. 197–98): *'Tis thus we must understand many places of Plato, Aristotle, Cicero, and others of the Antients, when they speak of "natural Instinct or Disposition in each Being, toward his own Preservation and highest Perfection, as the Spring of Virtue." 'Tis acknowledged by all, that we have such an Instinct, which must operate very indistinctly at first, till we come to consider our Constitution, and our several Powers. When we do so, we find, according to them, the natural Principles of Virtue, or the φυσικαὶ ἀρεταὶ [natural virtues], implanted in us: They appear to us the noblest Parts of our Nature; such are our Desires of Knowledge, our Relish for Beauty, especially of the Moral Kind, our Sociable Affections. These upon Reflection we find to be natural Parts of our Constitution, and we desire to bring them to Perfection from the first-mentioned general Instinct. We must not thence con-[198]clude, that all our Affections spring from Self-Love, or are ultimately pursuing private Good. Disinterested Affections are presupposed as natural Parts of our Constitution, and found in it upon Reflection, not raised by an Act of Choice for some private Good, nor ultimately pursuing it. (See Cicer. *De Finib.* Lib. iii. & Lib. v.) This would be manifestly contrary to the most express Words of these great Men on Friendship, Patriotism, and other Subjects. See Aristotle in the *Magn. Moral. & Nicom.* On Friendship; and Cicero *de Finib.* Lib. ii. & Lib. v.

164. D2, D3 (p. 198): From the preceding Reasonings we shall only draw this one Inference

165. A (p. 177): may

166. A (p. 177): 6, 7

167. A (p. 178): may only take

168. A (p. 178): be

169. Omitted in D2, D3 (p. 198).

Treatise II, Section IV

1. A (p. 179): see

2. Footnote not in A (p. 179).

3. D2, D3 (p. 200): universally

4. D2, D3 (p. 200): generally

5. Not in A (p. 179). Instruction for addition already in *Alterations and Additions* (pp. 16–17).

6. *Alterations and Additions* (pp. 16–17): occasion'd still

D2, D3 (p. 201): generally occasion'd

7. D2, D3 (p. 201): others.* [and the following footnote:] *Beside that moral Approbation or Commendation, we have also an immediate natural Relish for certain Powers and Abilitys, and the regular Exercise of them; and a Dislike and Contempt of a Person who wants them, or has not cultivated them; when we don't think of any Subserviency to a publick Good. But this is rather perceiving a vigorous or a mean Character, than a virtuous or vitious one.

8. A (p. 180): this

9. Omitted in D2, D3 (p. 201).

10. Not in A (p. 180).

11. A (p. 180): still

12. A (p. 180): Actions to tend

13. Omitted in D2, D3 (p. 202).

14. D2, D3 (p. 202): by stronger Motives of external Advantage

15. A (p. 181): yet does not cease

16. D2, D3 (p. 202): makes

17. A (p. 181): shall make

18. A (p. 181): command

19. A (p. 181): which in fact tend

20. A (p. 181): us

21. D2, D3 (p. 202): by their Moral

22. C (p. 202), D (p. 203): and conceive

23. C (p. 202), D (p. 203): to be

24. A (p. 182): Men may be blinded by Passion,

25. No new paragraph in A (p. 182): But to prove that some Men

26. C (p. 202), D (p. 203): without any Motive of Interest, real or apparent; and approved without any Opinion of Tendency to publick Good, or flowing from Good-will

27. A (p. 182): Person, of such Sentiments who

28. A (p. 182): touch

29. C (p. 203), D (p. 204): and the

30. A (p. 183): when Actions

31. No new paragraph in A (p. 184).

32. A (p. 184): antecedent to

33. A (p. 184): take away

34. D (p. 205): such

35. A (p. 185): shall certainly be

36. Not in A (p. 185). Instruction for addition of this paragraph already in *Alterations and Additions* (pp. 17–18).

37. C (p. 206), D (p. 206): They are sparing enough in Accounts

38. C (p. 206), D (p. 206): transiently

39. *Alterations and Additions* (p. 18): to Caution of Assent in other matters

40. A (p. 186): judge, and compare the Tendencys of

41. Not in A (p. 186).

42. A (p. 186): in the

43. A (p. 186): the

44. Omitted in C (p. 207), D (p. 208).

45. C (p. 208), D (p. 208): Deities

46. A (p. 187): amiable, gratefully

47. C (p. 208), D (p. 209): intimated

48. A (p. 187): us

49. The following two paragraphs not in A (p. 188). Instruction for addition of the following two paragraphs already in *Alterations and Additions* (pp. 18–21).

50. Footnote not in *Alterations and Additions* (p. 18).

51. *Alterations and Additions* (p. 18): Cabals, Factions

52. *Alterations and Additions* (p. 19): System."* [and the following footnote:]
*Ld. Shaftesbury's Essay on Wit and Humour, Part. 3. Sect. 2. p. 110. Vol. 1.

53. *Alterations and Additions* (p. 19): Notions

54. *Alterations and Additions* (p. 20): be very much

55. A (p. 188): as

56. No new paragraph in A (p. 188).

57. A (p. 188): with Peace a long Tract of Vice

58. B (p. 210): 1

    B [Errata, p. xxvi]: 2

    C (p. 212), D (p. 213): 1

59. A (p. 189): And hence

60. A (p. 190): conceiv'd as good

61. A (p. 190): are commonly observ'd to

62. A (p. 191): sometimes so,

63. A (p. 191): where yet there is nothing contrary to Benevolence apparent in the Actions

64. A (p. 191): Now we generally allow, that what is from Nature in one Nation, would be so in all.

65. A (p. 191): and yet we cannot find any necessary tendency of it to the detriment of Mankind, at least among Collaterals: Now this

66. Not in A (p. 191).

67. C (p. 215), D (p. 216): disapprove

68. A (p. 192): it is very hard to shew any

69. B [Errata, p. xxvi]: Persons

70. A (p. 192): Obligations; and this

71. A (p. 192): want of Benevolence, or Malice

72. A (p. 193): Incest, or prohibiting it; since it does not appear that any obvious natural Evils follow from it

73. A (p. 193): do so: but

Treatise II, Section V

1. D2, D3 (p. 218): of our Benevolent Instincts of various Kinds

2. D1 (p. 218): an

    D2, D3 (p. 218): a

3. D2, D3 (p. 218): all benevolent Affections are of one Kind, or alike strong.

4. Omitted in C (p. 218), D (p. 218).

5. D2, D3 (p. 218): Kinds

6. Omitted in D2, D3 (p. 218).

7. Omitted in D2, D3 (p. 218).

8. Omitted in C (p. 218), D (p. 218).

9. Not in A (p. 195).

10. Not in A (p. 195).

11. A (p. 195): may only further observe

12. No new paragraph in A (p. 196).

13. C (p. 219), D (p. 219): and

14. Omitted in C (p. 219), D (p. 219).

15. D2, D3 [Corrigenda, p. 310]: more strongly and constantly than it ascends

16. D2, D3 [Corrigenda, p. 310]: more

17. A (p. 197): But there is

18. A (p. 197): Part 2

19. C (p. 220), D (p. 220): great

20. C (p. 220), D (p. 220): great

21. D1 (p. 220): Maultiplicity

   D2 (p. 220): a Multiplicity

   D2 [Corrigenda, p. 310]: a Multiplicity

   D3 (p. 220): Maultiplicity

   D3 [Corrigenda, p. 310]: a Multiplicity

22. A (p. 197): be made useless towards multitudes, whose Interests, at vast distances, we could not understand

   D (p. 221): become useless, by being equally extended to Multitudes, whose Interest we could not understand

23. Omitted in D2, D3 (p. 221).

24. C (p. 221), D (p. 221): so well ordered it, that as our Attention is more raised by those good Offices which are done to our selves or our Friends, so they cause a stronger Sense of Approbation in us, and produce a stronger Benevolence toward (D1, p. 221: towards) the Authors of them

25. A (p. 198): towards

26. A (p. 198): selves; which we call Gratitude; and thus has laid a Foundation

27. A (p. 198): Part

28. Omitted in D2, D3 (p. 221).

29. Not in A (p. 198).

30. D2, D3 (p. 221): The

31. Omitted in D2, D3 (p. 222).

32. Omitted in D2, D3 (p. 222).

33. Omitted in D2, D3 (p. 222).

34. D2, D3 (p. 222): altogether. Beside this general Attraction, the Learned in these Subjects shew us a great many other Attractions among several Sorts of Bodys, answering to some particular Sorts of Passions, from some special Causes. And that Attraction or Force by which the Parts of each Body cohere, may represent the Self-Love of each Individual.

35. D2, D3 (p. 222): These different Sorts of Love to Persons

36. Not in A (p. 199).

37. D2, D3 (p. 222): natural

38. C (p. 223), D (p. 223): desire and delight

39. A (p. 200): as Honour, is constituted an immediate Evil.

40. C (pp. 223–24), D (pp. 223–24): an Opinion [224] of him as pernicious to his Neighbours; but what subjects his Ease to this Opinion of the World? Why, perhaps, he

41. A (p. 201): from Interest

42. A (p. 201): to be

43. A (p. 202): is founded on Self-Love

44. A (p. 202): our

45. No new paragraph in A (p. 202).

46. A (p. 202): but

47. D (p. 225): to

48. Footnote not in A (p. 202).

49. Not in A (p. 204).

50. New footnote in C (p. 227), D (p. 227): *This should be considered by those who talk much of Praise, high Opinion, or Value, Esteem, Glory, as Things much desired; while yet they allow no moral Sense.

51. C (p. 228), D (p. 228): be heartily approved and admired, when we know that Self-Love is

52. C (p. 228), D (p. 228): admire

53. D2, D3 [Corrigenda, p. 310]: No; we should distrust all Pretenders to such a Temper, and hate

54. B [Errata, p. xxvi]: to procure
      A (p. 205), C (p. 228), D (p. 228): to procure to

55. A (p. 205): form'd

56. A (p. 205): but

57. A (p. 206): any

58. D (p. 229): are

59. A (p. 206): did

60. C (p. 230), D (p. 230): all Men would look upon

61. C (p. 232), D (p. 232): hereafter

62. A (p. 209): And hence

63. A (p. 209): and they never

64. Not in A (p. 209).

65. A (p. 209): And the

66. A (p. 210): and

67. C (p. 233), D (p. 233): Desire of

68. A (p. 210): some of the

69. C (p. 233), D (p. 233) add: and of having been acquired by Virtue,

70. A (p. 211): And the

71. A (p. 211): Actions

72. D2, D3 [Corrigenda, p. 311]: strengthens the natural Modesty in civiliz'd Nations, as Habits and Education improve it

73. A (p. 213): many are there who

74. A (p. 214): the very

75. D2, D3 [Corrigenda, p. 311]: of

76. A (p. 214): We may also hence

77. D (p. 237): Pleasure

78. A (p. 214): as

79. A (p. 215): others, so no

80. A (p. 215): And therefore none are

81. A (p. 215): do not of themselves ever

82. Not in A (p. 215).

83. New footnote in C (p. 238), D (p. 238): *See another Reason of this, perhaps more probably true, in the *Essay on the Passions,* p. 6.

84. D2, D3 [Corrigenda, p. 311]: morally evil [an apparently incomplete correction]

85. Not in A (p. 216).

86. Not in A (p. 216).

87. A1 (p. 216): Misery and Distress immediately appear
    A1 [Errata]: Misery or Distress
    A2, A3 (p. 216): Misery and Distress immediately appears

88. A (p. 217): : Thus

89. Not in A (p. 217).

90. A (p. 217): and

91. A (p. 217): from Self-love we

92. A (p. 217): study

93. A (p. 218): pleas'd barely to

94. A (p. 219): meeting with

95. D2, D3 [Corrigenda, p. 311]: or Curiosity

96. A (p. 219): of all

97. Not in A (p. 219).

98. A (p. 219): do delight in some Actions which in fact

99. D2, D3 [Corrigenda, p. 308]: State. Some have alleged, That "however the Sight of another's Misery some way or other gives us Pain, yet the very feeling of Compassion is also attended with Pleasure: This Pleasure is superior to the Pain of Sympathy, and hence we desire to raise Compassion in ourselves, and incline to indulge it." Were this truly the Case, the Continuation of the Suffering would be the natural Desire of the Compassionate, in order to continue this State, not of pure Pleasure indeed, but of Pleasure superior to all Pains.

Treatise II, Section VI

1. A (p. 221): wherever it appears, that

2. A (p. 222): Mankind

3. A (p. 222): would

4. A (p. 222): when his
   C (p. 245), D (p. 245): whose

5. A (p. 222): Would

6. A (pp. 223–24): the external Sensations of Pleasure, or all the Opportunitys of seeing the most beautiful regular Prospects, and hearing the most harmonious Sounds, or [224] obtaining the most extensive Knowledge? These internal Pleasures of Beauty and Harmony, have a great Power to sooth

7. A (p. 224): would

8. A (p. 224): Nay

9. A (p. 225): Par. 5.

10. C (p. 248), D (p. 248) insert: as related by Cicero and some others,

11. C (p. 248), D (p. 248): better a

12. No new paragraph in A (p. 226).

13. A (p. 226): would

14. A (p. 227): of

15. A (p. 227): some Ideas are

16. Not in A (p. 227).

17. A (p. 227): such Pleasures

18. No new paragraph in A (p. 227).

19. A (pp. 227–28): obtain the solitary Perceptions [228] of

20. A (p. 228): 2

21. A (p. 228): universal Judgment of

22. Not in A (p. 229).

23. A (p. 229): 4

24. A (p. 229): any

25. A (p. 230): it is that such Forms

26. A (p. 230): toward

27. A (p. 230): for these Irregularitys of

28. D2, D3 (p. 253): upon some probable Foundation in Nature, and sometimes without any,

29. C (p. 253), D (p. 253): Is it

30. A (p. 231): those

31. A (p. 231): are

32. D2, D3 (p. 253) [no new paragraph]: Had Homer, in his Character of Helen, rais'd our Idea of her external Beauty to the greatest Height, yet

33. D2, D3 (p. 254): morally amiable

34. A (p. 234): even as

35. Not in A (p. 234).

36. A (p. 234): foresee all the

37. No new paragraph in A (p. 234).

38. New paragraph in A (p. 234).

39. C (p. 257), D (p. 257): and

40. A (p. 235): that it is not Love of sensible Pleasure which is

41. A (p. 235): we

42. A (p. 236): great

43. C (p. 258), D (p. 258): towards

44. Not in A (p. 236).

45. Omitted in D (p. 259).

46. Not in A (p. 239).

47. A (p. 239): how far does it go to

48. A (p. 240): the same moral

49. Not in A (p. 240).

50. D (p. 262): a more

51. D (p. 262): Representations

52. A (p. 241): hence it is that

53. A (p. 241): give

54. C (p. 263), D (p. 263): far

55. C (p. 263), D (p. 263): ver.

56. C (p. 264), D (p. 264): ver.

57. Not in A (p. 242).

58. A (p. 242): the

59. Not in A (p. 242).

60. A (p. 242): his

61. A (p. 243): with their rude throats counterfeiting

62. C (p. 266), D (p. 266): ver.

63. Not numbered in A (p. 244).

64. Not numbered, no new article in A (p. 244).

65. In A pages 244–48 follow articles VIII and IX, which in the later editions became articles III and IV of Section 7: B (pp. 270–74), C (pp. 271–74), D (pp. 271–75). Instruction for alteration already in *Alterations and Additions* (p. 21).

Treatise II, Section VII

1. A (p. 249): ; and that we have Ideas of Virtue and Vice, abstractly

2. A (p. 249): abstractly

3. A (p. 249): this Sense

4. Not in A (p. 250).

5. C (p. 268), D (p. 268): of

6. Omitted in D (p. 268).

7. C (p. 268), D (p. 268): beneficent

8. C (p. 268), D (p. 268): good

9. Not in A (p. 250).

10. Not in A (p. 250).

11. Not in A (p. 251).

12. A (p. 251): more promote our Advantage

13. C (p. 270), D (p. 270): virtuous Benevolence toward

14. A (p. 253): but are the Effect of the great Author of all things, who forms our Nature for them.

15. In A (p. 253) articles III and IV appear instead at the end of Section 6, numbered VIII and IX (pp. 244–48).

16. C (p. 272), D (p. 272): influence

17. A (p. 245): were

18. C (p. 273), D (p. 273): condemn

19. D2, D3 [Corrigenda, pp. 308–9]: contrary. Some also object, That according to this Account, Brutes may be capable of Virtue; and this is thought a great Absurdity. But 'tis manifest, that, 1. Brutes are not capable of that, in which this Scheme places the highest Virtue, to wit, the calm Motions of the Will toward the Good of others; if our common Accounts of Brutes are true, that they are merely led by particular Passions toward present Objects of Sense. Again, 'tis plain there is something in [309] certain Tempers of Brutes,* which engages our Liking, and some lower Good-will and Esteem, tho' we do not usually call it Virtue, nor do we call the sweeter Dispositions of Children Virtue; and yet they are so very like the lower Kinds of Virtue, that I see no harm in calling them Virtues. What if there are low Virtues in Creatures void of Reflection, incapable of knowing Laws, or of being moved by their Sanctions, or by Example of Rewards or Punishments? Such Creatures cannot be brought to a proper Trial or Judgment: Laws, Rewards, or Punishments won't have these Effects upon them, which they may have upon rational Agents. Perhaps they are no farther rewarded or punished than by the immediate Pleasure or Pain of their Actions, or what Men immediately inflict upon them. Where is the Harm of all this, That there are lower Virtues, and lower Vices, the Rewarding or Punishing of which, in Creatures void of Reason and Reflection, can answer no wise End of Government?

*Cicero is not ashamed to say of some Brutes, Videmus indicia pietatis, cognitionem, memoriam, desideria,—secreta à voluptate humanarum simulacra virtutum. De Finib. Lib. II. c. 33. [today: II, 110]. [Translation: *"In a certain class of birds* we see some traces of affection, and also recognition and recollection; and *in many we even notice* regret for a lost friend. *If animals therefore possess some* semblance of the human virtues unconnected with pleasure, . . ."* Cicero, *De finibus bonorum et malorum,* with an English translation by H. Rackham (Cambridge, Mass.: Harvard University Press, 1967), p. 202.]

20. Omitted in C (p. 273), D (p. 273).

21. A (p. 247): Interest do

22. A (p. 248): nothing else but

23. A (p. 253): wrongly numbered II (instead of III).

24. A (p. 253): Goodness, and Holiness

25. D2, D3 [Corrigenda, p. 311]: Or that his Will is conformable to his Will.

26. No new paragraph in A (p. 254).

27. C (p. 275), D (p. 275): Desire of

28. D2, D3 [Corrigenda p. 311]: morally good [an apparently incomplete correction]

29. C (p. 276), D (p. 276): Desire [In D1 and D3 pagination error: 267 instead of 276.]

30. Not in A (p. 255).

31. A (p. 255): altho

32. A (p. 255): Sanctions are join'd to co-operate

33. A (p. 255): Threatnings

34. A (p. 256): numbered IV.

35. C (p. 277), D (p. 277): one

36. A (p. 256): violated: And on

37. A (pp. 256–57): allowing

38. D2, D3 [Corrigenda, p. 311]: Natural Liberty

39. No new paragraph in A (p. 257).

40. Not in A (p. 257). Instruction for addition already in *Alterations and Additions* (p. 21).

41. D2, D3 [Corrigenda, p. 311]: Natural Liberty

42. C (p. 279), D (p. 279): naturally residing in the Persons injur'd, or their voluntary, or invited Assistants, to use force

43. Omitted in C (p. 279), D (p. 279).

44. Not in *Alterations and Additions* (p. 21).

45. *Alterations and Additions* (p. 21): injured Party

46. No new paragraph in A (p. 258).

47. A (p. 259): so the Power of

48. A (p. 259): is

49. A (p. 259): the Power of Compassion

50. A (p. 259): universal

51. A (p. 261): however

52. A (p. 261): Force: and hence

53. A (p. 261): War on both Sides just

54. A (p. 261): numbered V.

55. A (p. 261): a Power to transfer
    D2, D3 [Corrigenda, p. 311]: the Power of transferring

56. A (p. 262): pleases: and so

57. A (p. 262): serve

58. A (p. 262): numbered VI.

59. A (p. 262–63): all [263] Men are oblig'd to observe such a Tenour of Action as shall most effectually promote Industry; and to

Alterations and Additions (p. 21): when Men are so numerous, that the natural Product of the Earth is not sufficient for their Support, or Ease, or innocent Pleasure; all men are oblig'd to observe such a Tenour of Action as shall most effectually promote Industry; and to

60. A (p. 263): Whatever

61. Not in A (p. 263).

62. A (p. 264): of Self-Love from Industry, and leaves Benevolence alone; [Instruction for alteration already in *Alterations and Additions* (p. 22).]

63. Not in A (p. 264).

64. Omitted in D (p. 286).

65. A (p. 265): into

66. Not in A (p. 265). Instruction for addition of this paragraph already in *Alterations and Additions* (p. 22).

67. *Alterations and Additions* (p. 22): according to their Prudence

68. A (p. 265): numbered VII.

69. D2, D3 (p. 288): Rules

70. Not in A (p. 265).

71. A (p. 265): 2

72. Omitted in D2, D3 (p. 288).

73. Omitted in D2, D3 (p. 288).

74. A (p. 266): And so

75. A (p. 266): farther

76. A (p. 266): in as far

77. Omitted in D2, D3 (p. 289).

78. A (p. 267): Passions: And this

79. Omitted in D2, D3 (p. 289).

80. D2, D3 (p. 290): the Motives of private Interest are greater.

81. D2, D3 (p. 290): selfish Motives from

82. A (p. 268): has often

83. D2, D3 (p. 291): no new

84. Omitted in D (p. 291).

85. D2, D3 (p. 291): natural Liberty, or the Penalties of Law in Civil Society.

86. A (p. 269): perfect Rights, or even external ones,

87. D2, D3 (p. 291): A stronger and less extensive Tie of Benevolence, in equal Abilitys, must produce a greater Moment of Good to the Object of it, in equally good Characters, than the weaker Ties. Thus, natural Affection, Gratitude, Friendship, have greater Effects than general Benevolence: Or,

we do more Good to Friends, Children, Benefactors, than to Persons under no special Relation.

88. D2, D3 (p. 292): Benevolence alone

89. D2, D3 (p. 292): more extensive, but less passionate

90. D2, D3 (p. 292): more violent, or passionate

91. C (p. 292), D2, D3 (p. 292): more. The general Benevolence (C, p. 292, D1, p. 292: also) appears of itself a more amiable Principle, according to the Constitution of our moral Sense [C, p. 292, D1, p. 292 add after "Sense" a footnote: *See Sect. 3 Art. IX & Art. X § 2.]

D2, D3 (p. 292) add: , than any particular Passion. [and add a footnote after "Sense"]: *See Sect. 3. Art. ix. The Author all along supposes, that no Man acts without some Desire, or Instinct, or Affection, or Appetite; that of these Attachments of the Will, some are calm and unpassionate, others are passionate; some are extensive, and others confined to one, or to a few. The former Sort in each of these Divisions, manifestly appears more amiable; and consequently, caeteris paribus, the Virtue is less, in any given Quantity, of Good done from the violent, passionate, and narrow Attachment. A certain Remarker thence argues, "That then the Virtue is highest, when there is no Desire, Affection, or Attachment at all; or when we act solely from Reason, without any Affection to any Thing." One may retort this Reasoning in a like Case. In any given Momentum of Bodies, there the Velocity is greater, where there is least Matter; consequently, it is there greatest, where there is no Matter at all.

92. C (p. 293), D (p. 293): which

93. Not in A (p. 270). Instruction for addition of this paragraph already in *Alterations and Additions* (pp. 23–24).

94. *Alterations and Additions* (p. 23): ought

95. The following five paragraphs are not in A (pp. 270–71); instead: VIII. Let us not imagine, that from the above Idea of Right it will follow, [271] that the wise and benevolent have a perfect Right to dispose of the Labours or Goods of the weak or foolish, because perhaps they would better employ them for the publick Good than the unskilful Possessors can; for tho in some particular Cases this might happen to do good, as when a good-natur'd Octavius assum'd the Government of a distracted Commonwealth; yet what would be the Consequence of allowing this universally, while there is no acknowledg'd Standard, or Judge of superior Wisdom or Benevolence, which every one would be too apt to claim? And as each Man is more nearly engag'd for his own Good by Self-love, than another is by mere Benevolence, he will

scarcely be brought to believe, that another understands his Interest, or pursues it, better than he could himself. And what Happiness can remain to the Govern'd, while there is any Suspicion of either the Benevolence or Wisdom of the Governor? Especially when there are too great Presumptions, that Governors may be sway'd by Self-love against the publick Good. From this Consideration, as well as the natural Love of Liberty, and Inclination both to act and judge for our selves, we justly conclude, [Instruction for addition of the five paragraphs already in *Alterations and Additions* (pp. 24–30).]

  96. *Alterations and Additions* (p. 24) adds footnote: *See Art. v. of the first Edition.

   97. *Alterations and Additions* (p. 25): unawares, or in

   98. Not in *Alterations and Additions* (p. 25).

   99. Not in *Alterations and Additions* (p. 25).

  100. *Alterations and Additions* (p. 25): transferr'd

  101. *Alterations and Additions* (p. 25): ruining

  102. *Alterations and Additions* (p. 25): Forms of Civil Government

  103. *Alterations and Additions* (p. 26): or of both

  104. Not in *Alterations and Additions* (p. 27).

  105. *Alterations and Additions* (p. 27): toward the Repair

  106. *Alterations and Additions* (pp. 27–28): intirely

  107. D (p. 298): secure

  108. D2, D3 [Corrigenda, p. 311]: violent Usurper

  109. D2, D3 [Corrigenda, p. 311]: regard to a publick Good

  110. A (p. 271): Pleasure

  111. Not in A (p. 272).

  112. A (p. 272): we should be better guided by them than by our own utmost

  113. A (p. 273): numbered IX.

  114. Footnote not in A (p. 273).

  115. A (p. 273): But

  116. A (p. 273): (by his assuming Authority)

  117. A (p. 273): would

  118. D2, D3 [Corrigenda, p. 311]: as some ancient Hereticks did,

  119. A (p. 274): numbered X.

  120. C (p. 302), D (p. 302): There seems

  121. A (p. 274): Par.

  122. C (p. 302), D (p. 302): and desires

  123. Not in A (p. 274).

124. Not in A (p. 274).

125. A (p. 274): that a

126. A (p. 274): Course of such external
     D2, D3 [Corrigenda, p. 311]: or with a suitable Course of

127. C (p. 302), D (p. 302): Hobbes

128. A (p. 275): numbered XI.

129. A (p. 275): been often

130. A (p. 275): would know

131. Omitted in C (p. 303), D (p. 303).

132. A (p. 275): Yea

133. C (p. 303), D (p. 303): approve

134. No new paragraph in A (p. 275).

135. C (p. 303), D (p. 303): not

136. Omitted in C (p. 303), D (p. 303).

137. C (p. 304), D (p. 304): more than

138. C (p. 304), D (p. 304): more lovely

INDEX

This book is set in Adobe Garamond, a modern adaptation by Robert Slimbach of the typeface originally cut around 1540 by the French typographer and printer Claude Garamond. The Garamond face, with its small lowercase height and restrained contrast between thick and thin strokes, is a classic "old-style" face and has long been one of the most influential and widely used typefaces.

Printed on paper that is acid-free and meets the requirements of the American National Standard for Permanence of Paper for Printed Library Materials, z39.48-1992. ∞

Book design by Louise OFarrell
Gainesville, Florida
Typography by Apex CoVantage
Madison, Wisconsin
Printed and bound by Edwards Brothers, Inc.
Ann Arbor, Michigan